Charles E. Strom

18.95

ORGANIZATION DEVELOPMENT

Dr. Karl Albrecht is an internationally known management consultant, seminar leader, professional speaker, and author. He is the director of Albrecht & Associates, a consulting firm in San Diego, California, that specializes in organizational effectiveness through organization development and human resources development. Dr. Albrecht has consulted to or presented management seminars for organizations such as IBM, Xerox, Gould, M&M/Mars, Telefonos de Mexico, IRS, Air Force, Navy, and The University of California. He has been a resource speaker for the American Management Association, American Society for Training & Development, and the International Federation of Training & Development Organizations. He has written a number of other books for Prentice-Hall, including *Successful Management by Objectives, Stress and the Manager, Brain Power,* and *Executive Tune-Up.* He has also produced audio cassette programs, video programs, films, and training packages on various subjects. Dr. Albrecht is the creator of the Assessment Survey Kit (A.S.K.), a personal-computer software package used for processing OD survey questionnaires.

KARL ALBRECHT

ORGANIZATION DEVELOPMENT

A Total Systems Approach to Positive Change in Any Business Organization

A SPECTRUM BOOK

Prentice-Hall, Inc., Englewood Cliffs, New Jersey 07632

Library of Congress Cataloging in Publication Data

Albrecht, Karl.
   Organization development.

   "A Spectrum Book."
   Bibliography: p.
   Includes index.
   1. Organizational change.   I. Title.
HD58.7.A42 1983   658.4′06   8218603
ISBN 0-13-641696-9

This book is available at a special discount
when ordered in bulk quantities. For information,
contact: Prentice-Hall, Inc., General Book Marketing,
Special Sales Division, Englewood Cliffs, New Jersey 07632.

ISBN 0-13-641696-9

10   9   8   7   6   5   4   3   2   1

Editorial/production supervision by Alberta Boddy
Cover design © 1983 by Jeannette Jacobs
Manufacturing buyer: Barbara A. Frick

Prentice-Hall International, Inc., *London*
Prentice-Hall of Australia Pty. Limited, *Sydney*
Prentice-Hall Canada, Inc., *Toronto*
Prentice-Hall of India Private Limited, *New Delhi*
Prentice-Hall of Japan, Inc., *Tokyo*
Prentice-Hall of Southeast Asia Pte. Ltd., *Singapore*
Whitehall Books Limited, Wellington, New Zealand
Editora Prentice-Hall do Brasil Ltda, *Rio de Janeiro*

Contents

Foreword, xiii

Preface, xv

1

Basic Concepts, 1

WHY ORGANIZATION DEVELOPMENT?, *1*   "MAINLINING":
REACTIVE MANAGERS AND ADAPTIVE MANAGERS, *3*
PERCEIVED PAIN AND THE NEED FOR CHANGE, *7*
"PASSAGES" IN THE LIFE OF AN ORGANIZATION, *9*   HOW
ORGANIZATIONAL LEADERS RESPOND TO ENVIRONMENTAL
CHANGES, *14*   THE ATTENTION-SPAN PROBLEM, *16*

NINE SYNDROMES OF ORGANIZATIONAL MALADJUSTMENT, *18*
FOUR DIMENSIONS OF ORGANIZATIONAL HEALTH, *22*
ORGANIZATIONAL HEALTH THROUGH
ORGANIZATIONAL DEVELOPMENT, *24*

2

Approaches and Resources
for Developing Organizations, 29

A BRIEF HISTORY OF ORGANIZATION DEVELOPMENT, *29*
THE "ACTION-RESEARCH" TECHNIQUE, *35*   OTHER
CONTEMPORARY OD APPROACHES, *36*   THREE MAJOR
TRENDS IN OD PRACTICE, *37*   THE GROUP-DYNAMICS
SCHOOL OF OD, *40*   THE BEHAVIOR-MODIFICATION
SCHOOL OF OD, *41*   THE SYSTEMS SCHOOL OF OD, *42*

3

A New Systems View
of the Organization, 44

AN INTRODUCTION TO SYSTEMS THINKING, *44*   THE
CONCEPT OF A SOCIOTECHNICAL SYSTEM, *47*   THE FOUR
KEY SYSTEMS OF AN ORGANIZATION, *49*   THE
"MISPLACED FIX" SYNDROME, *51*   THE "PARADOXICAL
REWARD" SYNDROME, *53*   INTER-SYSTEM CONFLICTS, *56*
FADS, FACTS, AND FIXES, *58*   SPECIAL PROBLEMS
OF NONPROFIT ORGANIZATIONS, *59*

4

The Technical System, 63

COMPONENTS OF THE TECHNICAL SYSTEM, *64*   THE KEY
MEASURE: PRODUCTIVITY, *65*   INDIVIDUAL
PRODUCTIVITY AND COLLECTIVE PRODUCTIVITY, *67*
CAPITAL AND PRODUCTIVITY, *70*   MOTIVATION AND
PRODUCTIVITY, *71*   COMPETENCE-BASED TRAINING AND
DEVELOPMENT, *71*   PERFORMANCE APPRAISAL, *73*

5

The Social System, 75

COMPONENTS OF THE SOCIAL SYSTEM, *75*   THE KEY
MEASURE: QUALITY OF WORK LIFE, *76*   UNDERSTANDING
THE ORGANIZATION'S CULTURE AND CLIMATE, *78*

THE REWARD SYSTEM, *80*   RECOGNIZING ORGANIZATIONAL
VALUES, *82*   UNDERSTANDING THE PSYCHOLOGY OF
POWER, *84*   UNDERSTANDING ORGANIZATIONAL
POLITICS, *86*   UNDERSTANDING THE "GRAPEVINE," *88*
HOW A COMPANY GETS UNIONIZED, *91*   CULTURAL AND
CROSS-CULTURAL ISSUES, *92*

6

The Administrative System, 94

COMPONENTS OF THE ADMINISTRATIVE SYSTEM, *94*   THE
KEY MEASURE: RESPONSE TIME, *97*   MAINTAINING A
LOGICAL STRUCTURE, *98*   SYMPTOMS OF
MALORGANIZATION, *100*   COMMUNICATING THE
STRUCTURE, *103*   CLARIFYING POLICIES, PROCEDURES,
AND STANDARDS, *104*   MAINTAINING A HEALTHY
INFORMATION ENVIRONMENT, *106*

7

The Strategic System, 108

A SPECIAL COMMENT ABOUT THE STRATEGIC SYSTEM, *108*
COMPONENTS OF THE STRATEGIC SYSTEM, *111*   THE KEY
MEASURE: MANAGEMENT STRENGTH, *111*   UNDER-
STANDING "POWER PEOPLE," *113*   THE TOP MANAGEMENT
TEAM, *116*   THE EXTENDED MANAGEMENT FAMILY, *117*
UNDERSTANDING MANAGERIAL STYLES, *118*
EVALUATION, *122* ADAPTATION, *123*   GRADUATION, *124*
INNOVATION, *126*   THE THREE BOTTOM LINES, *127*
PUTTING IT ALL TOGETHER, *129*

8

A Systems Approach to Organization Development, 131

AVOIDING THE "HAMMER SYNDROME," *131*   SETTING A
CLIMATE FOR CANDID PROBLEM-SOLVING, *132*   THE
BASIC FOUR-PHASE OD PROCESS, *135*   THE CATALYST
FUNCTION, *138*   ENGAGING AN EXTERNAL CONSULTANT, *139*
SETTING UP AN OD TASK FORCE, *141*   THE INTERNAL
OD SPECIALIST, *144*   CLARIFYING THE ROLE OF TRAINING
IN ORGANIZATION DEVELOPMENT, *145*   ASSESSING
TOP MANAGEMENT "SUPPORT," *146*   OBJECTIVES-ORIENTED
OD, *148*   THE TIME LINE OF AN OD PROGRAM, *149*

9

The Assessment Phase, 154

ASSESSING ALL FOUR KEY SYSTEMS, *154*   FACT-FINDING
METHODS, *155*   ASSESSING THE TECHNICAL SYSTEM, *159*
ASSESSING THE SOCIAL SYSTEM, *161*   ASSESSING
THE ADMINISTRATIVE SYSTEM, *163*   ASSESSING THE
STRATEGIC SYSTEM, *166*   HOW TO ANALYZE MANAGERIAL
STYLES, *168*   HOW TO CONDUCT A CLIMATE SURVEY, *174*
BUILDING AN EMPLOYEE-SENSING SYSTEM, *177*

10

The Problem-Solving Phase, 179

A "CATALOG" OF OPTIONS FOR ORGANIZATION
DEVELOPMENT, *179*   TEAM BUILDING, *181*
DEVELOPING THE MANAGEMENT TEAM, *184*   CREATING
A PROCESS FOR COLLECTIVE PROBLEM-SOLVING, *186*
WHAT IS OUR BUSINESS? OD AND STRATEGIC PLANNING, *188*
STREAMLINING THE STRUCTURE, *190*
ORGANIZING AND MANAGING FOR INNOVATION, *193*
IMPROVING PRODUCTIVITY, *195*   IMPROVING THE
QUALITY OF WORK LIFE, *198*   IMPROVING THE UNION-
MANAGEMENT RELATIONSHIPS, *200*   DEVELOPING A
REALISTIC OD IMPLEMENTATION PLAN, *202*

11

The Implementation Phase, 206

THE "EXECUTIVE QUARTERBACK" CONCEPT, *206*
IDENTIFYING AND RESOLVING BARRIERS TO CHANGE, *209*
ANALYZING THE "FORCE FIELD," *212*   UNDERSTANDING
EMPLOYEE RESPONSES TO MANAGEMENT-INDUCED
CHANGE, *213*   DEVELOPING "OWNERSHIP" OF THE INTENDED
CHANGES, *216*   BUILDING A POSITIVE FEEDBACK SYSTEM, *219*

12

The Evaluation Phase, 222

CLOSING THE CYCLE, *222*   FORMAL PROGRAM REVIEWS, *224*
FACT FINDING REVISITED, *225*   ACCENTUATING
THE POSITIVE, *226*   SETTING A NEW DIRECTION, *227*

13

The Future
of Organization Development, 229

WHERE IS OD GOING?, *222*   SKILLS OD PEOPLE WILL
NEED, *232*   TEN COMMANDMENTS FOR AN OD PERSON, *234*

14

Case Studies
in Organization Development, 235

POLAROID CORPORATION, *235*   THE GENERAL MOTORS
QUALITY-OF-WORK-LIFE PROGRAM, *236*   SAAB-SCANIA
CORPORATION, *238*   THE U.S. DEPARTMENT OF ENERGY, *240*
A PRACTICE CASE STUDY, *242*

Appendix, 244

BIBLIOGRAPHY FOR OD, *244*
ORGANIZATIONS INVOLVED IN PROMOTING OD, *245*

Index, 247

Foreword

Karl Albrecht has made an important contribution to our understanding of organizations and how to improve their effectiveness. Given the fact that over 95 percent of the U.S. workforce is employed by a juridical entity, such as a bureaucracy, corporation, "group practice," or partnership, contrasted to the less-than-5 percent who are self-employed, this is no trivial matter. What Albrecht has accomplished in these pages is a book which is—at once—readable and practical. In addition, the book contains a seasoned, theoretical grasp of those issues facing both practitioners of organizational development and those executives who are striving for excellence. In short, Albrecht's book is written for and should be read by thinking managers and management thinkers.

What makes the book unique to me is Albrecht's basic orientation which he remains faithful to throughout: A systems orientation which not only provides a wholistic outlook, but which evaluates the practice and study of Organizational Development well beyond the gimmicky, the "quick fixes," and instant cures which have plagued the field since its inception about two decades ago. Albrecht doesn't just pay lip service to the venerable idea of "socio-technical" systems; he really rolls up his sleeves and gets into the significant day-to-day world of the manager, the work place. The heart of the book for me is the four chapters devoted to a pivotal feature of organizational systems: 1) technical, 2) social, 3) administrative, and 4) strategic. Nowhere in the literature I am familiar with is there such a perceptive and complete coverage of those elements which can make a difference. In this respect Albrecht deserves our congratulations for unskewing the field of OD away from narrow concerns—what Thorstein Veblen once warned us about many years ago: the "trained incapacity" of specialists.

Albrecht's main concern—*his* major preoccupation—is with people, processes, power, politics, technology, and how these exquisitely complex parts can be orchestrated to produce the best products with the most creative efforts of the personnel.

While there are a number of arguable points here and there and while Albrecht's version of OD's history differs in some respects from my own, I think he has made a valuable contribution both to the understanding of how to change and improve our organizations as well as to the underlying principles of organizational vitality and health.

Warren Bennis
Dubell Distinguished Professor
of Management
University of Southern California

Preface

This book will help you understand organizations and the management of organizations in an entirely new way. It will introduce you to the idea of managing an organization as a process of continuous development, which transcends the day-to-day patterns of simply "keeping things on track." Organization development, or "OD," is a comprehensive process of planned evolution and improvement in the total functioning of an organization. It is worth learning about by executives, managers at various levels, personnel people, training and development people, and all others who hope to prod organizations in the direction of increasing effectiveness.

The days are just about gone when executives could preoccupy themselves solely with the basic business of the organization—its primary productive axis—and ignore the other dimensions of strategy, administration, and social process. The manager who believes that "all you have to do is make a good product and sell it hard" is becoming a virtual dinosaur. To meet the demands of business in the future, managers must become better informed, think more broadly and comprehensively, and undertake problem-solving processes in all dimensions of their organizations, not just in the familiar "production" aspects. Today's manager must know the difference between running the train and running the railroad.

There is a critical need at his point for a practical and straight-forward approach to developing organizations. Managers need a workable perspective, or vantage point, from which to look at their organizations comprehensively and systematically, and they need a process for getting their organizations to move in the direction of adaptive change. The emerging management methodology known as organization development holds a promise of providing the needed perspective and process.

In the simplest terms, OD is a stage-wise process of assessing the organization, pinpointing those aspects of its functioning that need improvement, implementing the various changes according to a logical plan, and following through on them until they become part of a new way of life. This evolutionary process draws management's attention to the organization itself, rather than to the work of the organization. This is best done by a concerted effort on the part of the organiza-tion's leaders, although in many cases action people within an organi-zation can act as successful "change agents" in the absence of a high level of enthusiasm from the top managers.

For most of its short history, OD has unfortunately been in the hands of "human relations" people, most of whom have been external consultants with strong academic credentials but questionable ground-ing in the day-to-day realities of industrial organizations. Most of them have been psychologists of various types, heavily preoccupied with the social aspects of organizations to the neglect of the more concrete technical processes. Coming out of the "sensitivity training" setting of the middle 1950s, OD theory held that organizations got into trouble primarily because the people working there didn't get along well with one another. High-intensity training techniques, such as encounter group meetings, marathon sessions in sensitivity and self-discovery, and structured role-playing would presumably enable managers and other working people to deal with one another more effectively. This, it was believed by many, would lead to a revolution in organizational effectiveness.

Unfortunately, the revolution never came. After a number of years of attention-getting human relations programs, including some at large companies, OD simply had not gained widespread credibility with executives and managers. The human-relations "school" of OD has apparently reached a plateau in acceptance and probably will not gain much more ground in its present form.

This is not to say, however, that the need to develop organizations is any less pressing—quite the contrary. But the need is for a more believable process, which proceeds from a holistic perspective that top managers understand and can accept. This book answers that need. As a result of my experiences in working with many different kinds of organizations, in talking with executives and managers, and in observing various kinds of organizational change efforts, I have concluded that a total-systems approach to organization development makes the most sense. We need to look at the organization from the top-management perspective, understand it as a total system, and apply solutions that meet its real needs. Staff-support people, such as internal OD specialists, trainers, and personnel people, need this perspective just as much as executives and managers need it.

This book provides a straightforward systems approach to OD which will enable you to describe any organization in terms of four interlocking "systems," and to grasp the "big picture" of its operation. By using this simple systems model, you will know what things to look for in assessing an organization, gain an understanding of its key features and an appreciation of its "culture," identify its real developmental needs without getting sidetracked by false issues, and identify solutions that have the highest potential of improving its total effectiveness. You will know how to set up an OD program that will have the maximum likelihood of management commitment, and you will learn what it takes to carry it out successfully. You will also gain an understanding of the more significant OD techniques, such as productivity improvement, management team-building, and improvement of the quality of work life in the organization. Whether you are a manager or an internal OD practitioner, you can do your part more effectively by understanding your organization in all of its key dimensions, and by knowing what it takes to develop the organization as well as to operate it.

Karl Albrecht

NOTE: Some readers may want to contact Dr. Albrecht for consulting services, seminar presentations, or speaking engagements. You can do this by writing or calling:

Dr. Karl Albrecht & Associates·
P.O. Box 99097
San Diego, CA 92109
(619) 272-3776

1

Basic Concepts

WHY ORGANIZATION DEVELOPMENT?

There comes a time in the history of almost every organization, no matter what kind it is, when it becomes more or less "out of tune." A small out-of-kilter condition eventually becomes a large out-of-kilter condition because things change. The customers or clients change, their needs and attitudes change, the economic environment changes, the nature of the product or service has to change, the social conditions within the organization itself may change, or the management philosophy may change. What worked before no longer seems to be working so well. The passing years have a way of turning your assets into liabilities.

This out-of-tune condition does not necessarily result from weak or ineffective management, although it certainly can. More often than not, it results from the fundamental inertia that exists in virtually all human organizations—the tendencies of the people who work there to adopt a workable "status quo" mode of operating, and to refine it, cherish it, and eventually defend it against all outside forces that invite them to change it.

One of the most fascinating aspects of learning about management is seeing the ways in which organizations, as systems, adjust to these significant changes in their individual worlds. Some adapt quite well, some adapt poorly, and some adapt hardly at all. The ability to adapt, as an abstract feature of any organization, depends more on the skills and attitudes of its top management staff than on any other single factor. The ability to build an adaptive organization is becoming one of the key capabilities necessary for success among top managers.

As a practical matter, very few organizations really adapt to their changing environments in anything like a continuous, smoothly-flowing process. Instead, an organization will typically arrive at a "sticking point" of some kind—the "out-of-tune" condition just described. When the lack of adaptation becomes painful enough for the key people in the organization, they become highly aware of it and they take action to resolve it. So the history of almost any organization amounts to a succession of sticking points, each characterized by a buildup of pressure to change, followed by a kind of adaptive "lurch" into the future. If we take a realistic, accepting view of this process, we have the basis for an approach which we might call "management by lurch."

Usually, the sticking point calls for some fairly significant change in the organization itself. Rather than just an improvement in its product or service, the sticking point may force a change in the organization's administration procedures, the hiring of more people, or the like. Something about the organization itself—its structure, processes, functions, or internal relationships—has gotten in the way of the needed adaptation. At this point, an enlightened top management group intervenes in what has been an accepted, comfortable way of operating for the people of the organization and facilitates the needed changes to move the organization back toward a condition of reasonable harmony with its environment. They decide to develop the organization into a more effective enterprise. This process, very simply, is what we call organization development.

For the sake of greater clarity, let's adopt a working definition of organization development as a process of planned improvement in the overall functioning of an organization. The objective of this book is to provide managers, and the professional staff people who support them, with some basic concepts, methods, techniques, and tools which they can use to develop more effective organizations.

"MAINLINING": REACTIVE MANAGERS AND ADAPTIVE MANAGERS

What would you think of a manager of a field sales group, charged with the sales of a line of sophisticated electronic products, who, in response to a worsening turnover situation among his sales reps, simply hired more and more "green" people at minimum salary, gave them little or no training, threw them into a sink-or-swim situation, and kept plugging along? When asked about the effectiveness of his approach, he could say confidently, "Look, my cost-of-sales ratio (dollars of sales brought in per dollar of salary paid to the sales reps) is the best in the division. I'm getting good sales productivity." Perhaps you would tend to disagree with this as a long-term approach. You might contend that, by taking a broader view of the situation, and one that included training, developing, and retaining sales people, the manager might well have increased sales significantly and contributed a higher level of total profit to the company's operating statement. I would probably agree with you. We would probably agree in assessing this manager's approach as somewhat too narrow for the situation at hand.

Let's look at a different case, with an underlying similarity. An aggressive young executive, hired as a "turn-around" manager of a division of a company, jumps into the action with both feet. She takes charge of the lagging marketing process, selects several key products for high-priority promotion, and personally spearheads a campaign to increase sales to several of the biggest buyers in the company's industry. While she is traveling through ten major cities with an entourage of experts and support people, and giving briefings to potential customers, the organization at home is in a shambles. The marketing department is in tailspin, waiting for her to return and give them direction (she fired the marketing vice president), production is having a bitter feud with engineering, new-product development projects are stalled waiting for executive decisions, and a serious customer-relations problem in another area is going untended.

Would you say that this executive has lost control of the organization and is inappropriately preoccupied with one of its components (a crucial one, to be sure, but only one of a number of components)?

This kind of pitfall is common with managers who can't "see the forest for the trees." They fail to recognize the tremendously comprehensive nature of the executive job, and they fail to recognize the potential of managing all of the organization and of tending to all of its significant aspects. They don't realize that the effective executive must function something like the conductor of the symphony, who understands all of the instruments, but plays no instrument.

What shortcoming on the part of the manager is common to both these situations, and common to many other problem areas as well? Simply too narrow a view. These managers, and many others, have not broadened their outlook on the executive job sufficiently to include the variety of functions, approaches, problem-solving processes, and development processes that can play an extremely important part in the organization's total "health."

We can draw a useful analogy here to help us understand the nature of the managerial job and to see how organization development methods fit quite properly into it. Let's consider a manager as equivalent, for the moment, to an engineer who is driving a train. We often use the metaphor of a train in describing an organization, to talk about it as "going somewhere." This particular train engineer is rather narrow in his orientation: he drives the train, and that's that. He peers out through the front window, with one hand on the throttle and the other hand on the brake. So long as he sees the track out ahead and recognizes it to be in serviceable condition, he keeps the throttle forward. If anything seems improper about the track, he eases up on the throttle and uses the brake. He keeps to the main line, and so long as everything is in good condition, he drives the train adequately. This kind of a manager, one who merely keeps the train moving, we will call a "mainline" manager. "Mainlining," for a manager, is simply preoccupying one's self too narrowly with the primary productive axis of the organization, with little or no thought or energy given to the "second-order" aspects of the organization itself—its people, its processes, its structure, or its strategies.

When we speak of the primary productive axis, or "prime axis," of the organization, we are not limiting our discussion to organizations that manufacture tangible products. Every organization has some central process for which it exists. In a county welfare agency, the prime axis is the means for providing income support and social services to the needy. In an airline company, the prime axis is the process of transporting people from place to place and collecting their money in exchange for it. In a university, it is the process of giving scheduled courses to the students, testing them, and grading them.

To manage effectively means not only to understand and control the prime axis of the organization but also to facilitate all of the associated processes that are necessary to enable it to function. Here we can make a large conceptual leap with our train analogy. The mainline manager sees himself as running a train; the "comprehensivist" manager sees himself as running a railroad. The difference between the two points of view is enormous. For a railroad to function properly, not only must somebody drive the train, but somebody has to repair the track, keep the train working properly, put the food on the train, advertise, sell the tickets, hire and train the crew, pay them, keep the books, and carry out a host of other activities, without which the train itself would eventually grind to a halt. The effective manager, with a high degree of organizational awareness and a comprehensive mentality, understands that it is his or her job to direct and facilitate all of these processes and not to get swallowed up in any one of them.

Mainline management is all too common in American organizations today, both in the profit sector and the nonprofit sector, and even at top management levels. It is a relatively rare chief executive who has grown broad enough in his or her thinking to conceive of the organization in all of its major dimensions, and who can focus resources in a sophisticated, creative, unbiased way to keep the organization itself functioning at a high level of effectiveness.

This lopsidedness, when it exists in a manager, usually results from an incomplete developmental process during the years before he or she took office. It is a fact that relatively few company presidents, vice presidents, or nonprofit agency executives continue their own education as enthusiastically after their graduation into executive ranks as they did before that. The "I've made it" syndrome often sets in, with the implication that an executive who takes management courses or seminars must not be fully competent. Too many executives fall for this trap, cutting themselves off from valuable growth experiences and arresting their learning processes.

Most managers bring some specific set of experiences and technical qualifications with them when they arrive in the management ranks. A highly proficient engineer, for example, will find it very tempting to overcontrol the design activities of subordinates simply because he knows so much about the work. It will usually be a challenge for him to broaden his perspective to include the many other aspects of the engineering department that need managing. A vice president of manufacturing who becomes chief executive officer will likewise find it challenging to broaden his understanding to include unfamiliar functions such as product development, marketing, and finance. Most executives have some form of "learning lag" simply because they could not possibly learn all aspects of the organization as they were coming up. Executives who recognize this learning lag and undertake a developmental process to eliminate it will obviously approach their jobs more effectively than the ones who don't see the need. Most mainline managers suffer from just such a learning lag. They never had an opportunity to comprehend the management process in its broadest dimensions, and they may be protecting themselves from the recognition that they need to learn and grow.

Academic training does not necessarily keep a manager from falling into the mainlining mode. Many university programs that provide MBA degrees do not provide a well-rounded understanding of organizations. Presently, most MBA programs in the United States focus heavily on finance and accounting. Of course, it is fashionable to include a few courses in the behavioral sciences, but many MBA graduates still lack any kind of real grasp of the human element of business. Ironically, many universities with well-known business schools are among the most poorly managed organizations you will find anywhere.

All of the factors previously mentioned can contribute to a mainlining style of managing, on the part of a single executive, or among the entire membership of the management staff. Until mainline managers discover the possibilities of comprehensive management, they usually cannot grasp the significance of the organization development approach.

If you are presently a manager, at any level, I hope you have been thinking about your own approaches and philosophies of management. Would you confess to being a mainline manager? Or can you demonstrate, by your actions and organizational results, that you do indeed manage comprehensively? None of us ever learns all there is to learn, or even most of it, but a learning attitude is extremely valuable. I hope that the ideas in this book will help you to make a clear assessment of the way in which you now manage, and to identify new possibilities that can help you and your organization function more effectively.

PERCEIVED PAIN
AND THE NEED FOR CHANGE

To some extent, the very nature of an organization is to resist significant change. The basis for any organization is repeatability and routine. We have an accounts-payable unit in our organization because somebody decided we should have the same people paying our bills every day, in pretty much the same way, over the long run. Hardly anybody would want to work in an organization where the work was not divided up among the members in some logical way they could depend on. So inertia comes with the very structure of the organization.

Very few people in the organization are in touch with the "big picture." The top managers and a few key staff people preoccupy themselves with what the organization is all about and where it is supposed to be going, while the rest of the people tackle their individual, specialized jobs. This is, of course, as it should be. It does, however, mean that the working people of the organization have a very different outlook on things than the managers do. Although managers might see the need to do some things differently, workers tend to see management-imposed changes in their activities as disruptive and as causing at least some degree of psychological discomfort. Even the most adaptable of us want certain routines and processes we can trust and rely on; we want to work with a sense of momentum and continuity. It is this desire for momentum and continuity that confronts almost every significant change that management might seek to make in the organization itself, except for those cases where the people of the organization see such enormous personal advantages in the changes that they eagerly accept them (a pay raise, for example, or a move to much more attractive and comfortable offices).

Managers themselves also have needs for a sense of momentum and continuity; they need a feeling that their organizations and activities have a satisfying structure to them and that they can make them work. These feelings also tend to act as inertial resisting forces whenever significant change is at issue. The fact that the people in an organization, including managers, tend to operate as inertial resisting forces to significant change is not necessarily a good thing or a bad thing. It is simply a powerful, inescapable fact we must come to terms with if we want to make constructive changes. Every organization needs, within itself, the means for changing its own nature to deal with a relentlessly shifting environment. The means for this change rest ultimately with management, and the effectiveness of those means depends on the skills of the managers in facilitating change.

So, as a practical matter, we must recognize that a major adaptive shift in the way an organization operates seldom if ever comes spontaneously from the people working in the organization. The very nature of organizations tends to prevent this; the sum of the efforts of all of the people working in their own specialized areas, each seeking to maximize a sense of momentum and continuity, keeps the organization moving in pretty much the same direction. And the managers themselves, depending on their attitudes, skills, and levels of sophistication, can sometimes be the strongest of all the resisting forces.

What, then, causes the "adaptive lurch" mentioned previously? How does an organization actually begin to change in important and substantial ways? What motivates its leaders to get together and say, "We need to make some improvements in our organization. We need to develop it into a more effective enterprise"? The usual answer is, figuratively, "pain." As a general matter, people in an organization usually make major changes in the way they operate only in response to an immediate perception that something is seriously wrong. Someone in a key management position, and often several someones, must experience what I have come to call "primary pain." This means that these key managers must recognize some condition that is causing (or threatens to cause) problems that will affect an aspect of the organization that they hold dear. Something which the executives value highly (including, sometimes, their own jobs) must usually be in jeopardy for them to undertake a significant rearrangement of the organization's internal circumstances. This does not mean, of course, that actual physical or psychological agony must occur, but merely that their attention is arrested by a rather significant situation which spells to them the need for adaptive change.

This process of pain-induced change probably describes the large majority of organizations and their leaders, but by no means all of them. There are, indeed, managers who are so well in touch with the environments in which their organizations operate, and so perceptive of the internal phenomena that govern effectiveness, that they tend to anticipate the need for significant change and to get a head start on it. For their organizations, the occasional sticking points are not nearly so severe, so long-enduring, or so costly as for organizations managed by more reactive leaders. And their lurches into the future tend to be more efficient and more successfully adaptive.

The mentality behind organization development is the mentality of anticipatory management—the antithesis of reactive management. While the reactive manager backs into the future, the anticipatory manager navigates into the future. He studies the signals and studies the organization, and from the two he develops a view of how the organization must function to meet the probable future. This makes the effective manager a developer of organizations, as well as a developer of strategies and a developer of people.

"PASSAGES" IN THE LIFE OF AN ORGANIZATION

Many of the internal problems experienced by fast-growing organizations are really predictable side effects of unmanaged growth. As an organization emerges from its infancy, at a very small size, and proceeds to expand to a much larger size, there are certain inevitable obstacles it must surmount, problems it must solve, and adaptive "crises" it must survive. Every growing organization goes through certain distinct stages in its long-term growth, and each of these stages has distinct identifying characteristics.

Let's follow the course of an imaginary organization through the "passages" of its life, from its birth to the point where it has leveled off at a substantial size. Not all organizations grow to large size, of course, and many go extinct along the way. But for many, this progression accurately describes their development. We can trace five major stages of growth, which can be categorized by the approximate size of the organization as measured by the total number of employees. At each of these five growth stages, the organization takes on certain characteristic features. For each of the stages, the organization must successfully negotiate a characteristic "crisis" in order to break through to the next level of growth.

The term "growth crisis" is a very descriptive one, and not an exaggeration by any means. In the Chinese ideographic writing system, the character that represents the concept of "crisis" is a combination of the symbols for "danger" and "opportunity." In the same sense, the growing organization faces a combination of danger and opportunity at each of these major transitions in its life.

We can describe the organization at each of these growth stages in terms of metaphorical social structures, as follows:

Survivor Group

The "desert island" stage can be equated with the founding of an organization by a small band of entrepreneurs. For example, two or three electronic engineers may develop a new device, leave the company where they have been working, and set up a business to produce and market it. At this stage, the company is very small, possibly consisting only of themselves or at most five to ten people, with very simple roles and relationships, a simple leadership function, and a "share the work" style of operating. The adaptive crisis at this point is a crisis of resources. The business needs money and paying customers to survive.

Family

The company leaders are beginning to find customers for their new Franostat, and they're making some money. They've hired some people to help with the production, so they can devote their efforts to working out the final bugs in the product design and finding more customers. They've moved out of the President's garage and into a rented facility. Their group numbers anywhere from about ten people up to about twenty-five, and there still exists a relatively informal style of leadership and decision-making. Their adaptive crisis at this stage is a crisis of control. They've begun bumping into one another, and they must establish some semblance of leadership, divide up the responsibilities, and put someone squarely in charge.

Village

Now they're selling Franostats like the proverbial hotcakes and making a nice profit. They're hiring new people frantically, trying to fill orders, expanding their facilities, and struggling to get this rapidly growing adolescent of a company under some kind of control. The executives are overworked, don't have time to think, and are increasingly burdened by problems of coordination and administration. The organization will have up to 100 people or so by now. The adaptive crisis at this stage is a crisis in structure. The leaders must build a formal organization and a family of administrative systems which will serve as a framework for continued growth.

City

By this time, the organization has grown to several hundred people, possibly as many as 500. It has taken on a fully formalized structure, with departments reminiscent of "communities" within a city setting. Life for the founders has taken on a very different form by now. They are caught up in administrative matters, personnel matters, marketing problems, planning activities, facilities planning problems, and all the rest of the challenges that accompany rapid growth to such a size. They have had to become much more formal in their dealings with the employees, only a few of whom were there from the start. They face the realization that not everyone in the company lives and breathes Franostats, and as the president walks down the hall, he passes strangers whom he didn't hire and doesn't know. They are hiring and firing people on a regular basis, and the "one big happy family" feeling has faded significantly. The founders are far removed from product innovation and are now fully occupied with running a company. The adaptive crisis at this point is a crisis of strategy. The executives must decide what business they are going to be in for the next some years and how to develop and deploy their resources to meet the future.

Metropolis

Eventually, the company grows to large proportions, which means it might level out at anywhere from 500 people on up to several hundred thousand or more. Amalgamated Franostat is now an established, large, fully fossilized corporation, unlike anything it was in past years. What gives it the character of an urban metropolis, in figurative terms, is its diverse and highly "regionalized" structure. There are many people working in the company who will never come in contact with one another, simply because the enterprise is so large, or possibly because its operations are so geographically dispersed. In this respect, a small or medium-sized company can have a metropolitan orientation if the nature of its operation requires a geographic deployment into various regions or "communities."

At the metropolis stage, the company more or less runs itself, by virtue of its formal structure, delegation of authority to various executives, and the momentum of a well-established process for developing, marketing, selling, and delivering its products. The chief executive is generally more of a helmsman at this point than the straw-boss he was in the early years. Although the company's survival is probably no longer in jeopardy, the adaptive problem at this stage remains one of strategy. The executives must still play the game of positioning the company in the marketplace, with ever higher stakes. Many large companies also face an adaptive crisis of values. The executives need to think through what the organization's internal climate should be, how it should relate to its public and the community, and what ethical principles its leaders and employees should follow.

It may take many years for an organization to traverse all five of these growth stages, and, of course, many organizations will not go the entire route. Many of them will level off at various intermediate points along the way. Some will fold up, some will decline, and some will be swallowed up by others in mergers or acquisitions. Nonprofit organizations tend to traverse these same five growth stages, although they exist for different purposes and have different organizational problems. The adaptive side effects of growth tend to be very much the same for nonprofits as for companies.

Many of the adaptive difficulties experienced by growing companies result more or less directly from the inability or unwillingness of their executives to learn new roles and new styles of managing as their enterprises grow and develop. There are certain characteristic and predictable syndromes of management maladjustment during growth. Small, fast-growing companies in the electronics and semiconductor industries frequently epitomize these problems. In California's Santa Clara Valley area, near San Jose, there are many small high-technology firms, many of which have succeeded and grown rapidly. This area has such a high concentration of semiconductor firms, and firms that manufacture semiconductor-based products, that it has acquired the nickname of "Silicon Valley," after the raw material used to make semiconductor materials. Many of these firms have traced a very similar path during their rapid growth and have run headlong into a growth crunch. As a matter of fact, I've seen this happen so often among these kinds of companies that I've nicknamed this phenomenon the "Silicon Valley indigestion syndrome." Here's how it happens.

As in our classical example, a small band of entrepreneurs founds a company. During the survivor-group stage, they work as a tightly-knit team, with a heroic sense of commitment to one another as well as to their enterprise. Generally, one of them will emerge as the company president, usually the one who thought up the product or the one who put in the most money. Their relationships are very informal, and most of their problem-solving processes and decision processes are collaborative. The president is more of a doer than a manager, because the small unit doesn't need much management.

As the company grows to the family stage, life becomes more complex, but the managers try to keep their relationships simple. With employees to supervise and pay, they feel the pressure for a more "serious" way of operating. The engineer-leaders of the group probably have much more experience in engineering than in leading. Typically, they will be long on technical expertise and short on business experience, simply by virtue of their career histories. They continue to give most of their attention to matters of product design, production, and sales, which require the most guidance.

As the company progresses to the village stage, the first symptoms of indigestion usually start to show, but typically the leaders of the company are too preoccupied with technical matters to see the problem. They have little interest in administrative processes, forms, reports, plans, forecasts, cash-flow projections, salary schedules, and all the other "trivial" aspects of administration.

By the time the company has grown too big to operate as a village unit and verges on city-size, the mismatch between the way the leaders are leading and the form of leadership the organization needs is becoming painful. Many fast-growing firms have encountered very difficult and frustrating blockages because the leaders did not lay the groundwork for sudden expansion. They didn't lay out an effective structure, define goals and roles, build the administrative systems, train and place the proper people, delegate authority and responsibility, or set up a strategic planning process. Unconsciously, they believed they could somehow do it all themselves. They didn't realize that, at a certain point, they would need to amplify their own capabilities through other people.

When the crunch comes, the president of the company is still personally involved in engineering the products. He and the other engineer-executives are still trying out new design approaches, changing production processes, making sales calls on the big accounts, and in general, doing what engineers like to do—solve problems. Meanwhile, the people in the organization are increasingly confused about goals and roles. There are inter-unit feuds and misunderstandings. Communication of key information suffers from the lack of a workable administrative system. Mid-level leaders don't have the freedom to make their own decisions and take actions based on them. Morale takes a nose dive, and there is a general sense of frustration with an organization that is seriously out of kilter.

Instead of recognizing that the organization needs a comprehensive form of management from him, the president stubbornly continues to try to do what he does best—solve problems. He jumps on this personnel problem, or that production problem, or another pricing problem, scattering his energies and steadily losing ground. He can't or won't become the kind of comprehensivist manager the situation calls for. For this reason, the organization reaches an "indigestion" stage. Its further growth will be paced, not by the sales appeal of the product, but by the ability of the organization as a sociotechnical system to adapt to growth itself. In many cases, a fast-growing company cannot even process all of its current business for lack of a workable organizational structure and effective systems and administrative processes.

Many of the serious adaptational problems that arise in companies can be understood in the context of these five growth stages, or "passages," in the figurative life of the organization. Just as the organization evolves into something else at each new stage, the chief executive must evolve into something else as the demands of management shift dramatically. Few individuals, especially those with highly specialized backgrounds such as engineers, seem to be able to stretch to meet the requirements of these changing roles thrust on them by the dynamics of growth. This is one reason why the founder of a company may find himself eased out, bought out, forced out, or kicked out by a developing new leadership; the changing times have transformed him from a hero to an obstacle. Those founding executives who do recognize the changing nature of their roles, and who can stretch their capabilities to meet them, often create virtual "storybook" organizations, which grow rapidly and effectively, stay healthy and adaptive at each of the predictable growth crises along the way, and continue to be profitable both for the owners and for those who work there.

HOW ORGANIZATIONAL LEADERS RESPOND TO ENVIRONMENTAL CHANGES

We can analyze the attitudes and actions of a manager who is facing a serious and growing out-of-kilter situation, in terms of the extent to which he accepts and capitalizes on the reality which has presented itself. Of course, the need to change some aspect of the organization, or his way of managing it, is subject to judgment and opinion. If many observers of an organization hold the opinion that it is getting out of tune, this does not necessarily make the manager who disagrees with them wrong. There are often as many arguments he can muster for preserving the status quo as others can muster to support the need for change. In general, however, it often happens that a manager is stubbornly or inadvertently avoiding dealing with a significant problem when indeed there is abundant evidence that it needs dealing with.

A manager can deal with the need for change in roughly three ways:

1. *Deny* the need altogether.
2. Try to *accommodate* the problem; attempt to preserve as much as possible of the status quo, while trying to make some kind of a "quick fix."
3. *Accept* the significance of the problem and the need for adaptation and change, and begin seriously working on the solution.

These three modes of dealing with the pressure to change—denial, accommodation, and adaptation—give us a clearer notion of managerial styles, and a better way to observe and analyze the effectiveness of a manager's particular pattern.

For example, a hard-nosed chief executive of a small and profitable company making electronic components might have trouble dealing with the fact that, with a company of over 400 people, there isn't the "one big happy family" feeling there used to be with 40 people. He may not want to recognize that many of the people are less committed to the company and less loyal to him personally than were the members of the brave band who first came aboard when he and his colleagues were founding the company. He dismisses the rumors about a union being formed as so much grumbling. "My people would never do that," he contends. "They're just not that way. I know them." So, as a potentially explosive situation continues to brew, and as valuable time is lost, he turns his attention to other matters and refuses to hear of it. In the extreme case, he denounces any executive who takes the matter seriously and dares to bring it up. When he says, "I don't want to hear about it," he means just that, and they take him at his word. There is a collusion not to face the problem. This is the denial mode.

At a less extreme level, the executive may more or less acknowledge the problem, but he defines it or rationalizes it as one that can be patched up with a minimal amount of time, energy, and resources. In this mode, he says, "I don't know what they're grumbling about. We give them everything. Let's hold a company picnic. And, we'll give each of them a turkey at Christmas. Maybe that will get rid of these rumors." Or, he might take the unionism scuttlebutt seriously and try to nip it in the bud. He might take the primitive (and potentially illegal) approach of intimidating or firing the "ringleaders" of the union movement in order to bring the others in line. Or, he might make a number of promises in responses to his employees' list of complaints— things the company will do for them if they will just drop this union foolishness and get back to work. This is the mode of accommodation.

And at a more sophisticated level, the executive may take a broad view of the situation and recognize that it could be symptomatic of the need for a new look at things. If he is organization-minded, he will look into the matter further, taking seriously the indications that many of the employees feel dissatisfied with one or more aspects of the company. He may, for example, launch a fact-finding process to get a more accurate picture of what is going on. This might include the services of a consultant to provide an unbiased external perspective, and probably a survey to find out more about the perceptions, opinions, and wants of the employees. From these data, he would probably work out a problem-solving process, which could include any number of changes of various types in the way the oganization operates. He would not assume that any one approach, such as a raise in pay, turkeys at Christmas, or remodelling the cafeteria, would be the answer to the "attitude problem." This kind of an approach rests upon an investigative and adaptive attitude, and a respect for concrete evidence. This is the mode of adaptation.

This attitude, of course, is the attitude behind organization development. Not every problem calls for organization development, but many times the need for significant change in the interior processes of the organization does signal the need for an OD-type approach. The adaptive manager is open to the findings at hand and is willing to consider whatever actions it takes to improve the overall effectiveness of the organization.

THE ATTENTION-SPAN PROBLEM

One of the most common aspects of a perpetually out-of-kilter organization is simply a short attention span on the part of its leaders. Even highly professional managers can fall into this mode from time to time, but it is much more characteristic of relatively "underdeveloped" managers, i.e., those with practical experience but with no strong conceptual grasp of management practice or of organizational behavior.

The manager or the management team with a short attention span perpetually gets caught up in the day-to-day whirl of activities, paperwork, meetings, and crises going on in the organization, and can't seem to focus attention on the big picture long enough to achieve significant results. After all, the need to build morale among the professional staff managers of the organization, for example, is much less pressing, much less of a "noisy" problem, and certainly much less of a concrete and recognizable one than the need to staff up quickly to meet the requirements of a seasonal surge in demand for services. As a rule, in most organizations, management attention goes first and foremost to those problems that are the most immediate, the most directly cost-related, and the most concretely-experienced.

Closely related to the attention-span problem in many organizations is the follow-through problem. Because the big-picture solutions take a long time to carry out, they often fall by the wayside in the press of more immediate business. One of the most often-used terms in business organizations is "somebodyoughta." At almost any staff meeting, someone will say something like "That's right. We need a better way to get the service requests into the computer. It's costing us too much in time and money. Somebodyoughta look into that." And there the matter drops. It takes a highly disciplined management team to capture those "somebodyoughta's" and convert them into "somebodyisgonna's." Lack of disciplined follow-through on identified problems and solutions is one of the most costly management shortcomings of all.

The short attention-span syndrome often gives rise to faddism in the area of management approaches and developmental processes for the organization. A management team might spend a full week at an off-site retreat, going over the key issues and problems facing the organization, and then return to the office the next week and get sucked right back into the day-to-day quagmire of crisis. Last week they were ecstatic about the potential of situational leadership, or management by objectives, or transactional analysis, or creative problem-solving, or a new model for communication. This week they're floundering about with the same old habits they took with them to the workshop. Nothing has changed. Next year it will be a new fascination, with roughly the same degree of follow-through and implementation. It seems very difficult, and sometimes virtually impossible, for many managers to concentrate resources on a daily basis on a solution or a line of development whose payoff won't show up within the next few weeks or months, no matter how important they all agree it is during the excitement of the management retreat.

By developing a disciplined approach to payoffs and priorities, and by practicing effective time-management techniques, the managers of an organization can keep the high-payoff, longer-term solutions in sight, and can devote the resources to them which their value justifies.

NINE SYNDROMES OF ORGANIZATIONAL MALADJUSTMENT

A few years ago, I was having a luncheon conversation with a colleague of mine, who was describing to me an organization malfunction she was dealing with. I wisecracked something like, "That's Number Four on the list." She said, "List? What list?" I said, "Well, you know, there are really only about eight or ten basic syndromes we see over and over again in organizations. The circumstances and people vary quite a bit, but the underlying syndromes are pretty much the same. Life only has so many plots, you know." She called my bluff and said, "OK, name for me the top ten malfunction syndromes that occur in organizations." Pressed for an answer, I made a list on the paper placemat; I could only come up with nine of them that seemed to describe a wide variety of situations.

These nine situational syndromes, organizational malfunctions, or out-of-tune conditions do indeed seem to recur in many business organizations, both in the profit-making and nonprofit sectors. One could perhaps argue for one or two more than this number, or perhaps cut the list by one or two, but their general prevalence does seem indisputable. Here are the nine syndromes I identified, which signal a substantial level of organizational maladjustment.

Amoeba Syndrome

There is a virtual lack of strong direction from the executive of the organization: not enough structure, order, or guidance to enable middle managers and supervisors to give adequate direction to the managers of their staffs; the organization as a whole is in a tailspin, and top management cannot supply the leadership to get it moving in a constructive direction. The organization falls into the activity trap; a classic example of this was the U.S. Department of Energy.

Anarchy Syndrome

The organization's leadership is in dispute. This can come from a serious palace war, with executives getting axed left and right, or from a situational upheaval in which responsibilities, functions, and re- sources—"turf" issues, in other words—are in dispute. Ford Motor Company has had a colorful history of palace wars and executions. IBM went through an identity crisis many years ago when Thomas Watson was forced out of the company he founded by a younger group of managers.

Buggywhip Syndrome

The organization clings to an obsolete product or service which no longer has the potential for sustaining its livelihood. Chrysler Corpor- ation, right up to the time of its near-bankruptcy and rescue by the Federal Government, maintained its commitment to oversized cars which were being clobbered in the marketplace by Japanese imports. By the time the management of Chrysler—and the other American car makers, for that matter—came to their senses and recognized the realities of the marketplace, the Japanese were delivering nearly thirty percent of the new cars bought in the United States; this state of affairs would have been unthinkable before the era of expensive energy.

Deadlock Syndrome

A standoff condition exists between management and the leaders of the work force, usually the leaders of an officially recognized union. The adversary relationship between the two factions can become so toxic and so antagonistic that both sides lose. Some companies have, in fact, gone under, largely as a result of a union-management dead- lock and the inability to collaborate. American steel companies have for years had especially toxic union-management relationships in which productivity-improvement programs have been the center of bitter wrangling. Here, too, the Japanese captured nearly twenty-five percent of the American steel market, and a major contributing factor for this success has been the much more positive and collaborative relationship between workers and management of the Japanese steel companies.

Mom-and-Pop Syndrome

The small company managers can't or won't help the company grow past the awkward stage. It may be operating in a lucrative growth market, but if it lacks the adaptive mechanisms necessary to grow with the market, it will stagnate. Many small and growing firms in California's semiconductor industry, centered in the area around Santa Clara known as "Silicon Valley," have fallen into the same trap. Founded by engineers and scientists with little or no management training, these companies grew rapidly until they hit the sticking point of structure, leadership, and planning. Many of them got "indigestion"— they simply couldn't process the volume of business they might have been able to book because "Mom and Pop," the founders, couldn't figure out how to help them over the inevitable growth crisis. Nonlinear Systems, the much-publicized San Diego firm which Abraham Maslow and other psychologists studied so thoroughly and credited with the latest in "humanistic management" techniques, remained stagnant for many years under the control of an autocratic founder who couldn't or wouldn't build a management team to capitalize on a rapidly-growing market.

Myopia Syndrome

The organization's leaders are simply not future-oriented. They give very little thought to strategy, sense of direction, or planning processes. They live on a day-to-day, week-to-week, and possibly month-to-month basis. They are forever reacting to surprises brought about by their short-sighted approach to management. The myopia syndrome is often found together with the amoeba syndrome, although not necessarily. Managers might manage myopically, but with a strong and definite sense of priorities and activities. On the other hand, the prevalence of amoebic management more or less implies that myopic management will also be the case. In the grand view of management, most of the presidential administrations in the United States since the Second War have been relatively myopic about strategic matters and about questions concerning the future social and economic directions of the country. Most administrations tend to react to the immediately perceptible circumstances rather than to the foreseeable problems.

The inevitable collapse of the Social Security system is a case in point; a succession of Presidents and Congresses will probably continue to evade the issue until it finally becomes impossible to delay the day of reckoning any further.

Rat-Race Syndrome

A highly toxic social climate pervades the organization, which so undermines the morale and sense of commitment of the employees that it significantly diminishes the potential effectiveness of the organization. This toxic climate can result from oppressive or punitive managers at various levels, lack of top management interest in the legitimate concerns of the employees, or a "slave-driving" policy of executing the work which the employees perceive as unfair, inhumane, and unrewarding. It can also result from an indirect commitment on the part of management to dull, boring, unpleasant, or dehumanizing jobs designed for the sake of minimizing labor costs and maximizing productivity. Virtually all car manufacturers in the United States fall into this category, by virtue of the production-line techniques employed. The epitome of this syndrome is exemplified by the highly publicized walkout at General Motors' plant in Lordstown, Ohio, where plant management had the production lines moving so rapidly that workers finally rebelled.

Remote Control Syndrome

The organization must function with so much administrative or executive control from its parent organization that the decision-making autonomy of its managers is seriously impaired. This often happens in the case of a district office of a government agency, in which the head office hands down so many rules, regulations, policies, and procedures, that the field people wouldn't get anything done if they tried to follow them all. It also happens frequently after a merger or an acquisition when the executives of the acquiring company try to homogenize the new company and make its processes "compatible" with (i.e., controllable by) the parent's processes. The Federal Government's "CETA" program (Comprehensive Employment-Training Act) and a variety of others serve as good examples of the remote control syndrome. The agency or organization unfortunate enough to receive a grant from many of these sources finds itself strangled in red tape, procedures, and seemingly endless reporting requirements.

Rigor-Mortis Syndrome

In a rigor-mortis organization, conditions of inertia and constricted activity prevail, for the primary organizational value is structure and order. Military staff agencies and domestically-based commands are often classic examples of rigor mortis. The typical military organization, and to a great extent government organizations of many kinds, is constructed of so many "slots," or individual task-oriented jobs, which the managers must somehow try to combine into an effective enterprise. No matter that a certain kind of specialty is no longer needed by the organization; it's on the organization chart, it's approved by the higher-ups, and it would take a major upheaval to change it. In a rigor-mortis organization, the managers are not free to deploy their resources at will to adapt to the changing environment. This shows up as the "trapped administrator" syndrome. Often, the process of discharging an incompetent or unproductive employee is so cumbersome and protracted that many managers simply don't try. Universities, incidentally, are some of the most rigid, inflexible organizations found anywhere. Despite the outward appearances and proclamations, a typical academic department is quite rigid, status-dominated, and nearly unmanageable.

FOUR DIMENSIONS OF ORGANIZATIONAL HEALTH

Now that we have reviewed the major aspects and causes of organizational maladjustment, and we have a clearer picture of the reasons why organizations come to be in need of development or redevelopment, let's look at the positive side. What are the key features of a healthy organization? Are there certain characteristics of an organization, and of the way its managers manage it, that make for long-term success in adapting to the environment? Enlightened executives understand that attractive numbers on the balance sheet and income statement of a corporation are necessary for an optimistic view of its future, and that there are other, less-tangible factors that can be equally important.

For example, a company may be enjoying unusually high sales in one year, with good profitability figures, and yet be headed for disaster in a market about to make a drastic turn in a new direction. A labor strike, if not anticipated and forestalled, can virtually cripple a service-oriented firm, such as an airline or a major hotel. Obviously, it takes more than looking at the performance figures, which are simply historical, to assure the organization of a successful future. And the same point of view applies in managing the nonprofit organization; attractive cost and performance figures are necessary but not sufficient to conclude that it will fare well next year and the years after that.

If we study healthy organizations carefully, we can identify certain common features which tend to keep them healthy. Over and above the crucial operational aspects, such as having a product or service that somebody is willing to pay for, making or delivering it well, and getting adequate revenue in return for it, there need to be certain organizational aspects that ensure that these crucial conditions will continue to hold true.

We can sum up many of the features of a healthy organization in terms of just four key processes:

- Performance -

1. Evaluation—a periodic and systematic process of reviewing the entire functioning of the organization to answer the questions: What are the disparities between what is and what ought to be? What do we need to do differently? What changes do we have to make in the organization to meet the oncoming future?

2. Adaptation—a formal and disciplined planning process, which results in concrete decisions about the organization and its development and which leads to concrete actions assigned to specific individuals, together with specific outcomes and target dates.

3. Graduation—a systematic, relatively formal, and public process by which the organization identifies and develops its future leaders; a means for preparing management talent in advance of the need and having a pool of qualified people available to choose from.

4. Innovation—a conscious policy of encouraging the people of the organization, at all levels, to find new and better ways to accomplish the results for which management holds them accountable; a means for affirming and rewarding innovative thinking and innovative behavior, not just in product development, but in all aspects of the work.

Note that all four of these processes of a healthy organization depend to a great extent on the managers, and on the ways in which they manage. Note also that, in an extreme case of mainline management, as described previously, most of them are absent or are present in only a rudimentary state.

Most of the large and successful corporations meet all four of these conditions. Companies like IBM, Xerox, and Kodak, to name a famous few, all have highly disciplined and formal processes for evaluation and adaptation. They commit significant resources to training and developing people, and they have established an organizational climate, or internal "culture," which fosters newness, innovation, and a future orientation.

ORGANIZATIONAL HEALTH THROUGH ORGANIZATION DEVELOPMENT

The condition of organizational health described previously results from a relatively sophisticated level of professional management. It calls for the use of concepts and techniques that a typical manager, no matter how talented, is not likely to invent through sheer imagination or experience, at least not within any reasonably short period of time. These concepts and techniques have been developed over many years by many different thinkers and assembled into a body of management thought only within the past twenty years or so. It is no sin for a manager or executive to be new at the job, and to have come up through a career in which he or she learned a great deal about some special field but not very much about managing. In the study of organizational effectiveness and organization development, probably most managers reading this book will be on relatively new ground. We're dealing here with advanced management concepts.

If that is the case, it is worthwhile to pause at this point and clarify our direction for the remainder of the book. What are we going to explore, what do we want to find out, and—most importantly—what do we want to be able to do better after we complete this basic study of organization development? It is also important to understand how the approach presented in this book differs significantly from most of the approaches espoused by contemporary OD consultants and scholars. I will explain how and why shortly. The following observations, therefore, are offered to establish a "wavelength" for our thinking about OD, and to help you form a clear idea of where this book is taking you.

If you are not familiar with the literature and the language of OD, you probably want to know a little more of what it's all about. If you do know a fair amount about the subject, so much the better. This discussion assumes you are in the first category. First of all, there is a fairly large number of people who consider organization development a "field." Some people also call it a concept, a methodology, a type of management consulting practice, a philosophy, and a subject for academic study. As a field, OD has a respectable, although peculiar, history, which we will review briefly in the next chapter. There are several co-existing "schools of thought" about what OD is and is not, and about how people should apply it. There is a relatively large body of literature, consisting of journals, articles, and books, mostly oriented toward specialized practitioners who "do" OD. Until recently, hardly anyone bothered to try to explain OD concepts and methods to managers, which is a curious oversight in view of the fact that the manager is the person who signs the check to pay the expenses of the OD practitioner. There are consultants who specialize in OD processes, small firms that do the same, and at least one publishing company that publishes books and materials on the subject. A number of universities offer courses in OD or in various aspects of it, and several offer master's degrees in it. There is also an OD Network, a society made up of educators and practitioners.

So you can see that OD has come a long way, even though many managers know very little about it. The fact that OD has been around since the late 1950s but is not yet widely understood or accepted by managers is the reason why I have propounded a substantially new and different framework for it. OD needs to be comprehensible and useable by the chief change agents of our society—the managers. Making it comprehensible and useable is the purpose of this book.

At this point, it is crucially important that I declare certain biases I have about OD, and to sketch out the nature of the framework I am offering, which is very different from the traditional OD practice of the past ten to twenty years. First, while traditional OD philosophy contends that only highly-trained, highly-"qualified" specialists, usually with academic training in psychology, should "practice" OD, I believe that any manager can understand and apply OD methods in some legitimate way in his or her organization. The services of a consultant may be very helpful, but they are optional.

Second, while traditional OD teaching holds that this specialist must be an outside party, i.e., a person whose role places him or her in an external position from the ongoing processes of the organization, I believe that a well-qualified member of the organization can also practice an honest and legitimate form of OD. As a management consultant, I am naturally biased toward the advantages of the "catalyst" role, but nonetheless I feel that the members of an organization or of any unit within it can put OD methods to use with good results.

Indeed, the "field" of OD seems to be shifting rapidly as more and more professional staff people in organizations, such as trainers and personnel people, get interested in OD techniques. At a recent national OD conference, I discovered that almost 75 percent of the paid attendees listed themselves as "OD Specialists" and worked as employees for organizations of various kinds. Possibly some of the "elite" of the OD field, those with extensive academic credentials in psychology, are grieving that OD has been more or less given away to the "great unwashed"—ordinary working people in organizations who don't know much about it. This may run counter to OD tradition, but it is a powerful fact that will have a very strong influence in shaping the OD field over the next decade or so. People in organizations don't want to be fully dependent on outside experts and shamans for their solutions; they want to learn to use the magic themselves, and they are going to do it. I predict that the primary concepts and methods of OD will soon become an accepted part of management theory, and that managers will increasingly discover them and incorporate them into their management practice.

A third and very crucial point is that, until recently, OD tradition held that OD is primarily an application of behavioral sciences principles by behavioral scientists to the social dimension of an organization's operation. Many OD practitioners stand steadfastly by the conviction that OD should deal only with the "human element" of the organization—that it has no business dealing with the mundane technical, operational, or administrative aspects of the operation with which managers have typically preoccupied themselves. It is here that I depart most radically from traditionally accepted OD thought. I believe that the term "organization" should imply an organization in all of its dimensions, not just in one selected dimension. Just as many managers and management educators have tended to ignore or overlook the human element of the organization, so I believe do many OD practitioners overlook the other obvious aspects of the organization which are inseparably interlocked with the human element. Managers and the professional staff people who support them want a complete methodology, not one built around only one aspect of their problems.

It may well be that those who have devoted the most creative energy to the development of the OD field have been psychologists and others with a distinctive educational and experiential bias toward the behavioral sciences. Since many of them know very little about management itself, and very little about the concrete aspects of production, administration, product design, marketing, finance, and the like, they may have tended toward a convenient definition of OD as a methodology limited to the things they do well.

Let's summarize these key points to give a sharp focus to the "brand" of organization development we will be dealing with in this book:

1. OD, as we will deal with it, is a comprehensive process of planned improvement in the overall functioning of an organization.
2. It can be carried out by managers in their organizations, with or without the assistance of specialized resource people, including consultants.
3. It can be carried out in some legitimate way, and to some reasonable extent, by key people within the organization who act in the specialized capacity of change agents.
4. It deals with, and attempts to improve, any aspect of the organization that needs fixing; it is not limited to psychological, behavioral, social, or "cultural" aspects of the organization; it is comprehensive.

It is important to emphasize again that this approach to organization development does not square completely with traditional OD thinking as it has been propounded and written by the leading spokespeople of the field. I have constructed this framework because I believe the traditional approach is becoming obsolete, because it has never really gained credibility with managers, and because it is being bypassed by a large number of practical-minded organizational people who are in need of a more comprehensive and workable approach. My investigation of the field of OD has convinced me that the only plausible future direction for it is in the direction of a comprehensive systems approach which can be understood and used by managers, internal OD specialists, and other human resources development people. This is the approach, the definition, and the framework offered in this book.

So, what do we have at this point in our exploration? We have a simple and practical definition of what we are talking about, a comprehensive approach toward it, and a de-mystified point of view on how to go about it. How, then, does one actually do organization development? Where does one start? We will give a brief answer to that question here and develop it in much greater depth in the following chapters. For our purposes, we can say that one usually does organization development by carrying out some form of the following steps:

1. Assessment—One makes a comprehensive and realistic appraisal of the key aspects of the organization to establish a "baseline" or "point A" starting condition against which to compare future results.

2. Problem-Solving—Then one decides what organizational improvements to make, assigns priorities to them, and develops a project plan for carrying them out; the plan defines "point B" and spells out how to reach it.

3. Implementation—One then gets to work on making the changes, many of which may take a long time and require a patient process of selling and facilitation; one uses whatever specific techniques and strategies that are needed to bring about the planned improvements in the organization's functioning.

4. Evaluation—Periodically, one reviews results against expectations; on-going reviews of progress, and occasional large-scale reviews, tell us where we are on the path between point "A" and point "B." On a larger scale, the evaluation stage can become the assessment stage of a new cycle.

This overall process may take anywhere from months to years, depending on how ambitious the program of planned improvement is. When management undertakes the process in a comprehensive and deliberate way, it becomes a legitimate project or program like any other, with its long-term and intermediate objectives, milestones and checkpoints, budget, reporting requirements, and management expectations. There is much more to the process than what we've covered so far, but this brief description should serve to dispel the mystery of it and to give an overall impression of how straightforwardly managerial an OD program can be.

2

Approaches and Resources for Developing Organizations

A BRIEF HISTORY
OF ORGANIZATION DEVELOPMENT

Because the area of OD is growing rapidly, because approaches to it are becoming more and more diversified, and because practitioners of OD often disagree substantially on how to do it, it is valuable to have a general understanding of the history of the field. By understanding the development of OD, you will be better able to judge for yourself the relative merits of its various methods and techniques. Equally as important, when you discuss OD with other people interested in the field, you will better understand how they are thinking about it. You may occasionally encounter an OD practitioner who lets you know, in so many words or by implication, that you don't understand "what OD *really* is," as if there were some universal, cosmically valid definition which you somehow failed to learn. To avoid feeling intimidated by purists who may not want to acknowledge that OD is becoming increasingly secularized, you can assure yourself that you have the right to propound whatever approach to OD that you choose to. There is no one definition, no one right approach, and no one "correct" method. There are many roads to Mecca.

Let's review briefly the early work done by some highly skilled and respected practitioners, see how views and values have shifted since then, and see why we presently stand in need of a comprehensive systems-oriented approach to OD.

In the middle and late 1940s, various behavioral scientists in the eastern United States were experimenting with training methods that might be used to help managers and others working in organizations to collaborate more effectively. They wanted to find training techniques that would equip their students to work better as managers of their various departmental teams and allow them to communicate and cooperate more effectively across organizational lines. From this work emerged a very strong interest among industrial psychologists in what came to be known as group dynamics. Psychologists like Kurt Lewin, Kenneth Benne, Leland Bradford, and Ronald Lippitt began to put together a theory of effective intra-group action as well as a theory of inter-group action. One of their training innovations was to provide feedback to the seminar participants at the end of each day's session, by commenting on various aspects of the behavior of individual participants and offering opinions about which behaviors were helpful and which were hindering to the purposes of the group. They found that the seminar participants generally received this kind of feedback positively and enthusiastically and that it tended to augment the learning from the lectures and seminars very effectively.

From these early experiments, the training techniques evolved to include situations in which participants not only learned concepts by listening to lectures but also engaged in direct task-oriented interactions with one another, and then studied the various aspects of their interaction. This came to be called the "laboratory" training technique because of the attempt to simulate various aspects of the "live" work situation in the training room and to conduct experiments to find out useful things about human interaction. Trainees would work together to solve some simulated management problem involving group dynamics, and afterwards they would analyze and discuss the various key aspects of their own processes, usually with the assistance of a trained psychologist or facilitator.

A number of psychologists were so taken with the potential of the laboratory method that they set up more or less permanent training centers and applied-research projects to develop the techniques further. One of the first of these was the National Training Laboratory, at the Gould Academy in Bethel, Maine. This center conducted intensive basic-skill training programs in group dynamics, emphasizing the use of structured interaction, as well as analysis and feedback, to help the participants become more aware of themselves, their feelings, their interactions with others, and some of the cause-and-effect relationships between the behavior of individual group members and the success of the group in accomplishing the work it had set out to do. These skill-training groups came to be called "T-Groups," a name which has survived for many years. In OD parlance, a T-Group generally means a learning-oriented group, often meeting for a series of sessions, under the guidance of a trained facilitator, with the purpose of studying its own internal dynamics in hopes that the managers can learn things that will be useful to them in future group situations back on the job.

Up until this point, about the middle 1950s, organization development had not yet emerged. The work of Lewin and the others had attracted a fair share of attention, and a variety of universities and industrial firms had experimented with laboratory training and T-Group techniques. There had been some attempts at training entire units or teams from the same company, and some theoreticians such as Robert Blake, Herbert Shepard, and the highly respected Douglas McGregor from MIT were working on the problem of getting the individual learning process to carry over into the organization at large when the trainees went back home.

There followed a decade or so of popularization, false hopes, and finally substantial disillusionment with the T-Group. At about the same time that industrial psychologists were developing group-dynamics training techniques, the famed Carl Rogers was developing the encounter group as a therapeutic technique. In an encounter group, Rogers or other psychologists he had trained would meet with a group of patients in a minimally structured setting. There was no particular task or project for the group to accomplish, nor was there any formal designation of leadership or roles for any of the individuals. The purpose was simply to discuss whatever the participants wanted to discuss and, during the process, to become aware of the various levels of interaction going on among them in the group situation. Rogers believed that, in this setting, people could discover important aspects of their own behavior patterns, and they could find out first-hand how other people saw them and responded to them, all in the context of a supportive therapeutic setting facilitated by a trained psychologist. This encounter-group setting, and the Rogerian philosophy behind it, became quite popular among many therapists, particularly paraprofessionals and counsellors who were not strongly oriented toward orthodox methods or "schools" of therapy.

These two lines of activity, the T-Group for training purposes and the encounter group for individual growth, seemed to come together very compatibly in certain sectors of the business world. For a period of about ten years or so, ranging from the late 1950s to the late 1960s, it became somewhat fashionable to have attended "sensitivity training," as the technique was then known. While the number of managers and professional people who have actually attended sensitivity groups is probably much smaller than the attention given to the phenomenon would suggest, there was indeed a phase during which many people thought that group-dynamics training techniques would virtually revolutionize industrial organizations. The notion was that, by participating in an intensive learning experience, such as a five-day "marathon" session locked up at a mountain retreat with a small group of strangers from other organizations and other parts of the country, a manager would become more "sensitive" to the human aspects of life and work. He would become more aware of his own feelings and the feelings of others; he would become more caring and supportive of others; and he would become, in general, a more humane person. This, according to the hypothesis, would lead him to return to his organization and treat people in much more positive, constructive, and supportive ways, thereby causing a contagion of humanistic attitudes and behavior among the other members of his organization. Some very large organizations, such as Esso (now Exxon), Union Carbide, and TRW Inc., were among the most substantial supporters of the use of these training techniques.

Unfortunately (or fortunately, depending on your point of view), the "sensitivity movement" came and went. While the highly publicized "growth group" was taking the limelight in the popular-psychology arena, leading to the phenomenal self-preoccupation of the "Me Decade" of the 1970s, the sensitivity group in the business world was passing out of vogue. Very few of the hoped-for epidemics of humanitarianism came about in industrial organizations. The phenomenon of "re-entry shock" became well known, as a process in which a person returning from the atmosphere of personal intimacy and emotional immediacy of the T-Group simply could not apply the techniques he had learned in the business environment. He could "feel" more, but he couldn't transfer that heightened emotional sensitivity—which itself tended to subside within a few days to a few weeks after the experience—to other people or to the problem-solving processes facing him. This led to considerable disillusionment with the sensitivity group. It simply didn't pay its way in the minds of hard-nosed managers who were shelling out the money.

Meanwhile, some psychologists and trainers were embarking on a new tack, that of taking the group-dynamics training techniques directly into the organization itself, on a consulting basis. Whereas various practitioners had tried to modify the "stranger-group" setting of the T-Group by putting whole management teams through these sessions—again, largely without significant success—these people began to focus on the groups themselves, as opposed to focusing on the individual members. They began to speak of "team training," "team building," and "organizational development." The idea was to blend in various other training techniques and consulting methods with the basic group-dynamics processes, in hopes of producing more effective organizations by the direct route rather than by relying on the process of interpersonal contagion.

At this point, roughly the late 1960s and early 1970s, the history of OD becomes a bit fuzzy, because many practitioners moved into the field, many theorists began to theorize, many writers began to write, and many academics began to teach various approaches, models, and methods. Many of the methods developed were organizational in nature, rather than individual or small-group focused. There developed a more or less scientific orientation among some practitioners and client organizations, characterized by the use of fact-finding techniques, analysis of organizations as complete social systems, and goal-oriented change processes based on the findings. One of the best known of these approaches was the survey research technique developed and refined by Dr. Rensis Likert at the University of Michigan. Likert had founded by Social Research Center there in 1946, and for many years spearheaded the development of questionnaires and other instruments intended to "measure" the human climate in organizations as well as practical psychology would allow.

Using the survey method, Likert and others helped the managers of client organizations assess the social climate through the perceptions, opinions, and viewpoints of the employees. Customarily, the consultant drew up an "attitude survey" in collaboration with the managers. He or she then distributed the questionnaire to all employees, usually including members of management as well, and collected the anonymous results. By asking people to express their ideas in the form of a numerical value between 1 and 5, signifying relative agreement with a given statement about some aspect of the organization, the researchers were able to compile the results in statistical form. The use of this "Likert-type scale," named after its pioneer, Rensis Likert, caught on rapidly and has become a widely used technique in constructing organizational surveys. The consultant then presented these results to the organization's management and assisted in interpreting the results. In most cases, management then shared the findings with the members of the organization. In the most successful cases, the data served as a starting point for dialogues between managers and employees to identify needed changes in the organization.

During the 1970s, OD as a field of endeavor became somewhat more clearly defined and somewhat orthodox in its principles, largely due to the writings and teachings of a relatively small group of practitioners and scholars who had the strongest influence in shaping it. Most of these people were psychologists, and as mentioned previously, they gave OD a distinctive psychological flavor. The more orthodox of these people defined OD rather rigorously as something practiced by degreed psychologists (or at least recognized practitioners who had "paid their dues" by long association with the field), working as external consultants to organizations and aiming at making significant changes in the basic "culture" of the organization. They also defined organizational culture as the total arrangement of power, values, norms, and rewards existing in the organization at any given time. This gave OD a very strong sociological orientation, from which it has only recently begun to recover.

Presently, the field of OD seems to be undergoing a significant upheaval, as more and more people with diverse points of view lay claim to a stake in the concept and the methodology. One of the most significant, and so far unrecognized, elements of the new field of OD is the large number of organizational trainers and personnel people who have taken a liking to the overall notion of developing effective organizations and who are trying to invent and apply various techniques without the help of the orthodox practitioners. The needs and values of this large and growing group of people, very few of whom have formal credentials in the area, will probably become the strongest single factor shaping the field in the next decade.

As a result of the current upheaval, and the unprecedented involvement of all of these "amateurs," the field of OD is now up for grabs. Managers and internal human-resources-development specialists are becoming developers of organizations in their own ways, and the field will now probably develop and diversify rapidly.

THE "ACTION-RESEARCH" TECHNIQUE

The action-research technique gets frequent mention in discussion of OD by traditional scholars and practitioners, and it is well worth knowing about for anyone interested in OD. The term apparently arose during the early 1960s to fill the need for a practical, yet scientific-sounding name to describe what OD people did. Applying the action-research technique simply means carrying out a two-step cyclic process of:

1. Fact finding, or "diagnosis," through the use of surveys, interviews, and other forms of data-gathering; and then a process of—
2. Implementation, or administering the "prescription" for needed change, based on the evaluation of the results of the fact-finding process.

This is an especially useful concept, or "model" as behavioral scientists like to call it, because it introduces into management thinking a more or less scientific orientation. It legitimizes the process of investigating the current status of an organization, and of proceeding from facts and intelligent speculations rather than from pure "gut judgment."

This is no trivial point, in my view. It is remarkable how few practicing managers are truly committed to a fact-finding approach in dealing with organizational problems. Many managers will simply "sniff the wind" and proceed to make substantial changes in their organizations, without the slightest authoritative basis in facts. Often times a consultant, in working with such a manager, must insist on a careful first step of defining "point A," by a reasonably disciplined investigative process, before proceeding to prescribe solutions. Otherwise an impulsive manager may waste energy and resources trying to solve a nonexistent problem and, in the process, make an existing problem worse.

An OD truism holds that *"Prescription without diagnosis is malpractice, whether it be in medicine or management."*

OTHER CONTEMPORARY
OD APPROACHES

Although the action-research technique is by far the most widely known of the contemporary OD approaches, it is helpful to understand some of the other formulas used by OD people. Here we will review briefly several of them to get a better idea of how OD specialists think and talk. We can incorporate any or all of these approaches in our bag of tricks for systems-oriented OD.

The concept of *diffusion* involves the notion that, when someone implements a useful action, method, or procedure somewhere in an organization, other people who see it in action and who interact with the people doing it will take a liking to it and begin to use it themselves. Deliberate use of diffusion can play a very significant part in an overall organizational-change strategy. For example, if we want the professional staff members of a company to become more objectives-oriented in approaching their jobs, we might work together on a one-to-one basis with some of them, helping them to analyze their key result areas and set goals. In dealing with their colleagues, these key people can serve as effective role-models, and they can persuade others, to some extent, to adopt the same practices. Some organization development programs have used the diffusion approach very extensively as a primary means of change.

The concept of *linkages* is similar to the diffusion approach and is much more systematic and directed in the way it works. Using this technique, we enlist the help of certain willing people in various strategically chosen places in the organization to act as sales people or local change agents in promoting specific changes and introducing new practices. For example, the members of a special task force working on reducing conflict between two major divisions of a government agency might serve as local promoters of collaboration by getting specific individuals together occasionally, helping them to exchange information, and taking the initiative in getting agreement on key issues.

Another descriptive schema, dealing with the overall OD process, is well known to OD specialists although it is less directly useful to managers. This schema is based on the flow of events in an OD program as seen through the eyes of the external consultant, "catalyst" person, or change agent. Its five stages are:

1. Entry—The consultant becomes initially involved with the organization; the expectations surrounding his or her involvement are not yet established.

2. Sensing—The consultant proceeds to "look around," with the endorsement of the leaders of the organization; he or she tries to form an impression of the organization's present "culture" and to identify avenues for improving it.

3. Lock-on—The consultant and the organization's leaders jointly recognize one or more high-priority aspects of the organization's internal circumstances that they believe warrant a concentrated program of planned change.

4. Implementation—The organization, with the assistance of the consultant, undertakes a development program, using the action-research method or any equivalent approach that results in planned improvement.

5. Separation—On the notion that the eventual goal of the consultant is to eliminate the need for his presence, he works with the managers of the organization to make the new processes permanent and consultant-independent; this leads to an amicable separation, possibly with occasional return visits for long-term reassessment of the situation.

Each of these angles of view on the OD process has something to recommend it. These and others of the many concepts and techniques developed over the years will serve us well as we integrate a systems-oriented approach to OD throughout the rest of this book. When we have completed the trip, we can expect to have a comprehensive, easy-to-understand, practical, and useable approach which managers and staff people in organizations can learn and apply.

THREE MAJOR TRENDS IN OD PRACTICE

At this point, we must begin to make choices about how we will go about formulating our own brand of OD. We have reviewed the development of OD as it has come to its present style in the hands of contemporary specialists, and we have looked at a variety of their approaches and techniques. In order to make sense of the many other techniques the field has to offer, and to bring in other useful techniques, we need to choose some framework for our thinking. We need some organizing system, which can incorporate a large part of what we know about organizations and help us decide what we want to do with it.

This organizing framework has been missing in OD ever since its inception. This, in my view, is the primary reason it has failed to catch on in a significant way with executives and managers of many organizations over the past thirty years. Many managers, staff professionals, trainers, and personnel people say, "I don't think I really understand OD. What is it, really? I have a hard time getting a handle on it." They know, of course, that it is a method for bringing about planned changes in organizations, but beyond that it seems to have a frustratingly fuzzy character. It seems to be basically a consulting specialty rather than a management technology. Unless they read a fair amount of the literature of the subject, they can't really picture it in action.

Probably, the behavioral scientists who developed much of the early OD practice saw little need to explain it in lay terms or to relate it to managerial perceptions of the organization. Many of them did indeed conceive of it as a process they brought to the organization—something no one in the organization was qualified to do or understand. I call this the "shaman syndrome." As a matter of fact, many of the early OD efforts by consultants, and possibly a number of recent ones, were really research projects aimed at learning about group dynamics in general, more than they were aimed at helping managers manage better. I suspect that some of these projects were more important to the consultants (especially to some who were academics) because of the papers they could write about them, than because of the needs of the people in the organizations they were supposed to serve.

I have also noted a trace of intellectual arrogance from time to time in much of the OD literature written by academics and scholarly practitioners. Many books and articles describe OD programs and activities with very little reference to the managers of the client organizations and thereby give the impression that the managers are virtually insignificant. One of the popular slogans among some practitioners is "The system is the client." Taken to extremes, this can become a snobbish attitude that says, "I, the OD consultant, know what is best for this organization: I will make the necessary repairs to this needy human system, and the part its management plays in the process is minimal." I call this the "messiah complex." If my appraisal is correct, it means that this very attitude toward managers, who after all are the primary sources of authority and resources in the organization, has prevented the traditional OD approach from gaining acceptance as a potential management technology.

The decision we have to make at this point, in working out an approach to OD for our purposes, is the choice between a priest-centered form of OD and a secular form of OD. Does OD belong to the behavioral scientist or to the manager? All of the comments offered so far should give a pretty clear impression of the avenue I recommend: the secular approach. But to go this way, we will have to recognize clearly that we are breaking away once and for all from the mainstream of OD history and contemporary OD practice. I've predicted that this new secularized form of OD will rapidly outgrow and outpace the traditional form, but let's keep in mind that at this point the strongest voices are saying that OD belongs to the high priests of the field.

My investigation of current trends in OD leads me to speculate that the field is figuratively "flying apart" into three major "pieces," or, if you prefer, three "schools of thought." Three relatively disparate points of view are separately coalescing and becoming more clearly identified. Two of them are predominantly priest-centered, and the third is management-centered. The third, or management-centered approach, is the one I am propounding in this book. Let's review the three major trends as they seem to be developing:

1. The *Group-Dynamics School*—the historical and traditional approach to OD; a consultant works at the small-group level, using T-Group methods, encounter techniques, sensitivity training, and related approaches aiming at changing behavior in these situations.

2. The *Behavior-Modification School*—an emerging new trend in which trained psychologists work with managers to rearrange the reward system in the organization in order to reinforce selected "target" behaviors on the part of the employees; this approach to OD uses the behavior-shaping principles as operant conditioning, that were developed by Harvard psychologist B.F. Skinner.

3. The *Systems School*—a very new and secularized approach to OD in which managers or other change agents examine the organization in all of its important dimensions, not merely the social dimension, and undertake whatever constructive changes in its functioning they are able to bring about, considering the realities of their authority, resources, and expertise.

As a consultant, trainer, and author, I place myself squarely in the systems school of OD. Although most people do not, at this point, realize that there even is a systems school, nevertheless this is what many of them have been craving—the development of a systematic methodology for comprehensive organizational improvement. This book, I believe is one of the first efforts to propound the systems approach, especially an approach not considered constrained to behavioral science techniques, and to prescribe methods for implementing it. I believe that this systems school, or some version of it, will become the primary approach to OD over the next decade.

Let's examine each of these three schools of OD in somewhat greater depth.

THE GROUP-DYNAMICS SCHOOL OF OD

The group-dynamics school has the longest history as an OD approach, and it currently enjoys the widest acceptance. It has by far the most extensive body of literature. Adherents of this school consider the primary OD activity to be process consultation to the small group. This means that the consultant sits in on group meetings with people, observes their interpersonal processes, and offers comments on significant aspects of their interactions. This may also extend to facilitating certain more skillful ways of working together. The techniques used may range from psychologically "safe" activities such as guided discussion all the way to highly intensive, emotionally charged encounter-group activities.

The group-dynamics school does not necessarily exclude or reject from its approaches the broader aspects of organizational problem-solving. However, adherents of this avenue of consulting tend to arrive sooner or later at small-group activity as their preferred method for attacking the problems that surface during the diagnosis phase. The more orthodox practitioners of this school tend to approach what is commonly called team building by means of encounter—or sensitivity—group techniques. They prefer the emotional immediacy of the encounter setting to the "cognitive" processes involved in discussion, analysis of problems, and conventional skill-building.

The most influential institutions in this particular arena seem to be the NTL Institute for Applied Behavioral Science (originally founded as National Training Laboratories) and the publishing firm of University Associates, which distributes by far the largest share of OD literature.

The technique of behavior modification, widely nicknamed "be-mod," was pioneered by B.F. Skinner at Harvard University, during the 1930s and 1940s. Skinner extended the findings of the Russian psychologist Ivan Pavlov, who became famous for his study of the conditioned-response phenomenon. Pavlov's research showed that a dog could be trained to salivate at the sound of a bell. Of course, the dog had heard the bell ring and simultaneously had been presented with food many times before, and it was the food that originally made it salivate. Skinner's research with rats and other laboratory animals led him to the point of view that *all behavior is, in the long term, a function of its consequences.* By simply observing which of the immediate consequences of an animal's behavior led to more or less of that particular behavior (a pigeon pecking at a colored button, for example), he felt one could identify certain controllable consequences (such as having the button trigger the dispensing of a grain of corn for the pigeon to eat) which could be used to shape the behavior. Skinner spent many years working out the particulars of this theory and developed a set of principles that psychologists widely acknowledge as workable in deliberately shaping the behavior of human beings as well as laboratory animals. Skinnerian conditioning has found its way into theories of child-raising, therapy for severely disturbed people, rehabilitation of delinquents and criminals, and—only recently–changing the behavior of people in organizations.

The ethical ramifications of applying these techniques in managing the activities of human beings in the industrial setting are beyond the scope of this discussion, although they are indeed profound. For the sake of this discussion, we will simply review the basic process of behavior shaping as it is currently being applied in a small number of organizations, usually through the services of a consulting psychologist. The be-mod technique usually works in the following way:

1. Specifying—The consultants identify the specific employee behaviors that they and the managers choose to change; this usually involves increasing some observable behavior, such as arriving on time, filling out shipping documents accurately, protecting products from damage during handling, or keypunching a larger number of cards per shift.

2. Observing—The consultants (and possibly trained managers or staff people) study current behavior of the employees and construct graphs and tables which show the frequency and extent of the behavior (for example, how many people arrive before the starting bell each day?).

3. Changing Consequences—The consultants and managers then systematically introduce "reinforcers," such as recognition, comments by supervisors in praise of the new behavior, or even concrete rewards such as money or incentive items, all of which are aimed at increasing the frequency of the desired behavior.

The approach is cyclic; that is, the psychologist and the managers continue to observe the behavior and keep changing the consequences until they find the most effective reinforcer—the thing they can say, do, or provide that has the strongest positive effect on the employees' behavior.

Recently, a number of consulting psychologists have begun to adapt these techniques to organizations in ways similar to those just described and to train managers in using them. A major objective in this field is to develop approaches for changing employee behavior on a large scale, as an OD approach, i.e., a methodology for improving overall organizational effectiveness by scientifically shaping the behavior of the members of the work force.

My prediction for the behavior-modification school of OD is that it will gain favor in some limited circles, but that its essentially manipulative overtones will make it forever suspect among most business managers. It may shift into a less clinical, more humane orientation, or it may merge with other avenues of OD practice.

THE SYSTEMS SCHOOL OF OD

The newly emerging point of view on organization development, which forms the basis for this book, is that we can apply a straightforward "systems approach" to improving the overall effectiveness of the organization. Such a systems approach would have several advantages over the forms of OD practiced historically and discussed so far in this book. These advantages include:

1. Less of a preoccupation with emotionality and more attention given to the familiar forms of activity actually found among business people engaged in their day's work.

2. Approaching OD in the form of a concrete project, or program, like any other development program that is part of the legitimate activity of the organization; less reliance on ad hoc "groping" approaches with few pre-established goals or outcomes.

3. A broader scope of effort, which takes into account all kinds of problem-solving activities, including those dealing with "technical" problems, productivity, profit-oriented improvements, organizational strategy, administrative efficiency, and organizational structure, in addition to the traditional specialized focus on the human climate and on interpersonal relationships.

4. A procedure and a set of methods that managers and staff-support people, including internal OD specialists with modest training in the behavioral sciences, can put to use with good results; a step-wise process which the leaders of the organization can recognize, appreciate, and endorse.

5. A vocabulary which is comprehensible to managers, and a simple "theory" which they can explain in their own words.

6. A means for thinking about the organization in a systematic and comprehensive way, and for discussing it in management-oriented terms.

This systems school of OD is based, first, on a view of the organization as a total system composed of several basic subsystems (one of which is traditional OD's "human" or "social" system); and second, on a way of describing and evaluating these subsystems to determine what constructive changes we need to make in them in order to improve their functioning. It leads naturally to the four-step process previously described: assessment, problem-solving, implementation, and evaluation. We can, without too great a risk of oversimplification, regard these four steps or phases as a basic "recipe" for organization development. They form a closed cycle, and they can become the readily manageable stages of an OD program which management can carry out.

As previously mentioned, the rapidly increasing appetite for a readily applied form of secular OD technique, especially among internal OD people working in staff positions in organizations, suggests that this systems approach will become the mainstream of organization development within the next decade.

3

A New Systems View of the Organization

AN INTRODUCTION TO SYSTEMS THINKING

In this chapter we will develop a way of thinking about an organization—any organization—that will serve as a foundation for a systems approach to OD. This particular thinking process is crucial to an effective understanding of organizations and of the many possibilities open to us in developing them. Therefore, it behooves us to proceed carefully and deliberately at this point.

Let's assume for a moment that you are a manager in an organization. You might be located anywhere between the first level of the executive family and the chief executive officer's chair. Whether or not this is true of you, or whether you even aspire in that direction is less important than the kind of perspective that imaginary position will give you in understanding OD. Even if you are an internal OD specialist or a human resources person, looking at the organization through the eyes of top management can be most instructive.

To understand the systems approach, you must first ask yourself how comfortable you are with the term "system" and how familiar you are with the idea of a system. If you tend to be a highly concrete thinker, you might find the idea of an organization as a system somewhat awkward and mechanical, since you may only be familiar with tangible physical systems such as computer systems, plumbing systems, or filing systems. If you do not presently think fluently in terms of other, more abstract systems, now is the time to learn. If you are familiar with systems thinking, so much the better. For the purposes of this discussion, I will make the safest assumption—that you are a little rusty at this kind of systems thinking, and that a conceptual warm-up will help.

You probably use the term "system" more freely than you realize to describe many different kinds of systems of which you are more or less aware. You may speak of your own body, for example, as a system. You have probably often said something like, "My system is a little out of kilter today," meaning, of course, one of your subsystems, such as your digestive tract. It is perfectly reasonable to use the terms system and subsystem interchangeably, as long as no confusion results. So, you can indeed conceive of a part of your body as a system, even though you have probably never seen it.

You might also say, "I've worked out a good system for keeping track of the projects I have to accomplish." In this case, your system is likely to be somewhat abstract; it might consist of a checklist or a diagram, as well as a few other thinking tools, and probably a well-defined set of functions which they help you perform. If someone asked to see your system in that case, you could probably show them a few tangible aspects of it, but a large portion of it would be abstractly represented, consisting of procedures, sequences of action, and relationships among them. So, you probably already feel competent to think about systems in somewhat larger terms, such as organizations, involving somewhat abstract features.

What is a system anyway, just for the record? We can define a system as having:

1. Some components, usually tangible but not always, that comprise it.
2. Functions and processes performed by these various components.
3. Relationships among the components that uniquely bind them together into a conceptual assembly which you are willing to call a system.

4. An "organizing principle," which is an overall concept that gives it a purpose.

Let's take, for example, the "registration system" for students at a college. We could list its components as the course catalog, the enrollment forms, the file cabinets that contain the records, the computer program that matches student requests with available classes, the key people who handle the various steps involved, enrollment lists, and student class-verification notices. We can include other components in this perceived system if we like, depending on what aspects we want to study and what we intend to do with the results.

The functions going on in this particular system include receiving student requests, making file copies of them, entering the data into the computer system, retrieving the results and reviewing them, preparing enrollment lists, and sending class-verification notices to the students. The relationships among the components of the system are more abstract than the functions, but still comprehensible. These include relationships such as one person providing data to another, i.e., the two of them relate to one another as giver and receiver in distinctive roles. Similarly, the student class-verification notice has a specific relationship to the enrollment lists for the various classes; the data for one of them comes directly from the others. Note that, without necessarily being cold-blooded, we include the people as "components" of the system. This just gives us an easy way to think comprehensively about what is going on in the situation we are studying.

Why is this systems-oriented way of looking at the student-registration process useful? Because it gives us a way to analyze and evaluate all of the important aspects of student registration in logical relationship to one another. If the director of registration asked you to analyze the registration process and to make recommendations for improving its efficiency, you could diagram all of the aspects in relationship to one another on a piece of paper and use it as a thinking tool, a discussion tool, and a problem-solving rool. You could inspect each of the components, review each of the functions, and examine all of the key relationships, looking for missing pieces, malfunctioning processes, or important relationships in need of rearranging. Then you could improve or redefine the system to make it accomplish its purposes better. This process, in its simplest form, is "systems analysis." It is the very same process we will apply in our systems approach to organization development.

I hope the preceding tutorial discussion of systems thinking has not insulted your intelligence. If you are one of the relatively small number of readers who have had extensive exposure to systems thinking and systems analysis, you may have found it amusingly simplified. However, if you are like the majority of professional people, you can probably grasp the reasoning process readily enough, but you might not have come up with it on your own.

Systems thinking is a comparatively rare phenomenon in the business world, and it is a skill well worth developing. Many managers proceed habitually on a "seat-of-the-pants" basis, dealing with whatever concrete aspects of their organizations they can readily perceive, disinclined to lay out a systematic description of the entire enterprise and its processes. As we noted previously in the discussion of the pitfalls of mainline management, too narrow a view leads to too narrow a range of solutions to the problems at hand. The manager who cannot conceive of an organization as a system in its entirety, who cannot think systematically about its human dimensions as well as its more tangible technical processes, and who is not comfortable in dealing with its abstract features as well as its concrete features will be limited to solutions that are concrete, familiar, and obvious. The manager who can figuratively step back and look at the entire enterprise as an interesting, multifarious, interconnected system can deal with its problems more effectively, manage it more effectively, and change it more effectively when it is in need of change.

THE CONCEPT OF A SOCIOTECHNICAL SYSTEM

For a long time, managers and management theorists have felt fairly comfortable in thinking about organizations as more or less "technical" systems. Much of management education in universities and in industrial training programs portrays the organization as a unified collection of "boxes" on a chart. The boxes, which have names to describe their general functions, are arranged to show hierarchical relationships (the "chain of command") among one another. The chart invites one to think of the entire enterprise as a logical framework for allocating resources. The familiar organization chart is actually a systems diagram, very much like the kinds of diagrams systems analysts use. So, the technical-systems view of management has been around for quite some time.

Since the late 1930s and 1940s, behavioral scientists interested in organizational behavior—the behavior of people as organizational creatures—have been trying to make a case for teaching managers to perceive and think about a "human system" as well. This human or social system would include all of the people as "components," and it would account for their activities and relationships toward one another over and above their job functions which are described in the context of the technical system. The key variables in the social system are authority, values, norms, and rewards. The idea is to conceive of the social system as intertwined with the technical system, and sharing many of its components, so that one can think about one system or the other, or both, depending on the kind of problem one is trying to solve.

All of this systems talk might seem a bit abstract to you if you are not accustomed to discussing organizations this way. But it becomes very clear and concrete when you take a close look at an actual business organization, say a large hotel. As a traveling customer of the hotel, you may not have conceived of it as an organization, but indeed it is. A major hotel is much more than a building. It typically has a sales staff, an administrative department, a housekeeping department, a maintenance department and a full-fledged chief executive officer with a support staff. Organizing and managing all of these activities so that you and several hundred other guests are properly taken care of is quite an undertaking, and it requires a highly systematic form of management. The next time you find yourself in a large hotel, take a few moments to look around. Study the operation from the business standpoint, and trace out the technical system that forms its primary productive axis. Then look for evidence of the social system—the people, and the ways in which they relate to one another and to the management. This kind of an investigation can help you make the bridge between the abstract level, where you can think about the organization from the broadest point of view, to the concrete level, where you directly experience its realities. You will find it helpful to train yourself to switch fluently between these two levels: the level of systems thinking and the level of direct experience.

The dominant trend emerging in the management field since the beginning of the 1970s has been the approach that attempts to combine these two systems views into the single notion of a "sociotechnical system." The compound word "sociotechnical" implies that we want to think of the two key aspects of the organization, the human and the technical, as closely interrelated. We want to keep them both in mind and remember that a change in one may have an important effect on the other. So far, these two systems don't seem to stay too well "glued" together of their own accord in management thinking, probably because of the extensive history of management education which has stressed the technical view almost to the exclusion of the human view. Also, the primary spokespeople for the human view have been mostly psychologists rather than managers, and they have largely lacked the credibility necessary to put the point across.

Management education and training has begun to shift markedly since the 1970s, and the sociotechnical view is becoming much more prevalent. More and more managers have begun to learn about the applied behavioral sciences and concern themselves in a serious way with merging this knowledge with the more conventional management concepts. We will draw extensively on the concept of the sociotechnical system in this book, as we explore the systems-oriented approach to organization development.

THE FOUR KEY SYSTEMS OF AN ORGANIZATION

Now we come to the foundation of the systems approach to organization development: a way of describing the organization as an overall system, composed of four subsystems, so that we can think about it effectively, analyze it, identify needed improvements in its overall functioning, and put them into effect. For our discussion, we will use the terms "system" and "subsystem" interchangeably; that is, we will refer to the overall organization as a system, and we will also call each of the four components a system. This will keep our terminology simple, without running any great risk of confusion.

A word of caution is in order, before we proceed, to make sure we avoid going off on an intellectual tangent in describing organizations as systems. A person with a rather compulsive orientation to systems thinking could easily become engrossed for the rest of his or her life in diagramming out an organization in terms of all of its perceptible components, functions, and relationships. Some people do indeed thrive on this kind of activity, but our needs are much more modest. Rather than take the systems view to great levels of detail, we will simply sketch out the general nature of each of the four organizational systems and then proceed to use practical judgment, intuition, and common sense in putting these general descriptions to use. So, we are not seeking a highly elaborate, detailed description of each system. Rather, we will use the notion of a system somewhat loosely, more along the lines of a metaphor, or a figurative way of talking. Our emphasis will be more on getting a clear understanding of these four key dimensions of the organization than on intellectualizing about their details.

The next several chapters will describe the four key systems fairly comprehensively. At this point, we shall simply list them and define them briefly. They are:

1. The Technical System—the elements, activities, and relationships that make up the primary productive axis of the organization; this system may include physical facilities, machinery, special equipment, work processes, methods and procedures, work-oriented information and various media for handling it, and the people themselves from the point of view of the parts they play in the processes. This is the concrete, "un-human" view of the organization, which we need to integrate with the human and other aspects.

2. The Social System—the people of the organization, including the managers, and the activities they engage in over and above the work processes of the technical system; their roles and relationships with one another, including forms of authority and status; this system also includes the values, norms for behavior, and reward/punishment processes—basically, all the aspects of their "citizenship" in the organization. If the term "system" sounds too mechanistic or inhuman in this case, just call this the social "dimension" of the organization.

3. The Administrative System—the information media and the paths along which information flows; policies, procedures, instructions, reports, and the like, that are required to operate the organization itself, over and above those required to operate the technical system; also, those people who participate in and directly operate the administrative apparatus.

4. The Strategic System—the management "family" of the organization, from the chief executive to the lowest formally-appointed supervisor; the chain of command, reporting relationships, and the power values of the leaders of the organization; also plans, the planning process, and the procedures these people use in governing the organization and adapting it to the future.

Figure 3–1 diagrams the interrelationships of these four overlapping and interlocking systems. Note that a manager belongs to each of the four systems, either by virtue of his or her special role, or simply by

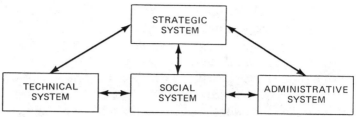

FIGURE 3–1   An Organization Is Composed of Four Interlocking "Systems"

virtue of being a member of the organization. The strategic system is basically the "moving force" for the organization. This is why managers are potentially the most effective change agents and organization developers; they control the resources, the plans, and the priorities. What the managers do affects all of the organization's systems.

THE "MISPLACED FIX" SYNDROME

Let's begin to put this systems view of the organization to practical use. Throughout the book we will be studying one or more of the key systems most of the time, and we will be searching for ways to diagnose their needs to improve their functioning. Let's look at some of the ways this systems view can help managers manage more effectively.

One of the most common causes of organizational ineffectiveness, and one of the most common ways in which managers can make a bad situation worse, is by trying to repair the wrong system. I call this the "misplaced fix syndrome."

Without an accurate understanding of the systems in the organization, a manager may be tempted to make changes that not only fail to relieve the pain, but in some cases may actually aggravate it. A case in point comes to mind: a large county agency, staffed by over 2000 professional and clerical workers. I was engaged by the director of one of the two major divisions of the agency to undertake a program to bring the philosophy and practice of management by objectives into the organization. Management saw the possibility of clarifying the sense of direction (strategic system), communicating the direction more clearly to the work force in order to improve organizational performance (technical system), and improving a disastrously low level of

*(social system)

51

morale by fostering a participative and candid problem-solving atmosphere (social system).

So far, so good. As this program was getting under way, the director of the other major division of the agency decided to implement an "MBO system" in his organization without consulting support. He formed a small task force to set up a system of written performance measures, operational goals, unit plans, and progress reports. This executive was described by his colleagues and subordinate executives as a "professional administrator." With a strong administrative background, and relatively little management training or training in the applied behavioral sciences, he approached the organizational "fix" through the administrative system, rather than through the strategic, social, and technical systems. He perceived "MBO" as an administrative solution to an administrative problem. I learned later, after morale in that division had taken a further nose dive, that his primary motive in implementing the system was to increase the centralization of his authority over the geographically-dispersed community offices and to bring a group of young and aggressive district directors into line. Here was an organization in which the social system desperately needed fixing. One executive applied a social solution—fairly successfully, under the prevailing circumstances—while the other executive applied an administrative solution—with disastrous results.

You can find many similar cases of misplaced emphasis in organizations. The phenomenon seems to stem from a relative lack of management awareness of the four key systems of the organization and a lack of appreciation of the impact each of them can have on the organization's overall effectiveness if it is out of kilter. When the organization's managers lack the broad view, they tend to center their attention on the most familiar, most demanding, and most readily "repairable" system—the technical system. More than one time-and-motion study (technical system) has triggered a walkout by angry production workers (social system).

Instances of misapplying a social fix to a technical problem are considerably more rare than the inverse case and are generally confined to OD practitioners. This is reminiscent of what Abraham Maslow called the "hammer syndrome." According to Maslow, *"When the only tool you have is a hammer, you tend to treat everything as if it were a nail."* This commonly happens in OD when a person with an overspecialized set of qualifications—the T-Group "hammer," for example—goes looking for things to pound on. In a certain number of cases, the social fix is what the organization needs, and the T-Group method may fill the bill, or at least form a part of the solution. In other cases, a T-Group specialist might sell the managers of an organization on a sensitivity training program (social fix) when what they need is to divest themselves of an entire division of their operation (strategic fix), or to redesign certain manufacturing processes (technical fix), or to reorganize the company (administrative fix). The existence of conflict among the people in an organization does not prove that the social system needs fixing directly, despite what some traditional OD practitioners might insist. Many kinds of system malfunctions can give rise to inter-unit and interpersonal conflict, which have side effects in the social system.

I hope, from the foregoing discussion, that you have extracted one key point: common sense and the scientific method dictate that we first find out which system really needs adjustment before we start trying to apply solutions. Please reflect, again and again, on the significance of this point. An accurate diagnosis of the need is absolutely essential to organization development.

To repeat the basic OD truism: "Prescription without diagnosis is malpractice, whether it be in medicine or in management."

THE "PARADOXICAL REWARD" SYNDROME

One of the aspects of organizations that management consultants find most intriguing is the reward system. The reward system can be considered a subsystem, actually, of the social system. For convenience, we shall continue to use the simplified term "system" to refer to both. It is at one and the same time fascinating and flabbergasting to see how often the managers of organizations inadvertently construct or evolve punishment systems rather than reward systems, and how often they are dangerously out of touch with the real reward and punishment dynamics of their organizations as perceived by the employees.

A case in point: in the midst of a hectic project undertaken by an aerospace firm, which involved putting together an extensive and elaborate technical proposal in a competition for a multi-million-dollar defense contract, the proposal team leaders discovered that the manufacturing department literally could not estimate with any degree of confidence how many hours of manufacturing labor would be required to fabricate the various subassemblies of the system they were proposing. This was true even though the system they were proposing to the government was a modified version of a production unit they were currently manufacturing for the same agency. How could this be? One would think that, with modern methods of production scheduling, record-keeping, and cost accounting, a manufacturing supervisor would be able to produce hourly labor figures for the various printed-circuit boards, amplifiers, and antennas they had made over the previous several years. Surely, with these data, they could look at a new or modified unit and say, "This circuit card is similar to card number LMN in System B. Allowing for 5 percent more labor and 5 percent more in materials cost, we can use the historical data to arrive at an estimate of the manufacturing cost of this new item." They couldn't.

This sounds like a problem in the technical system, right? Wrong. The team leaders traced it to a malfunction in the social system, specifically in the reward system. A close investigation showed that the manufacturing supervisors had not been keeping accurate labor-hour records for a good (to them) reason. Whenever they had periods of slack work in their departments, usually due to irregularities in the production schedules and back-ups due to occasional production problems downstream of their units, they would have a certain number of their employees relatively idle, without production work to do. The manufacturing vice president criticized the supervisors severely for having these people "on overhead," i.e., charging their time to the division overhead account which came out of the vice president's budget rather than direct-charging them to the product work orders which came out of the product-line managers' budgets. He threatened layoffs if the supervisors couldn't keep their people off the overhead account. The supervisors, knowing that they couldn't locate and hire highly-skilled electronic assemblers on a few days' notice to meet the expected upsurge in work when the production jam cleared, did the best thing they knew.

You probably guessed it. They simply allocated the total number of labor hours they had on the staff each day to the total number of parts that passed through their units, divided the total number of hours by the total number of parts, and recorded this data as the fictional labor-cost of making each unit. This defense tactic, aimed at protecting their workers (social system), resulted in completely corrupting labor-cost data (technical system). In some cases the phoney "cost" to produce the same item varied by as much as 200 percent, depending on the intensity of the production workload.

This is a classic case of "asking for A and rewarding B," a phenomenon known to organizational psychologists as *paradoxical reward*. The executives wanted accurate and reliable cost data, yet they had constructed a reward system—or, more accurately, a punishment system—that incentivized the creation of dangerously unreliable data. A more enlightened approach would have been for top management to allocate to the manufacturing budget a category for labor slack, based on reasonable historical estimates of the need. This administrative fix would have prevented a problem in the technical system, and it would have improved the climate in the social system.

Think about the organization in which you work. Have you seen similar or equivalent instances of paradoxical reward—asking for A and incentivizing B? This kind of schizophrenic value system is all too common in organizations. It is no exaggeration to say that, in probably well over half of the organizations in the business world, the overall reward system—the sum total of what you get for what you do—is seriously out of whack. It is also reasonable to contend that relatively few managers, including chief executives, have ever taken a comprehensive and systematic look at the overall reward system they have created (or allowed to evolve), including social and psychological rewards as well as monetary rewards.

For the purposes of understanding the reward-system concept, let's state the obvious, which obviously isn't obvious to many managers: whatever people do in an organization over the long term is what their environment has incentivized them to do; whatever they fail to do or have stopped doing is what their environment has punished, discouraged, or prevented them from doing.

One of the hallmarks of the manager who doesn't understand organizational reward and punishment is the statement, "You just can't get good people any more." He is willing to assume that all of the people in this particular work force are somehow inferior to the general populace and that he was simply unlucky enough to get stuck with them. A more reasonable statement would be, "We need to eliminate the organizational circumstances that push people into acting in such-and-such a way and substitute new circumstances that will invite them to act in this new way." An understanding of these aspects of reward systems is essential to an understanding of the organization as a sociotechnical system, and it forms a very important part of the systems approach to OD.

INTER-SYSTEM CONFLICTS

The systems approach to thinking about the organization helps to clarify certain situations in which the priorities of one of the four systems conflict with the priorities of another. We have had an inkling of this in the preceding discussion of paradoxical reward. Some additional concrete examples will help to lend emphasis to the notion that each of the systems is important in its own right, and that none should be continually ignored or given undue preference over another.

A common form of inter-system conflict, and often an unnecessary one, is the question of people versus profit. For example, the owner of a small company may adhere rigorously to a policy of paying the absolute minimum wages possible and accepting turnover among the employees as a part of the package. The profit line (technical system) gets top priority, and the people-dimension can go hang. However, the choice is not really so simple in the long run, even in terms of strict bottom-line consequences.

For example, a condition of low wages generally leads to low commitment on the part of the employees toward the company and its executives, and usually high turnover as well, unless jobs are in short supply. High turnover means that, if the company is in a growth mode or at least situated in a growth market, there will be a shortage of well-developed leaders to choose from as it expands in size. The owner will probably always be able to find somebody willing to take a supervisory job, but not many people with very much background, experience in the company's work, and commitment to the enterprise. We could argue, although admittedly without concrete proof, that this technical-system policy of minimizing labor costs will have social-system effects that will impinge on the other systems, such as weak management, low morale, limited productivity, and possibly personnel shortages during growth surges. These social effects will reflect back to the technical system in terms of higher overall operating costs due to ineffectiveness, and lost profits due to the inability of the organization to respond well to its market.

Some of the classical blunders committed in the name of "management by objectives" fall into the category of conflicts between the administrative system and the strategic system. When managers get fascinated with the idea of an "MBO system," conceiving of it as some kind of an administrative apparatus, they often fall into the trap of creating a ponderous paper process that, ironically, cripples the energetic and creative process of strategizing and planning for the future.

They can get so caught up in the tangible attributes of their new system—the forms, written goal-statements, plans, timetables, and reports—that they lose track of the purpose they had in mind when they started it. Also, when "rigor mortis" sets in, i.e., when the system just about grinds to a halt and people become exasperated with it, it usually has some toxic effects on the social system as well. Employees lose respect for their managers, conclude they don't know where they are going with the organization (frequently a well-founded conviction), and become exasperated with the ritual and procedure. The system can also have some serious negative impacts on the technical system if many people are distracted from productive work while they have to fill out forms, write meaningless objectives, and prepare reviews and reports.

In some cases two or more systems may conflict with one another simply because the people and processes that comprise them operate to differing priorities. For example, in a military headquarters where I worked many years ago, there was a small administrative unit in charge of keeping track of all classified documents, of which there were many, coming into the staff section where I worked. The various military and civilian staff people had ordered these documents from various government agencies and needed them for the conduct of their work (technical system). The people in the documentation-control unit (administrative system) were responsible to the leaders of the organization to make sure that all of the incoming documents were accounted for and that any of them could be located on demand. The administrative unit set up a virtually foolproof system that was unfortunately so ponderous that it took several days from the time a document arrived in the unit until it got into the hands of the person who needed it. In this case, the legitimate priorities of the two systems, as perceived by the two different groups, were in conflict. One system was attempting to maximize security and control, while the other system was attempting to maximize response time to information needs. After a great deal of conflict and haggling, the two groups worked out a compromise arrangement that enabled each of them to settle for less than they ideally wanted but to have more than they had been getting.

One of the first useful areas to investigate during an organizational diagnosis is frequently this area of inter-system conflict. Many of the brouhahas that people call "personality conflicts" turn out to be role conflicts, or the focal points of inter-system differences in priority.

FADS, FACTS, AND FIXES

One of the most useful rules you can adopt in managing an organization, and in working as an organizational change agent is—*don't fall for fads*. The systems approach to OD is a scientific approach. It proceeds from investigation, information seeking, and logical diagnosis. The corrective measures you employ or propose for the consideration of management need to be grounded in a factual assessment of the organization's processes, and they need to have a clear-cut relationship to the causes of the problem.

Personnel people and training people are often especially prone to jumping at the latest technique or fad in trying to improve circumstances in their organization. Top managers can also fall into this trap, often by reading an article about a provocative new method or hearing from their colleagues about something they've tried.

Diagnosis must come before prescription. Don't assume that what your organization needs is T-Group training, management by objectives, transactional analysis, zero-based budgeting, behavior modification, or Zen Buddhism, until you have made a reasonably comprehensive review of the four basic systems—technical, social, administrative, and strategic. Only after you have made the assessment and have a fairly good idea of how the systems are functioning and interacting can you select one or more intervention strategies or modes with a high probability that it will indeed contribute to solving the problem.

SPECIAL PROBLEMS OF NONPROFIT ORGANIZATIONS

Nonprofit management has for many years been one of the greatest sources of frustration and disillusionment among management theorists. It has always seemed that federal agencies, state and local government units, military organizations, universities, community service agencies and the like are somehow "unmanageable." Some managers in organizations such as these will even go so far as to say so. Even the renowned Peter F. Drucker, dean of management consultants, has had relatively little to say about the management of nonprofits. It is as if something about the deployment of resources in a not-for-profit mode removes some essential element from the situation that makes for an effective, adaptive organization.

We have many unfortunate stereotypes about "government workers," "civil servants," and the like. C. Northcote Parkinson, the originator of "Parkinson's Law," even observed, "If there's anything a public servant hates to do, it's something for the public." Yet, many of these stereotypes, unfortunately, are true in many cases. History provides abundant evidence of the wastefulness and ineffectiveness of government organizations as problem-solving entities. We have learned that, in the majority of cases, throwing a government agency at a problem—especially a newly created agency—is one of the least effective of our options for getting it solved. There is a ring of truth in the stereotype. Yet, the problem does not lie with the people of the nonprofit organization, who, after all, simply respond to their circumstances, but in the strategy and structure underlying the operation.

There have been some notable exceptions to the "bureaucracy syndrome." The Tennessee Valley Authority, for example, is a quasi-government agency that accomplished a significant economic end. And the National Aeronautics and Space Administration (NASA) is an outstanding example of a large government agency that orchestrated the American space program from its inception in 1959 through the successful moon landing in 1969 and afterward. These kinds of organizations are notable by their rarity, but they do indeed exist.

It is generally conceded that a corporation, as a problem-solving entity, will usually outperform a government agency, and usually most other nonprofit structures as well, when given a clear-cut mission. This suggests that, as a broad matter of social policy, we should minimize the number of people who are deployed in governmental and other nonprofit structures if we want to get high levels of human-resource efficiency. But what is the missing ingredient? What is it about the corporate structure and operational mode that gives it an advantage?

I think we can isolate two primary factors that usually distinguish between profit-making and nonprofit enterprises, neither of which has anything to do directly with profit. The first and crucial factor is the presence of competition—predatory forces in the organization's environment that threaten its livelihood and force its leaders to keep adapting to the wants and needs of the marketplace. It is the presence of competition and the possibility of extinction, not the love of profit, that fundamentally drives the managers of the profit-making organization, or "PMO" as we shall call it here.

We see many cases in point. The American public school system seems almost pledged to mediocrity and the pursuit of irrelevance in education, largely, I believe, because it has no plausible competition.

The American Federation of Teachers and the National Education Association, the two largest unions of civil-service teachers, have succeeded for years in derailing Congressional initiatives aimed at giving tax credits to parents for private-school expenses. Very few school superintendents, principals, or other administrators seem to have any substantial management experience or any particular commitment to the strategic issues inherent in their relationship to the community. For the typical high school, there is little or no real competition; it is the only game in town. For most parents, it a choice of this or nothing. Picture an alternative deployment of resources in which every school operates as a profit-and-loss center, in competition with others for the business of the families they are supposed to serve. This is admittedly a bizarre concept in the context of several generations of government-provided schooling, but it is no less logical for being unfamiliar.

The second critical factor in the effectiveness of PMO's and NPO's (nonprofit organizations) is the presence or absence of clear-cut measures of performance—outcomes which connect directly to the values and desires of those who provide the money to support them. In the United States, government agencies typically take on the more vaguely stated missions, perhaps by default or perhaps because they are generally set up as part of a political process which values big promises and inspiring commitments to social welfare. The U.S. Department of Education in the 70's, and its predecessor agency, the Department of Health, Education, and Welfare, were both ponderous beasts, subject to argument about the legitimacy of their missions and the nature of the valued outcomes they could produce. The typical county welfare department, an organization with a very tenuous charter and an organization often considered a necessary—or unnecessary—evil, is expected to simply hand out money. Municipal service departments generally have more of a focused mission and often make more sense internally. In sharp contrast to the typical government organization, NASA operated from a clearly defined charter and had a very concrete objective that President John Kennedy announced in 1960: "We are going to put a man on the moon in this decade, and bring him back safely to Earth."

In contrast to the typical nonprofit organization, the profit-making organization usually has a well-defined outcome or set of outcomes: sell as many or as much of what it produces or does as it can. The PMO operates by a direct chain of cause and effect with its customers or clients. If a company can't or won't provide goods or services comparable to those of its competition, the customers tell it so by going to the competitors more often and coming to it less often. The government agency, on the other hand, and likewise many other nonprofits, gets its revenue from a source which is not the same as the customer or client. While the PMO has only the customer to please, the NPO has a customer and a benefactor as well. In most such cases, they are not the same people, at least in the sense of immediate give-and-take between them. Indeed, for the county welfare department, the benefactor is the board of supervisors, and indirectly the taxpayer, while the "customer" is usually someone who does not pay taxes. This division of roles amounts to a splitting of the "customer" personality into two disparate entities, often with conflicting desires and values.

I think the message is fairly simple: profit-sector managers are not basically smarter or more skilled than nonprofit managers, and corporate employees are not basically smarter or more self-motivated than civil service employees. It is just that the profit sector imposes very real forces on the corporation that oblige its leaders to learn to adapt, at least to a great extent. The nonprofit environment, generally speaking, provides much less of this pressure for survival and adaptation.

As a consequence, we find the typical nonprofit organization much more "introverted," i.e., with the attention of the managers turned inward, than we find in a PMO. Also, NPO managers typically preoccupy themselves more with process, procedure, administrative matters, inter-unit transactions, and organizational rules and regulations than profit-sector managers do. Profit-sector managers tend to pay more attention to the primary technical axis of the organization and to problem-solve around the issues they encounter there. In some nonprofit organizations, you can find highly strategically minded managers, who manage with a strong sense of direction and outcome, just as you can find some amoeba-like managers in corporations, who don't seem to know where they are going. In general, however, the general population of managers represents the cross-section of the society in terms of personal competence and the ability to manage, and the vast majority of them are simply shaped by the environments in which they operate.

If we take this reasoning process to heart, it means that we need to find ways to shape the internal processes of the nonprofit organization so that it places value on two things: an external focus of attention and recognizable outcomes. Both, unfortunately, usually depend on the personal qualifications of the chief executive. If he or she understands the need for an external focus and manages accordingly, the organization is much more likely to adapt successfully to its environment than otherwise. A "caretaker" executive, or one who is a "career administrator," is likely to get caught up in "administrivia" at the expense of the larger issues. The second requirement also depends on the executive's competence, but to a lesser extent. It calls for a commitment to managing by objectives, i.e., clearly-specified key result areas and concrete outcomes pegged as objectives in each of those areas. The biggest challenge for the nonprofit manager is to avoid getting seduced and sedated by the organization itself, and by its orientation toward introversion. He or she must constantly think in terms of outcomes and adaptation to the environment.

4

The Technical System

Now we shall embark on a fairly comprehensive exploration of the four organizational systems, technical, social, administrative, and strategic, taking them one by one. In each case, we will identify the primary components or elements of the system, identify some of the key measures of "health" for it, and examine the more important processes that go on and that can go wrong. As we proceed through the four systems, it will become increasingly clear that they share various components amongst them and that they do not have sharply defined boundaries separating them. Indeed, if we take the matter to the logical extreme, we must recognize that these systems are actually figments of our own perception rather than obvious subdivisions existing in nature. So, when we speak of an organizational system, we speak of a set of features that we choose to perceive as interconnected and worthy of thinking about as an entity.

We will define these systems as widely as possible to account for as many kinds of organizations as we can. As you read through the catalog of components and functions for each system, you will find it necessary—and, I hope, enlightening—to think in specific terms about your own organization. If you work in a manufacturing company, your technical system will look much different than it would if you worked in a hospital, a college, a research laboratory, or a government agency. I will offer some examples to clarify the nature of the systems we are discussing, but for the most part I must rely on you, the reader, to make these systems real in your own experience.

COMPONENTS OF THE TECHNICAL SYSTEM

The technical system is basically synonymous with the primary productive axis of the organization. It includes the first-order arrangement of resources—human, physical, and intangible resources that actually execute the primary function for which the outfit exists. The elements of the technical system usually include at least the following:

1. The "production" people—those directly involved in developing the product or service, building it or performing it, selling it, and delivering it.

2. The primary facility or facilities where the action occurs; this might be a production building, a department store, a hotel, or a group of college classrooms.

3. The capital resources—money and related forms of wealth; machinery and special equipment; specially equipped facilities such as a radiation-therapy lab, a wind tunnel, a prison compound, or a language learning lab.

4. Raw material, if any, and the means for handling it; in a printing firm, this includes paper, ink, glue, solvents, photographic plates, and the like; in some organizations, such as data-processing firms or those heavily involved in "knowledge" work, information may literally serve as a basic raw material.

5. The flow of activity—the chain of processes you can trace out and diagram to show how the product or service moves from creation to delivery; this flow can be very simple in some organizations and very complex in others.

6. Methods and procedures, either in writing or in people's heads, that prescribe how the technical system should operate.

7. Standards of performance, in writing or in people's heads, that tell what constitutes a job well done.

8. Media of all kinds used to record information which is central to the work itself; examples are production schedules, patient records, computer programs, teller cash reports, and research project plans; as a matter of choice, certain items, such as employee work and vacation schedules, can be classified as part of the technical or the administrative system—take your choice, so long as you account for them somewhere.

THE KEY MEASURE: PRODUCTIVITY

It helps to think of each of the four organizational systems in terms of one or, at most, a few key features that define its effectiveness. Thinking for the moment only of the "un-human" technical system, and agreeing that we will later account for human values and concerns, we will deal here with the one key variable that sums up the health of the technical system: productivity.

The notion of productivity is getting a great deal of attention in manufacturing organizations today, and rightfully so. It is getting less attention in many other organizations, where it rightfully could. Although many union people, and many people who do not work in organizations, seem to think that managers only eat, sleep, and live for productivity, this is far from the case. There are many "production"-type organizations, i.e., those with highly-programmed, repetitive processes, in which the managers don't really have a good grasp on productivity measures.

We will deal with productivity measures and productivity-improvement programs in greater depth later. At this point, let's settle for a reasonable working definition of productivity as a numerical measure that relates the value of what the technical system produces to the cost incurred in producing it. Cost can include many factors, not just dollar measures. The same holds true for value.

In the United States as well as in other industrialized countries, there is an increasing preoccupation in the news media with the phenomenon of "declining productivity." There are many misconceptions and fuzzy notions circulating about concerning the so-called "productivity crisis," many of them unwittingly created and reinforced by magazine and newspaper writers who lack the technical knowledge to understand it in depth. Many national economists use a customary definition of a country's overall productivity as the ratio of the dollar value of all goods sold to the total number of labor hours expended. This is a very gross figure, with a vast number of peculiarities and arguable factors reflected in it. It is nearly useless at the sociopolitical level for setting government policy, and it is almost meaningless at the company level for deciding how to manage and how to adapt. It includes the effects of variations in the money supply, buying habits, level of unemployment, and a very arbitrary definition of the consumer price index used to adjust for inflation.

Actually, "productivity" in the United States has not been declining even by this grossly oversimplified measure. It is merely the *rate of increase* in productivity that is declining. In addition to these considerations, we have the larger philosophical question facing American society and the other major consumer societies of the world, namely, is more necessarily better? Do the industrialized nations of the world have to be locked in an economic race to see who can convert natural resources into garbage the fastest? There is likely to be a natural limit to the trajectory of consumption, and the major industrialized nations—America in particular, which still outstrips all other nations—may be rapidly approaching it. When we think about productivity at the organizational level, we had best not let ourselves get dragged into these kinds of global philosophical arguments. What we need is a way of thinking about productivity at the organizational level that will help us understand the possibilities of the technical system and develop management strategies to realize those possibilities as well as we can.

The most important thing you should know about productivity at the organizational level is that there is no one "right" measurement of it. If you think through all of the direct inputs to your organization's product or service, you will see that relating them to the outputs can be somewhat complex. For example, do you want to include the costs of raw materials, energy, and machine wear-and-tear, or do you want to confine your productivity measure to labor-hour inputs? The simple notion of productivity as the ratio of "output over input" gets pretty slippery when you go into detail. In a labor-intensive operation such as mining, the variable of "tons of coal per labor hour" may be a good choice. In a capital-intensive operation such as oil drilling, the better measure might be "barrels of oil recovered per dollar spent." No one variable can capture the whole picture, so it usually makes sense to choose a family of productivity measures that best reflect the health of the technical system we have at hand.

Some of our ready choices for productivity measures in a production-type organization include the following:

1. Number of units of output produced per labor hour.
2. Dollars of sales generated per labor hour, or dollars of annual sales per employee.
3. Dollars of profit per labor hour.
4. Dollars of annual sales generated per dollar of invested capital, i.e., capital productivity, or "turnover."
5. Dollars of profit generated per dollar of invested capital, i.e., net return on investment.

Looking at these various measures should make it clear that productivity does not depend solely on how hard or how well the employees work. It is a much more complex concept than that. For example, labor productivity figures will fluctuate in a manufacturing organization according to the production workload. When the customers are buying less of the product, as in the case of a seasonal market, management must usually cut back on production to minimize inventory carrying costs. This causes the computed value of units of production per hour of labor to drop, unless management hires and fires people sporadically as sales fluctuate. So it is important to understand the concept behind productivity, to develop useful measures, and to use them intelligently and humanely.

INDIVIDUAL PRODUCTIVITY AND COLLECTIVE PRODUCTIVITY

Although some people, notably professional and staff workers, balk at the notion that what they do can be measured and assessed, nevertheless it makes sense to try to develop some basis for deciding how well the job is getting done, and indeed if there is any worthwhile outcome. It is important to avoid an oppressive, "Gestapo" approach to productivity assessment so as not to cause counter-productive reactions on the part of workers who feel they are getting the blacksnake whip treatment. And at the same time, it is important to maintain a commitment to results.

We can consider productivity measures in two broad categories: individual measures and collective measures. Individual productivity is the input-output ratio for one person, considering a situation in which he or she has control of all of the key variables involved. It only makes sense to measure individual productivity when the individual can do something to maintain a level of excellence. Collective productivity deals with broader, more "global" measures, which usually take into account other key components of the technical system.

It is also helpful to think through the reasons for gathering and using productivity data. We want to avoid a "rat-race" syndrome in which the employees conclude that management is about to impose controls or demands on them, or that they will be bludgeoned with a punitive, "no-win" system of numerical standards. Many managers mistakenly use productivity measures for this purpose.

There are two excellent uses for productivity measures that do not relate directly to employee evaluation and that are generally nonthreatening. Both deal with collective productivity. One is using productivity figures as a general indication of the overall health of the technical system. The second is using them as planning variables.

The second use probably merits additional explanation. In a software development company, for example, managers can compile statistics over many projects that tell them roughly how many hours of programmer time it takes to develop a typical software system of a certain size. These figures come out as nominal rules of thumb, much like the figures that builders use in estimating the cost of a building in terms of dollars per square foot of floor space. In a software firm, the productivity figure may take the form of the number of lines of code (computer instructions) per hour that a programming team can turn out over the long run. In bidding on competitive contracts, the company managers have some moderately reliable parameter on which to base their cost estimate and their price to the potential customer. These estimating rules of thumb are really measures of collective productivity, and they include all of the miscellaneous factors such as the effects of vacations, sick leave, errors, false starts, project delays, and the like. They are global figures, useful in large-scale analysis.

In addition to using productivity figures as planning data, the managers can also compare their company's productivity levels to those of the industry at large, if they are available, and know where they stand competitively. A significant increase in productivity in an area such as this translates fairly directly to higher profitability.

It also makes sense to use individual productivity measures in first-line supervision, provided the supervisor knows how to use them fairly and positively. Most people like to have feedback on the results of their work; they like to know how they are doing. It is a fairly simple first step to begin a program of measurement and feedback, to establish a setting in which people can discuss performance based on facts and logic. Even with vaguely defined jobs, it is often possible to develop a useful notion of productivity by thinking imaginatively about the nature of the work.

For example, when I write books, although there is no objective way to measure the "quality" I turn out, I can indeed measure my performance at the general task of writing. The marketplace will tell how well I have met the needs of the prospective readers, but I can tell how many hours of work it will take me to complete the manuscript. I know, for example, that I can average about two to three pages of manuscript text per hour, counting flashbacks to see what I said, on-the-spot revisions, sketching figures for the draft, changing disks on the word processor memory, and the like. So, when I plan a book project, I use a figure of about two and a half pages per hour to estimate the number of hours it will take to complete the job, considering the estimated length of the manuscript. The *content* of the job is creative, and not subject to simple means of measurement. But the *process* of the job is highly measurable in the long run.

This content-process distinction is an important one, especially for white-collar productivity considerations, which are becoming more and more pressing as time goes on. It is important for a manager, in working with an employee, to acknowledge that the quality of the work is subject to a separate reasoning process and that the productivity measures are simply a means for evaluating the process. For example, an executive assistant might seem to be a person with a job that almost defies definition or analysis. The content varies widely, but at the process level it is easy to describe. The assistant carries out tasks and projects. Without getting compulsive about the need for measures, still the executive can confer with the assistant about the nature and number of these projects, and get agreement about priorities, number of projects completed in a given review period, and the average length of time to complete one. The projects may vary extensively, but over the long pull certain rules of thumb will emerge. An assessment of a staff person's productivity in this way, and positive feedback of the results, can lead to a marked improvement in his or her effectiveness in getting results.

CAPITAL AND PRODUCTIVITY

There are two basic ways to improve productivity if we conceive of it broadly in terms of getting more of what the technical system delivers—more patients treated, more integrated circuits manufactured, more fires put out, more pages of typeset text produced, or more lines of computer code written—in proportion to what we put into it. One major way is to use capital improvements, such as machinery or special facilities, to multiply the effectiveness of the individual working person. The other way is to help or enable the working person to do his or her job more skillfully or effectively, thereby getting more impact per person than we got before. This section describes the capital-effectiveness approach. The next section describes the human-effectiveness approach. Both are often needed and are mutually compatible if introduced properly.

Capital effectiveness simply means using special machinery, equipment, or facilities to expand the capabilities of the person doing a job. A worker with a jackhammer can open up a hole in a street much faster than one using a sledgehammer. With a motorized conveyor-belt system bringing the products to him, an order clerk in a mail-order company can fill and package more orders for shipment than one can who has to walk up and down the warehouse aisles finding the items on the shelves. Whenever we can augment human effort with machines or special equipment, without negative side-effects on the people who do the job, we can usually improve productivity.

Many people feel that the executives of industrial companies in America have taken the capital-improvement approach to extremes, dehumanizing the workplace in the process. While that point of view does have merit, and while we need to repair a great deal of the damage caused by that process, nevertheless it is helpful to reflect on the enormous multiplication of human effort that effective use of capital has brought about. A very simple example: General Motors corporation has over 700,000 employees. Without the use of computers, an industrial organization of that size simply wouldn't be possible. Take a pen and paper, and estimate the number of employees that would be needed just to prepare the paychecks for the rest of them, without data-processing equipment.

MOTIVATION AND PRODUCTIVITY

We've known most of what we need to know about motivation and productivity for several thousand years. There is only one basic finding: people working in an organization tend to work harder and more productively when they feel personally involved, connected, important, affirmed, appreciated, and rewarded for the work that they contribute.

The human-effectiveness approach to productivity depends not so much on sophisticated techniques or advanced psychological knowledge as on enlightenment and education among the managers of the organization. Motivation is a prime example of the overlapping of two organizational systems—the technical system and the social system. When the social system is working well, and specifically when the reward system is working well, the technical system benefits from the greater level of energy and commitment people bring to their jobs.

A great deal of research and a great deal of common sense shows that employee motivation, both at the individual level and at the collective level, responds more to the attitudes and actions of supervisors than to any other single variable. The quality of the supervision that a working person receives plays an enormous part in how productively he or she works. The place to start, therefore, in understanding motivation and productivity in your organization, is the reward system and the behavior of those who are the keepers of the reward system—the managers.

COMPETENCE-BASED
TRAINING AND DEVELOPMENT

The process of training and development can play a very important part in the effectiveness of the technical system. Some organizations have a strong commitment to developing their employees' work skills and related capabilities, while others seem to get by with little or no training investment. It is very difficult, in many cases, to evaluate the effects of not training people, since the technical system can usually get along in some way or other; it seldom comes to a halt solely for lack of training.

In many organizations, the incoming employee does not even get an effective orientation to the overall system. He or she may receive the perfunctory briefing from the personnel clerk about insurance, benefits, and the location of the nurse's office, and little more in the way of an effective introduction to what the organization is all about. Of course, the supervisor is responsible for helping the new employee get adjusted and become productive as rapidly as possible, but the skill of supervisors at this process varies widely. The customary orientation process seems to be a short meeting with the supervisor, a few friendly and encouraging remarks, and the assignment of a desk and some harmless task to get started on. It is generally assumed in most business organizations that the new employee will simply catch on over a period of months and become one of the folks. This usually does happen, but usually at the expense of considerable lost potential productivity during this period. Many employees who go through this process acquire a basic survival knowledge of the organization and seldom ever learn anything more than the rudiments of the organization, because their jobs don't present them with broad-scale learning opportunities.

A more effective approach is for the organization's managers to have a training plan as part of their process of continually maintaining and upgrading the capabilities of the people in the organization. Technical training, i.e., building the job-skills of people engaged in the technical system, usually deserves a high priority, especially in an organization where the jobs are fairly complex and require high skill levels. Management training is another important area for a potential training plan, because it can have such a strong influence on the strategic system by developing the management strength of the organization.

Training can play a very useful role in a typical organization development program. It can serve as a resource for improving the technical system through skills training, the administrative system through skills training for people who work in those functions, the strategic system through management development, and the social system through improving the skills of managers in developing a positive organizational climate.

Training programs make most sense in the OD process when they are competence-based. That means that they need to focus on specific, comparatively concrete, and observable skills that people can acquire and put to use. This sounds obvious, yet it is by no means widely practiced in industrial organizations. Much of industrial training follows the high-school and college models, which revolve around people learning "content," or information, rather than skills. People who educate or train by following the "content" route assume that the trainees will more or less develop the competencies they need by putting the concepts they learn to use.

A healthy and rapidly developing trend in the training and development field involves the use of *competence models* for teaching people various jobs and capabilities. A competence model is simply an itemized list of selected concrete skills, expressed in action-oriented or behavior-oriented terms. It may take the form of a categorical list, or a "tree" diagram showing various logical groupings of skills. This becomes the basis not only for training, but also for skill testing, placement and promotion, and performance appraisal. This kind of competence thinking is gaining in importance in business organizations, and it will probably be a major development of the 1980s.

PERFORMANCE APPRAISAL

The problem of performance appraisal has created frustration for personnel people for many years, and for managers as well. Quite a few organizations, especially small and medium-sized ones, have no systematic means of appraising employee performance; others have formal systems that hardly work at all; and a relatively few have useful systems that actually do appraise performance and serve as a basis for management decision-making.

Typically, a performance appraisal "system" in an organization will consist of a personnel form which managers are supposed to fill out, one for each employee. Once a year, twice a year, or however often the schedule dictates, the personnel office sends the forms out to all managers, asking them to fill them out, discuss them with the employees on an individual basis, and send the completed forms back. Just as typically, a manager will fill out the form for each person, giving most of the people high marks and complimentary comments, and giving the people he doesn't like average or only slightly-above-average marks. He sits down with the employee, shows him the form, and after a few minutes of strained and carefully controlled conversation, they both ritualistically sign the form and that's all there is to it. For most organizations, the performance appraisal process is not really an appraisal of performance at all—it is simply an administrative ritual. Most of the time, the appraisal is misplaced; managers and personnel people alike see it as belonging to the administrative system, when it really should belong to the technical system.

If we're going to call it <u>a performance</u> appraisal, let's use it to do just that—<u>determine a working person's performance, as measured by</u> <u>results achieved</u> instead of by personal traits like "punctuality," "grooming," and "cooperativeness," <u>and use that</u> information in <u>making management</u> decisions about <u>the technical system</u>. If we want to tie the compensation of each individual to his or her accomplishment, we have to get the evaluation process out of the administrative system and back into the technical system where it belongs.

5

The Social System

COMPONENTS OF THE SOCIAL SYSTEM

Now we come to the system that has interested traditional OD practitioners the most, and indeed it is a fascinating one. The social system in an organization represents a very different point of view on the operation than the technical system. Coexisting with the technical system, and inseparably intertwined with it, is the fabric of roles, relationships, values, norms, and rewards that bind certain people together and make them citizens of a particular miniature society. To understand the social system of an organization is to understand how people function as interconnected human beings rather than as elements of a production process.

The components of the social system are fairly simple:

1. All of the people who belong to the organization, including the managers and other people in positions of influence.

2. The formal power hierarchy, or chain of command, usually portrayed by the organization chart.

3. The various values of the organization, expressed formally by proclamations and informally through the actions of the leaders and the people at large.

4. The various recognized norms for individual behavior, both spoken and unspoken, fair and unfair.

5. The tangible and intangible rewards available to people and the means for dispensing them, whether these rewards support the purposes of the organization properly or not; the entire reward system of the organization taken as a whole.

6. The overall social climate in the organization, i.e., the composite perceptions of the employees of how they are treated by their managers and their peers; how they get along with one another.

7. The organization's "grapevine," or informal communication network, which exists outside the channels of the technical and administrative systems.

THE KEY MEASURE: QUALITY OF WORK LIFE

The term "quality of work life" is becoming widely used in organizations, largely because it seems to capture, in distinctly human terms, a key human concern. We can describe the quality of work life in an organization as the perceived quality, in the minds of the employees, of all aspects of their citizenship in the organization. This definition is deliberately broad because it attempts to capture a wide range of aspects of living and working in the organization. The notion of quality of work life—"QWL" for short, hereafter—enables us to think comprehensively and systematically about what is going on in the social system. More and more organizations are instituting what are called QWL programs, aimed at improving various aspects of the organization that affect the morale, commitment, and psychological well-being of the people who work there.

This notion aligns with, and mirrors to a great extent, a developing concern in the United States ever since the beginning of the 1960s. This is the idea that, in a wealthy technological society, we can easily mistake the "quantity" of life for the quality of it. More cars, more refrigerators, more mobile homes, more electric butter knives, and more throw-away items may not be the answer to the human need for high-quality living. Many people in the United States are rejecting the more extreme consumerist values and are moving toward life styles that emphasize high-quality personal experience and a graceful mode of living within the human and natural environments. Similarly in organizations, more and more working people and more and more managers are emphasizing the broader view of work and working, which includes personal and psychological satisfaction. All of these satisfaction factors taken together add up to the concept of quality of working life.

From the point of view of the desires, needs, and values of the individual working person, QWL has at least these aspects:

1. *A job worth doing*; one that makes a worthwhile contribution to the objectives of the organization and that calls upon a reasonable share of the employee's skills, knowledge, and capabilities.

2. *Adequate working conditions*; a safe and reasonably humane set of physical and psychological conditions immediately surrounding the performance of the job.

3. *Adequate pay and benefits* in return for competent work.

4. *Job security*; knowing that one has a reasonable assurance of a job tomorrow if one is willing to work.

5. *Competent supervision*; positive, supportive, and affirmative treatment by one's boss and by higher levels of management.

6. *Feedback on the results of one's work*; recognition and appreciation of one's contributions to the objectives of the organization.

7. *Opportunities for growth and development* in work skills and in responsibilities; progressively more challenging work which develops or activates progressively larger skills.

8. *A fair chance to get ahead on merit*; access to training, visibility to upper management, and competitive opportunities to win promotion to higher levels.

9. *A positive social climate*; a work setting that is stable, psychologically reinforcing, and humane in terms of values and interpersonal processes.

10. *Justice and fair play*; a sense that those in charge value and emphasize fairness and equitable treatment of all employees, regardless of social or ethnic concerns.

These are fairly concrete aspects of the social system, which we can detect and measure at least in qualitative terms. We can even take this assessment as far as a numerical rating for each of these factors, say on scales ranging from 1 to 5. It is a fairly simple and enlightening process to present these ten QWL factors to the employees of the organization in the form of rating scales on a questionnaire and analyze the results in numerical form. Quality of work life does indeed sum up the health of the social system.

We must also remember a key point: the quality of work life in the organization is a matter of the perceptions of the employees, not the judgments of the managers. People respond to their own perceptions, and the only way to find out about the current quality level of life in the organization is to find out what their perceptions are. Further, we must validate any improvements we try to make in quality of work life by re-examining those perceptions after the change.

UNDERSTANDING THE ORGANIZATION'S CULTURE AND CLIMATE

The term "organizational culture" originated many years ago in the OD field, and it has become a very useful metaphor for thinking about and describing the social system. We will use it here in the broad sense to mean the overall social setting of the organization as determined by the four key aspects of power, values, norms, and rewards. Here we use the term "power" without any sinister or negative connotation. One of the obvious facts of organizational life is that somebody has to be in charge, and being in charge means having power in the sense of controlling the punishment-and-reward processes of the organization. So, in order to understand organizations fully, and to develop them comprehensively, we can't afford to be shy about dealing with the realities of power, authority, and influence. Let's review each of these four aspects of organizational culture in turn.

Power

Power is present in every organization, of course, but managers vary widely in the styles with which they use it. A great deal of what organizational behaviorists study when they study managerial style is the mode of deployment of formal authority. Managers, from the lowest-ranking supervisor up to the chief executive, have their own distinctive ways of being in charge. Some of them tend to manage autocratically, controlling as many aspects of the work as possible, reserving many decisions for themselves, and emphasizing through many different signals that they are firmly in charge. Their physical bearing and demeanor, the way they talk, the kinds of directives they give, and even the ways they arrange their offices and departments spell out their attitudes about being in charge. Other managers deploy their authority much more deftly and conservatively, granting more autonomy and derivative authority to their subordinates, inviting much more participation by them in problem-solving and decision-making, and de-emphasizing differences in status and position in the hierarchy. In every case, the styles with which the managers in an organization deploy their formal authority have a fundamental and profound influence on its culture.

Values

Every organization also has a distinctive set of values, spoken and unspoken, which govern the way people do business with one another. Although there might not always be a monolithic, unquestioned, and universally accepted set of standards, nevertheless most of the people working in an organization seem to have a pretty accurate idea of what the culture at large considers important. Many of these value standards stem from the words and deeds of the managers, and much of a manager's day-to-day behavior serves to create or reinforce certain definite values. A later section will deal with values in somewhat greater depth.

Norms

Behavioral norms are usually so well known and well accepted in an organization that people don't pay them much conscious attention. Only when someone violates a strongly emplaced norm, or threatens to, do the onlookers become highly aware of the norm. There are probably too many behavioral norms in a typical organization to count, and most of them are unconsciously understood and unconsciously enforced. A few illustrative examples of the many kinds of norms include these: ways to speak to persons in authority; styles of dress; who signs what; patterns of protocol in staff meetings; interactions between men and women; degrees of cooperation or antagonism between neighboring departments; established methods for disagreeing with the boss (or avoiding doing so); protocol for young people deferring to the judgment of "old timers"; and the considerations of arriving and leaving on time, and working extra hours without pay.

Rewards

Rewards, as previously discussed, consist of all the possible forms of return to the individual on his or her invested work energy—the sum total of what you get for what you do. These include financial rewards, such as pay and benefits, and intangible or psychological rewards, such as recognition, praise, or increased responsibility. A later section treats the reward system in greater depth.

Think about your own organization in connection with these four features of a culture—power, values, norms, and rewards. How would you assess the culture you live in? Each organization has a very distinctive—and indeed unique—culture, evolved from all of the many interactions people have had with one another and with those in authority. By spending a relatively short period of time in an organization, and watching people deal with one another, you can form a fairly reliable assessment of its culture. This is what we do in OD, and we use the findings of the culture assessment for the purposes of planned change aimed at enhancing it.

We have also been using the term "climate" in referring to the social conditions prevailing inside an organization. How does climate relate to culture? For our purposes, let's simply consider the climate to be the emotional state of the culture—the "mood" of the organization, so to speak. We find out about the climate existing among the people by gaining access to their perceptions of it, simply by asking them in an honest and straightforward way how they feel about various aspects of working there.

THE REWARD SYSTEM

An elementary-school teacher took her class on a field trip to the zoo. They made their first stop at the monkey cage, a large fenced compound. However, they didn't see a single monkey anywhere inside the compound. Puzzled, the teacher went to one of the attendants for help. "Where are the monkeys?" she asked him. He said, "Oh, don't you know? It's mating season, and the monkeys are all over there behind that big stone wall, mating with one another. They don't usually come out." "Oh," she said. "The children will be so disappointed. Well, do you suppose they'd come out if we offered them some peanuts?" The zookeeper looked at her for a moment, shrugged, and then said, "I don't know, ma'am. Would you?"

It is remarkable how many managers lack any practical grasp of human motivation and how many naive assumptions they make about what it takes to influence human beings. If you want to change somebody's behavior, you've got to have something more to offer than peanuts.

The reward system in the organization is, for the most part, the consequence of managerial action—partly conscious, and sometimes largely unconscious. The things that managers say and do often constitute rewards and punishments in themselves, and in the larger sense the systems they set up to determine who gets ahead and how far they get become for the employees the basic realities of compensation for their efforts. For our discussion, we will consider punishment as well as reward under the heading of the reward system, although we will emphasize the use of rewards.

We can think of the reward system as having at least the following elements:

1. Pay, benefits, and other forms of compensation.
2. Desirable work assignments or special high-status roles in the organization.
3. Private praise for well-done work.
4. Public recognition for well-done work.
5. Promotions.
6. Perquisites, such as parking places, office furniture, and the like.
7. Personal privileges, such as time off, opportunities for desirable business travel, attendance at professional symposia or training programs, and reimbursement for educational expenses.

The punishment side of the ledger also relates to these seven factors in inverse fashion. For example, a person can be punished by a reduction in pay or other compensation, receiving undesirable work assignments, getting criticized privately or publicly, getting demoted or discharged, and having perquisites or personal privileges taken away.

Since, as noted previously, the managers are the builders and keepers of the reward system, it behooves them to know just what kind of a reward system they have created. Understanding the reward system is crucial to understanding the social system. Many of the important changes managers would like to make in the social system depend to some extent or other on revising the reward system.

RECOGNIZING
ORGANIZATIONAL VALUES

In much the same way that an individual human being has a value system, an organization also has a value system, or actually a collection of value systems. Just as a person's values guide his or her behavior, so the values in the organization govern the behavior of the people who work there. Values, both at the individual level and the organizational level, are inseparably intertwined with behavior, so it makes sense to define a value system in terms of its influence on behavior.

For our purposes, we can define an organizational value as a condition or a state of affairs that people habitually act to create or to preserve. Just as the evidence of our personal values is in our actions, so the evidence of organizational values is in day-to-day collective behavior.

There are, of course, many kinds of values and value systems, and anything like a complete accounting of them would probably get us into a verbal quagmire of labels. However, we can identify some of the primary value systems we see operating routinely in organizations, and these will give us a fairly good grasp of that aspect of the social system. We also need to recognize the importance of values operating in the other three organizational systems: the technical, the administrative, and the strategic. For example, a key technical-system value would be product quality. For this discussion, we will focus only on social values, especially since an understanding of them has received relatively little emphasis in the traditional study of management.

Here is a selection of some of the most significant and influential value systems operating in organizations:

1. *Authority*—the matter of who is in charge, how authority is parceled out and distributed through the leadership hierarchy, and the prerogatives that go with power.

2. *Subordination*—the degree of obedience to authority and conformance to rules expected of the individual employee; the relative extent to which he or she is expected to conform to certain patterns of behavior.

3. *Status*—the means of defining, signalling, and reinforcing levels in the informal social hierarchy; what it takes to have influence and recognition over and above formal authority; for example, academic.

degrees, graduation from certain universities, specialist-roles such as physician or psychiatrist, or a position of leadership in a union.

4. *Social Distance*—the relative psychological and social separation between "ordinary" people and those in charge; the degree of closeness with which an individual employee can approach an executive, and the relative amount of deference that he or she is expected to exhibit.

5. *Business Ethics*—the accepted relationship between profit and human values; what constitutes an acceptable way of making money, competing with other organizations, and treating customers or clients.

6. *Pressure and Pace*—the relative tempo of work activity, usually as enforced by the managers.

7. *Jurisdiction*—the extent to which administrative subdivisions of the organization—the organization chart—dominate working relationships; the importance of "turf," proprietorship of certain aspects of the work, and role-oriented interactions.

8. *Collaboration*—the extent to which people emphasize cooperation and compromise in their daily interactions; the extent to which they compete against one another in preference to helping one another.

9. *Structure and Order*—the importance of the formal organization and its processes, and the significance of having things thoroughly and unambiguously defined; reliance on systems, methods, procedures, and forms in structuring the work; preference for precise definition of responsibilities, authority, and day-to-day work of various units.

10. *Change and Innovation*—the appetite of the key people in the organization for finding new and better ways to accomplish results; seeking new products or services, new ways to organize resources, and new possibilities for effectiveness versus preoccupation with tried-and-true methods and comfortable ways of working.

For the most part, the managers of the organization are the builders and keepers of the value systems, whether they realize it or not. Although the employees themselves do bring many personal values to the organizational setting, and many values are more or less "standard" within the society, the day-to-day actions and words of those in management tend to reinforce certain values much more than others.

For example, if managers tend to push the workers very hard for "production," whatever that may be, then clearly pressure-and-pace becomes a key organizational value. If the managers foster and reward initiative and independent thinking, and invite workers to develop new and better ways to do the work, then change-and-innovation becomes a key value.

By simply looking around awhile in an organization, you can get a fairly representative picture of what is important in the social system. And you can usually trace these important features fairly closely to what the managers do or neglect to do. When you understand the organization's value system, you know a great deal about what goes on there, and you have a fairly clear picture of the reactions that the people and managers in the organization will probably exhibit to any comprehensive attempt at planned change.

UNDERSTANDING THE PSYCHOLOGY OF POWER

In virtually any human organization that has permanency and well-defined patterns of activity, the matter of authority gets accounted for first and foremost. If the authority structure should come into jeopardy, it usually gets top priority over other matters. It seems that not only those who are in charge, but the other citizens of the organization as well, want a relatively clear definition of control relationships.

Think this over for a moment. Human beings are organizing creatures. From the most primitive families, tribes, and clans, to the most complex corporations, universities, professional associations, and even governments, people tend to want to function within well-established social frameworks. And one of the essential features of an organization is its authority structure. This we can take as virtually a defining characteristic of human society.

Nevertheless, most people seem to have a curious reluctance to talk openly about the authority structure in their organizations, and when they do they usually seem to talk in one of two ways: abstractly, as if they were discussing an apparatus rather than a group of people, and covertly, in private "political" conversations. Most of them particularly avoid mentioning the matter of authority in the presence of people in high authority. The subject is handled rather lightly whenever possible. It is as if people have a strong ambivalence about authority. They want to belong to an established structure with a hierarchy and with people in charge, and yet they don't like to be reminded too emphatically that they are subordinate to someone else and that part of their role involves taking orders from another human being.

New supervisors in particular usually face some difficult challenges in adjusting to their newly acquired authority. Some of them get carried away with these power feelings, and they use their authority at the expense of their staff members as a way to build their own egos. Others feel reluctant to accept the power that comes with their jobs and tend to avoid giving direct instructions and making firm decisions. It usually takes a while for someone new to management to become comfortable with authority and to learn to use it gracefully; some never do. If you presently have a managerial job, you might find it helpful to think over the matter of how you handle your authority. Do you tend to confuse your ego with your authority, using the status and power of your position to reinforce your feelings of personal significance and self-esteem? Or can you honestly say you have enough self-confidence and maturity to use your authority gracefully and effectively?

One of the key issues we have to deal with in organization development is the way in which managers use their authority, a topic we will explore more thoroughly later. A typical problem in organizations is the fairly highly placed executive who uses authority in an oppressive, toxic sort of a way, with many negative side effects for the organization as well as for the people. Managers like this have relatively weak egos and spend a great deal of their attention and energy in ego-building and ego-protection. Since this is the case, they aren't likely to want to sit down with an OD specialist, consultant, task-force member, or anybody else and talk frankly and logically about the way they use power. And very few subordinates, no matter what their assignments, would feel safe in telling them in so many words that they, the executives themselves, are sources of problems and organizational pain. This has turned out to be one of the classical dilemmas of the OD field—how to get an authoritarian manager to understand that he or she is causing serious problems, without losing your job or your contract? There are techniques for getting at this dilemma to some extent, and we will explore some of them later, but let's recognize that they typically don't happen spontaneously in most organizations.

While we're discussing the matter of authority and managerial ego-strength, it's worthwhile to introduce a concept widely discussed among OD consultants, but not necessarily widely discussed with managers. This is the concept of "OD-readiness" on the part of a given organization. Typically, an OD practitioner will refer to an organization as "OD-ready" if certain conditions prevail. Most of these conditions have to do with a frame of mind on the part of the key managers in the organization. If they are sufficiently confident in themselves and psychologically disposed to assess their own management processes with a view toward improving the organizations, then most of the things that need to happen can indeed happen. But if the chief executive, or a majority of the members of the management team, are not mature in the uses of power, and are defensive about examining their own practices, then very few of the enabling conditions will prevail. Many a potential OD program, advocated by a trainer, personnel manager, or a particular line manager, has died in its infancy because the power people of the organization were not psychologically equipped to accept it. This one factor has probably caused more frustration for human-resources people in organizations than any other. OD-readiness is mostly management readiness, and without it the most well-intentioned OD program usually won't get very far.

If you function in a potential change-agent capacity, or intend to, you will sooner or later find it necessary to understand the psychology of power. For in organizations as we know them, the most influential change agent of all is the manager. Just as a manager can act as an effective change agent, so he or she can act as a resistance agent. And one managerial resistance agent can sometimes counteract the efforts of ten change agents who don't have any formal authority. This is why OD people working within the organization must be realistic about the kinds of change they can probably bring about, and why they must aim their shots with a great deal of forethought and consideration for the realities of their organization's social system.

UNDERSTANDING ORGANIZATIONAL POLITICS

Every organization has its own distinctive processes of internal "politics," whether we like to accept the fact or not. Probably the most effective way for a person involved in organization development to understand and come to terms with political processes is to stop thinking of the term "politics" as having a fundamentally negative or sinister connotation. Let's define politics with a completely neutral connotation, as simply the forms of informal influence people exert in dealing with one another and in getting work done.

Given what we know about basic human behavior, we must recognize that it would be impossible to have an organization without an internal political process. The tremendous complexity of inter-action even among a relatively small number of people guarantees that there will be differences of opinion, and these will lead to attempts to influence and persuade the people in authority by means of informal coalitions among certain members. It is a mistake to think that all political acts on the part of people working in an organization are completely self-serving. Many of the things people do when they "play politics" are aimed at accomplishing organizational purposes they believe in. While there certainly are people who seem to have little regard for anything other than their careers, the best politicians seem to get ahead by using political strategies to promote solutions, to persuade others to accept them, and to sell them to upper manage-ment. The fact that they enhance their careers in the process does not detract from the value of their results.

Indeed, one of the topics I enjoy teaching in management seminars is the skill of "positive politics," defined as the process of getting ahead in the organization while keeping your value system intact. I show managers that they can indeed use political strategies honestly, effectively, and in good faith to get things done, thereby achieving the kind of results-oriented track record that helps to get them promoted.

For the purposes of OD, a realistic assessment of the social system must include a matter-of-fact description of its politics. Of course, this does not mean a brass-band kind of a disclosure of what's going on behind closed doors all over the organization. This is the kind of information that tends to make people uneasy, and as a promoter of constructive change you need to have a healthy respect for their reaction processes. At the same time, you must have a working knowledge, at least in your own mind, of the basic political landscape of the organization.

Actually, you can describe an organization's political setting quite handily by investigating and analyzing five basic aspects of the day-to-day interplay among its formal and informal leaders:

1. The quality of the relationships among the members of the inner circle; relative equality in their de facto status with the boss: openness and friendly personal relationships, or the lack of them; existence of any smaller "in-group" within the executive circle; tendency to ostracize or shut out one or more members; degree of honesty, trust, and open collaboration among them.

2. The existence of any particular "axis of influence," usually running from a mid-level manager, through an executive to the chief executive; if it exists, it may run along some natural line within the organization, such as a functional area in which the chief executive takes a great interest.

3. The existence of any informal centers of power, usually individual action people who, by virtue of circumstance, expertise, or relationship to top management, carry more informal "clout" than their positions would ordinarily confer.

4. The existence of any organizational "fences," splits, or feuds that tend to polarize departments or executives and their subordinates, and consequently to incentivize "gamey" interactions among them.

5. The existence of informal coalitions among middle managers and others in action roles, in such a way that a certain few key people usually show up on the same side of various technical issues or matters requiring discussion and decisions.

To a great extent, any two people define the political relationship between them in terms of whether they intend to collaborate most of the time or to clash most of the time. And whenever possible, if they can assemble a coalition of several collaborators, they can usually sell their ideas and approaches better and consequently form more favorable personal relationships with the executives. Treaties and feuds make up most of organizational politics.

Everything said here about politics in the organization at large also applies on the scale of an individual division, department, branch, or other unit, with appropriate allowance for the smaller size and less formal way of doing business on a day-to-day basis.

UNDERSTANDING THE "GRAPEVINE"

The "grapevine," or informal communication network that exists in any organization, is a critical part of the social system. Some managers, and even some textbooks on management, claim that a properly managed organization has no grapevine and doesn't need one. This, in my opinion, is absurd. It is a characteristically self-centered point of view on the part of some managers and some "old-school" management theorists to think that the only information of any consequence to the employees is that which the managers, in their all-encompassing wisdom, choose to pass down. This point of view assumes, probably unconsciously, that people are creatures without initiative, without curiosity, and without resourcefulness in looking after their own personal interests.

Any organization, healthy or not, has a grapevine. The "tribal drums" are always beating, sending bits of hot news along the way. People who car-pool to work together, friends or relatives in different departments or on different shifts, single people who date one another, members of the bowling club—all of these relationships provide opportunities for people to compare notes about what's going on in the organization. The function of the grapevine is to pass around *information of direct personal interest to the people who work there—* information that the managers don't generally consider "business" information. Whenever people working together consider some aspect of the organization or their managers as important to their personal well-being, they quite naturally take steps to find out whatever they can about it. If, for example, the president of a company retires, just about everybody wants to know who the next president will be and what that person will be like. Each person checks his or her own "connections" to see if the information is yet available. If the company is having business troubles and seems headed for a large layoff, naturally the people want to know about it.

The grapevine can be amazingly speedy, accurate, and efficient at times, since it generally isn't cluttered up with "useless" information about production schedules, changes in procedures, accounting data, and the other kinds of mundane topics with which managers concern themselves. It carries only the hot, new, useful, and emotionally significant information.

Indeed, the grapevine can serve as a compatible information network to the conventional administrative pathways by which information travels, although many managers might feel a bit uneasy about deliberately recognizing it and putting it to use. Quite a few managers, however, do indeed rely on the presence of the grapevine, sometimes without even consciously realizing that they do. For example, in many organizations the managers will "leak" impending bad news through the grapevine, not necessarily deliberately, but simply by discussing it freely among themselves and their immediate staff and letting the drums pick it up and carry it through the organization. Thus the possibility of a layoff, for example, becomes known to the workers without management having made any formal announcements. Later, when the time comes for the action, the workers don't see it as a surprise, and they have already adapted to it to some extent. Interestingly enough, many managers will try very hard to keep sudden good news from getting into the grapevine, so they can gain the psychological benefits of giving a pleasant surprise to the workers at an assembly meeting or special celebration.

Effective organization development requires that we first be able to identify and trace out the grapevine, find out how it is currently working, and take steps to assure that it supports the overall well-being of the organization, and that it doesn't become a more trustworthy source of general information for people than their day-to-day dealings with their leaders.

HOW A COMPANY GETS UNIONIZED

When we understand the social system of an organization, when we have a fairly clear idea of its culture, and when we know the prevailing social climate as seen by the people working there, we have a pretty good idea of how the workers relate to management. Many cases in which a company gets unionized turn out to be cases of myopic management, in which the managers got dangerously out of touch with the social system. They simply didn't grasp the significance of the social climate and the needs of working people to feel fairly treated.

While one can make a case, in some instances, for an advantage on the part of an outside union, say in a traditionally heavily unionized industry, or a large and powerful union going after a small company, nevertheless in most cases we can attribute unionization of a company to a failure of management to meet the needs of the workers. To working people, joining a union essentially means bringing in a third party between themselves and the management group in hopes of getting better wages, hours, or working conditions. An additional factor that often plays a key part in unionization is the feeling on the part of a majority of employees that management literally doesn't care about their concerns. Many a unionizing campaign centers on the attitudes of top management as perceived by the workers. For many workers, forming a union becomes a way to "punish" management and to retaliate for what they see as oppressive, degrading, or inconsiderate treatment.

Many company executives, contrary to popular belief, have proven that unionization of their work forces is not inevitable, including some very large companies. Eastman Kodak, for example, a company with 125,000 people and sales of $8 billion, is a nonunion company. Similarly, M&M/Mars, one of the largest and oldest manufacturers of chocolate, candy, and related products, is completely nonunion. Both of these companies have policies on wages, hours, and working conditions that make typical union wage settlements in their industries look pale by comparison. They prevent unionization by making it unnecessary and unattractive for their employees.

You may have sensed an underlying bias about unionization in the foregoing discussion. I openly concede that, for the most part, I regard a unionized company as evidence of ineffective management, from the comprehensive point of view of managing the railroad instead of just the train. In my experience, a company after unionization can be likened to a person after a heart attack. The patient may survive, but life is seldom ever the same again. Although I am not categorically against unions, I do believe it is possible for managers to manage in such a way as to make unionization an unattractive and unnecessary option for the employees of the company.

In general, if a company's workers, or a substantial portion of them, vote in favor of having a union represent them, a number of enabling conditions probably prevail. Although not all of them will be present in all situations, and not in equal proportions, nevertheless they tend to correlate closely with the decision of workers to unionize. These are the most common conditions:

1. A feeling of profound alienation on the part of the workers from the people in the management group; a "we-they" attitude, probably reciprocated by top management; a conviction that "they don't give a damn about us."
2. Oppressive, punitive, or otherwise toxic treatment by supervisors.
3. Dissatisfaction with perceived fairness of wages, hours, or working conditions; a feeling of entitlement to better treatment on the job.
4. The lack of any workable mechanism by which workers can make themselves heard by top management.
5. The presence of a strong national union, whose leaders are interested in unionizing this particular work force.
6. One or more strong leaders in the work force, who can persuade,

organize, and unite people in the belief that the union will give them a better shake.

One of the objectives of an OD program in a nonunion company may be to keep it as a nonunion company. This almost always centers attention on the social system. If you find yourself in such a situation, for example, you will find it very important to make an effective assessment of the social system, its culture, the climate as perceived by the employees, and the extent to which any of the previously mentioned union-enabling factors exist. Given this diagnosis, you can then propose whatever changes may be warranted to keep the climate of the organization healthy. Note that the union-enabling conditions enumerated above relate directly or indirectly to the quality of work life in the organization as defined by the ten key factors given in a previous section. By focusing on these key factors, and systematically improving them, the executives of an organization have the best chance of preventing unionization, and even—in some rare cases—of facilitating the de-certification of a union if one exists.

CULTURAL AND CROSS-CULTURAL ISSUES

Before leaving the subject of the social system, it is worthwhile to touch on a factor which is highly characteristic of American organizations, and becoming more so. This is the coexistence, within one organization, of distinctive social groupings that ally people in terms of "cultural" factors.

First, of course, we have racial and ethnic similarities. About twelve percent of the American work force is black. Rapidly approaching that proportion is the Hispanic subculture, consisting of Spanish, Mexican, Cuban, Puerto Rican, and other people who trace their ancestry to Spanish-speaking countries. Asians also represent a significant population, although smaller in proportion than blacks and Hispanics.

Since the civil-rights movement of the 1960s, and the Civil Rights Act of 1964, ethnic differences and needs have become increasingly important. It is a fact of life that white, Anglo-Saxon, Protestant ("WASP") males outnumber all other segments of the population in supervisory, management, and professional jobs, far in excess of the extent to which they outnumber them in the society at large. This is what the equal-employment-opportunity (EEO) movement and issue is all about, and it is an aspect of the social system with which OD needs to concern itself.

An even more significant issue than the treatment of ethnic minorities in organizations is the treatment of women if only because they constitute nearly half of the American work force, and because they bridge across all the minority categories. The issue of women in management is emerging rapidly and will probably become one of the key social issues in business for the rest of the century.

Add to these concerns the fact that more and more American companies are doing business in foreign countries, and you can see that cross-cultural cooperation and cross-cultural synergy are likely to become significant OD concerns in the future.

6

The Administrative System

COMPONENTS OF THE ADMINISTRATIVE SYSTEM

Although many managers may consider it mundane, uninteresting, and a necessary evil, the administrative system often offers a very high potential for improving the overall effectiveness of the organization. Seldom do managers really think in comprehensive terms about the administrative processes in the organization, and typically they only make major changes to them when they cause significant pain.

It is probably quite safe to say that, in the vast majority of organizations, the administrative system simply "grew like Topsy," with little rhyme or reason to its design and little compatibility among its many components. As people create file systems, adopt local procedures, organize reports in certain ways, design forms, distribute information, write computer programs, and all the rest, they are assembling an administrative system whether they know it or not. Like the other three systems, the social, the strategic, and (perhaps to a lesser degree) the technical, the administrative system seems to be less designed than patched together. And characteristically, people who use the components and processes of the administrative system as part of their daily work tend to resist ferociously any attempts by others to change the system. "It works OK, so why mess around with it?" seems to be one of the most common defenses of the status quo, even in those cases where it obviously doesn't work in the larger scheme of things.

Reminding ourselves of the OD truism that diagnosis must come before prescription, we will find it useful to be able to recognize the administrative system, assess its workings, and determine whether it is in need of significant improvement. To some extent, administrative improvements are easier to make than improvements in the other three key systems, if only because there is usually less emotionality attached to the ingredients of the systems themselves. So, let's make sure we give the administrative system proper attention as a potential avenue for planned improvement.

First, let's make sure we recognize the administrative system when we see it. It consists mainly of the components we need to manage the flow of information in the organization, over and above the technical information handled within the technical system. We can see the administrative system figuratively as the nerve pathways and the blood vessels of the organization. Here are at least the basic components we can consider as belonging to it:

1. The people who have as their primary jobs the production, manipulation, and distribution of administrative information, that is, the information which serves to make the overall organization itself work.

2. The abstract structure of the organization to the extent that it conveys the lines of direction down through the hierarchy, and the flow paths over which formal communication takes place, i.e., from managers to workers, and from workers to managers. Note that we can conceive of the organization chart as playing a part in all four systems, conveying a different set of ideas in each; in the social system it conveys power and authority; in the technical system it explains the allocation and grouping of work activities; in the administrative system it shows how information flows; and in the strategic system, which we will discuss later, it shows how the managers guide and control the overall enterprise.

3. Any specific facilities or organizational units that process the organization's data, except for purely technical, scientific, or management data; this can include a large number of possibilities, such as the computer center, local computer terminals or systems, a reproduction facility, a records storage facility, and the like; it could also include the finance department, the personnel department, and the organizational library if it has one.

4. The routine media that people use to move information about amongst them: forms, lists, tabulations, reports, computer printouts, and the like—but not the information itself.

5. The routine flow paths over which the information travels as it passes from person to person or from unit to unit.

If you have been following the development of these system descriptions closely as we've proceeded so far, and if you've been trying to classify various aspects of your own familiar organization, you might have found yourself having a little difficulty in deciding where to place certain components or processes. For example, does a certain kind of a report, which your colleagues think is extremely important, go under the administrative system or under the technical system? Or is it really part of the strategic system since managers mostly use it? The answer to that question comes in several satisfying parts. For one part, you can classify it in any one of a variety of ways without worrying too much because the only purpose of the system framework we're developing is to help you think about it logically. If it seems to fit comfortably in several systems, then any of them will do just fine as its "home" system. The dividing lines between the four systems will often be somewhat blurred because the systems are figments of our deliberate perceptions rather than part of the natural order of the world.

The second part of the answer to the question of where to put something is provided by the following guideline: feel free to classify it simultaneously as a component of more than one system. The organization chart, as previously cited, is a good example of this. People, at least some of them, are another example. Every person belongs to the social system, including managers; each person also belongs to at least one of the other systems. We can treat managers, in fact, as belonging potentially to all four systems, except possibly those who manage purely administrative units.

And the third part of the answer is this: it often doesn't matter. If some aspect of the organization seems to defy classification, let's not get too disturbed about it. If it isn't distinctly technical, then throw it in with the administrative system and be done with it. Again, the primary purpose of the systems approach is enlightenment and understanding, not compulsive classification.

THE KEY MEASURE: RESPONSE TIME

As with each of the other systems, we need to choose a primary variable for measuring the health of the administrative system. I propose a simple and very straightforward measure—response time. If the purpose of the administrative system is to carry the nerve impulses of the organization from one organ to another, i.e., to move information about reliably from those who have it to those who need it, then it should do so reliably, accurately, and quickly.

A useful "end-to-end" system test of the administrative system is for a manager to ask a question, for example, "How many people do we have working in this entire organization as of today?" and see how long it takes for a reliable answer to come back. The term "reliable" is important, because if the manager has reason to believe the answer may be untrustworthy, then he or she really doesn't have an answer, and the clock keeps ticking. Of course, in many cases, the manager simply doesn't know how trustworthy the information is, which is part of a more fundamental question about the system: not how well does it work, but does it work at all?

Did you know that the President of the United States doesn't know how many civilian employees the Federal Government has? And he can't find out? President Jimmy Carter attempted to get an accurate count of the number of employees and simply couldn't get a number he could trust. There are so many branches, agencies, departments, commissions, boards, panels, and the like, that the process of totaling them up introduced so many uncertainties that the counters had to settle for an estimate. Makes you stop and think, doesn't it?

A similar test is for an executive to put out an item of information and to ask to have it conveyed to every single employee in the organization. How would you best go about it, and how long would it take? "Well," you might say, "just put a slip in everyone's pay envelope." But how long before the next payday? If payday is tomorrow, can the administrative system respond fast enough to get that many slips printed? How about the extra work of stuffing them into pay envelopes? How about shift workers? Those in the field offices? People on vacation? People on sick leave or in the hospital? One of the realities that a manager must accept is that it takes time for information to travel. And the response time of the administrative system is one of the best measures of how well it is serving the needs of the organization.

MAINTAINING A LOGICAL STRUCTURE

The decision about how to organize—the abstract structure we are going to create in order to allocate tasks and resources—is one of the most critical of all decisions to the overall effectiveness of the enterprise. Given this critical importance, it is remarkable how many organizations go along for years in a state of profound malorganization before their managers take drastic action to rearrange them. Curiously, there seem to be some organizations in which the top managers seem to make a hobby of reorganizing, whereas managers in others keep the same structure for years and years.

Make no mistake—just reorganizing does not guarantee that you will improve things. I have seen quite a few companies and government agencies where the executives made a bad situation almost disastrous by reorganizing the outfit into an even less workable configuration. I have seen relatively few reorganizations that proceeded from an objective and dispassionate analysis of purposes and options. I have seen reorganizations that came about in order to reward a key executive, to satisfy a disgruntled owner, to push someone out of the organization as part of a "palace war," or simply to stir things up a bit. One executive remarked, "I like to stir things up now and then, just to prove I own the spoon."

Quite often, executives who reorganize to eliminate some pain factor will choose an organizational arrangement without thinking it through and end up with a new set of problems that are no better than the old ones. It makes sense in reorganizing, or in establishing a brand-new structure, to analyze the purposes of the organization, to review a variety of options, and to select a structure that satisfies the widest range of requirements and constraints. This element of careful analysis can pay off in huge dividends. As management consultant Peter Drucker puts it, "Reorganization is surgery. One doesn't just cut."

There are some definite principles and strategies in defining a workable organizational structure, and although they won't guarantee success, they can go a long way toward creating an effective arrangement of resources. Architects and designers have a long standing axiom: "Form follows function." By this they mean that the designer must have a clear idea of what the design must accomplish, or its basic function and purpose. In management, we have a similar axiom: "*Structure follows strategy.*" This means that top management needs to clarify the overall "thrust" of the organization; the grand design; and the highest-level strategy that will take the organization into the future. This is sometimes fairly straightforward, and sometimes an extremely difficult process. In any case, the effectiveness of the organization in the long run depends on having it. Once this strategy is available, management needs to choose a structure that actualizes the possibilities inherent in it.

This is a very different point of view than simply splitting one department into two, or combining two functions into one, or declining to replace the head of a division once he or she leaves by having a higher-level executive control it as "acting" manager, or any of a number of other ad hoc fixes. A serious definition of the organization's structure requires a clear understanding of where the organization should be going.

Take some time to think through the implications of this notion—structure follows strategy. When we create an organizational structure, we are predefining how a large number of people will relate to one another. We are establishing the lines of control, the primary channels of information flow, and the various functional roles that will govern their interactions. If we choose this overall pattern wisely, we maximize the "natural" forms of cooperation and collaboration amongst them, and we become much less dependent than we otherwise would be on individual personalities and attitudes.

The same principles that apply to reorganization from the very top of the organization also apply in reorganizing any part of it. Some of the factors to use in evaluating various options for organizing are as follows:

1. The extent to which a particular option creates and clarifies a primary productive axis for the organization; one that we can define clearly, manage effectively, and assess accurately in terms of whatever productivity measures we can identify.

2. The span of control offered to the executive, i.e., the number of subfunctions reporting directly to that executive; too small a span of control implies the possibility of an unnecessary layer of management; too wide a span implies that the executive would be spread too thin to give adequate guidance to the second-level executives.

3. The need for a logical, compatible, and psychologically satisfying grouping of functions or activities; a "natural" structure that most people think they can make work.

4. A structure that does not depend on certain executives, or certain personalities, or certain peculiar capabilities of those who manage it; an arrangement that more or less makes sense regardless of who occupies the various spots, provided they have the basic competencies required.

5. A high degree of *role freedom*; a set of relationships among the various divisions of the organization that minimizes unnecessary interdependence, interlocking of information-flow functions, and excessive "back-and-forth" interaction in handling routine matters.

The matter of appropriate organizational structure, and the question of whether the enterprise might be malorganized, present difficult issues sometimes. An OD program, if it focuses on this question, needs to approach it in terms of a careful assessment of the current structure; a review of the design factors that go into creating an effective organization, such as those listed above; and a selection from well-examined options of the approach that management considers most workable for the future. It is, of course, the first and final prerogative of top management to determine the structure.

SYMPTOMS OF MALORGANIZATION

Malorganization is much more common in business enterprises than one might suppose. Because organizations tend to "grow like Topsy" and because executives always include their personal and interpersonal needs in their decisions about deploying and controlling resources, many organizations appear to be organized in irrational ways. Actually, they are indeed rational if you consider the various subterranean factors involved; they only seem irrational if you insist on seeing a reorganization as strictly as administrative proposition. It is helpful to keep in mind some of the key symptoms of malorganization, so you can recognize it or begin to sense it when you encounter it.

Probably the most common form of malorganization is the span-of-control problem. This may involve far too many people reporting to the chief executive, or it may involve a very "tall" and "narrow" organization in which only a few functions report to the chief, with an inordinate number of levels running down through the organization. The primary symptom of a span-of-control problem of either sort is usually the same: the chief executive cannot "activate" the structure √ effectively and becomes increasingly frustrated at not being able to make things happen.

With an overly large span of control, on the order of twelve to fifteen functions or more, the executive is trying to overcontrol. By trying to keep one finger on every single project and problem, the executive runs out of fingers and runs out of time. The most common indication of this is a line of people waiting to see the boss, all frustrated at how long it takes to get into the front office. People in this "flat" organization tend to become exasperated and de-motivated, because they are forever dependent on the boss for direction. They can't get the boss's attention without a great deal of effort, and yet they aren't allowed to proceed on their own initiative. The organization just struggles along with only the essential things getting done. Such an executive doesn't realize that, after a certain point, the larger the span of control is, *the less real control he has*.

Too narrow a span of control slows things down as well in a different way. In this case, there are so many levels in the hierarchy between the working level and the chief executive that, as a result, he finds himself comparatively isolated from the day-to-day happenings. He may function as more of a caretaker than a manager, and the decisions and policy determinations get made at various levels of the structure without any central theme or philosophy. People may complain about not knowing what the chief is thinking or what his policies or objectives are. The "tall" organization takes on a distinctively "bureaucratic" style of operating.

Another common form of malorganization is, of course, having certain boxes misplaced on the chart. In some cases, a needed function doesn't show up on the chart at all, indicating that top management hasn't seen fit to give it a significant emphasis. In small and growing companies, for example, the personnel function is often the last to be fully developed. The head of personnel may be a "retreaded" purchasing agent, the chief executive's ex-secretary, or someone else with no training and preparation. In the early stages, the personnel function might land under the vice president for finance, or the chief of administration, or wherever else the president sees fit to place it. Only when the personnel needs of the organization become pressing and highly visible does the function get moved on line with the other major functions. The training function is another one that sometimes gets misplaced, or sometimes split up into several factions, often with a great deal of disagreement about how they should operate.

A frequent symptom of misplaced functions is the interdepartment squabble over turf. Two department heads vie with each other for the same mission, function, or project. Each can explain energetically why it falls logically into his or her organization. Chances are that the executives are in need of clarification of goals and roles, and possibly a rethinking of their organization chart.

Another form of malorganization, usually a less obvious one, is a severe imbalance of power among the executives who report to the chief. Occasionally, for any of a number of reasons, the chief executive will arrange things so that one favored executive gets a much larger "stick" than the others. This might include decision-making control over most of the resources, a physical location that gives advantageous access to the chief's office on a daily basis, a higher formal rank than other executives at the same level, or perhaps just a tendency toward favoring one individual. When this happens, the balance of power will usually shift gradually so that the strong get stronger and the weak get weaker. The result may well be a lopsided organization without enough checks and balances to keep the various divisions or departments working together.

Besides the possibility of being malorganized, we need to consider the question of whether the enterprise might be inappropriately organized. This means that it has no obvious glaring structural malfunctions, but that its primary deployment of resources no longer matches the natural structure of its market or the buying patterns of its customers or clients. This happens most commonly when an organization's environment has changed substantially or when something about the way it does business has made an extreme shift.

For example, a small company that manufactures specialty components may be appropriately organized along functional lines, with marketing done primarily through catalog sales. As it grows, begins to take on larger jobs involving custom orders, and eventually gets into aerospace or government/military markets, the executives may find a very large portion of the work taking the form of large contracts and special orders, with less routine manufacturing for inventory. Because the organization's way of doing business has changed, it may indeed have become inappropriately organized. It may be time for them to shift—in a carefully planned way—to a project-oriented structure or to a matrix-type structure. Similarly, at some point in a company's development, it may make sense to shift from a functional arrangement to a product-line arrangement.

Of course, the question of the appropriateness of the structure is a matter of opinion. We have no objective way of proving that one structural option is obviously better than another without trying them all and measuring the results. In a sense, any organizational arrangement is "wrong," in that it sacrifices the advantages of other arrangements in favor of its own distinctive advantages. Sooner or later, the decision about how to organize depends on judgment, fact finding, and careful consideration of the key factors affecting the particular organization in question.

COMMUNICATING THE STRUCTURE

It usually helps if the largest practical number of people in the organization understand the structure and know how to navigate within it. This would seem to go without saying, except that in many organizations, one can find quite a few staff people who "should" know how the system is supposed to work, but don't. It is not at all uncommon for a person to work in a staff position in one division of an organization, having come up through the ranks there in specialized assignments, to have daily dealings with a few counterpart people in another division, and yet have only a fuzzy idea of what goes on over there.

Some executives institute programs of cross-departmental exchanges, or cross-educational meetings and workshops, in which staff people get a better idea of what goes on in parts of the organization with which they haven't had a chance to become familiar.

There are some companies, however, in which the executives deliberately maintain a level of "creative confusion" about organizational structure and reporting relationships. Some of them believe this contributes to a more dynamic organization and prevents it from becoming fossilized. Another motive may be to maintain a closer form of control, by means of the additional dependency on the part of the workers that comes about when they have to rely heavily on the managers to know what to do. In general, a policy of organizational clarity seems to have the most benefits. It simply means making a clear definition of organizational structure, roles and goals, reporting relationships, interfaces between divisions of the organization, and pathways for the flow of information. On the average, this helps people to function in self-directing, self-managing ways, and it tends to aim their collective effort effectively in the direction of increased organizational effectiveness.

CLARIFYING POLICIES, PROCEDURES, AND STANDARDS

Policies are widely used, widely misused, and widely misunderstood aspects of running an organization; so are written procedures, and so are standards. Many people seem to get the three terms, and the concepts behind them, tangled up in discussing administrative forms of guidance in the organization. It will be helpful to our purposes here to adopt specific, concrete, and non-overlapping definitions of the three forms of guidance and to account for them in diagnosing and improving the administrative system.

Often, when people use one of the three terms given above, they have in mind a specific written implementation—a published document, possibly formally signed and released by someone in authority, which is distributed to various key people in the organization for compliance. Let's use that connotation here. When we refer to a policy, a procedure, or a standard, we will be talking about a written form of guidance. Let's use the term "guidance media" to suggest that they do exist on paper.

You may find it interesting to ask people for their definitions of the term "policy," and to ask them to explain to you the difference between a policy and a procedure, again referring to them as documents. You might find that they, and perhaps you yourself, have trouble making a distinction between the two. If so, that probably means that the concepts behind them are somewhat fuzzy in your minds. By clarifying the concepts of what the organizational guidance media are supposed to accomplish, we can use them more effectively.

I will offer a set of definitions here that are not necessarily widely known or widely used in the study of management, but that nevertheless come closer to making things understandable than any others

I've read or heard. The remainder of the treatment given to the administrative system in this book uses these following definitions, so please take care to understand them accurately.

A *policy*, according to my definition, is a guideline for management action, not for employee action. A *procedure*, by that token, is a guideline for employee action. And a *standard* is a specific measure of performance against which the manager and the employees can evaluate the employee's work. Let's take these terms one at a time, in somewhat greater depth.

The distinction given here between a policy and a procedure may surprise you to some extent, especially if you have become accustomed to using the two terms almost interchangeably. Your organization might have a "Policy and Procedure Manual," and you might sometimes have difficulty deciding which of the documents are really policies and which are really procedures. Of course, they "are" whatever people choose to call them, but many times the administrative specialists who write them get their purposes mixed up. The purpose of a policy, according to my definition, is for *management to go on record as promising to behave in certain ways under certain circumstances.* This is a way in which management can become relatively predictable to the employees, and it usually helps them understand what management considers important.

For example, most American organizations have policies about equal employment opportunity—"EEO." When the chief executive says in writing, "It is our policy to recruit, hire, place, train, promote, and pay people without regard to their race, color, religion, sex, age, or national origin, and to hire people based on ability to do the job," he or she is committing the managers of the organization to a very specific pattern of action. Another example: an organization may have a policy about personal work habits. Part of it might say, "Coming to work intoxicated is grounds for immediate dismissal." While one could argue that this is an instruction to the employee—"don't come to work drunk"—under our scheme of definitions it is a promise, or a warning, that management will take a prescribed action under certain circumstances.

This approach to policies very quickly clears up any confusion about what they do and about how to use them. People like to know the rules of the game and to have the assurance that management will apply them fairly and uniformly. A capricious style of managing, with frequent changes in the way the manager approaches the same situation, and with little consistency people can depend on, creates confusion, apprehension, defensive behavior, and above all a lack of respect, confidence, and faith in the manager. Think over this approach to policies, and you will see how valuable policies really can be. We don't have to churn out policies on every little matter, but it does help to have a family of well-thought-out, clearly-written, and widely-understood policies for the organization on matters of consequence.

If a policy is a promise by management to behave in certain ways under certain circumstances, then a procedure is an instruction to the employees requiring them to behave in certain ways under certain circumstances. An effective procedure should be specific, brief, concise, easy to understand, and generally easy and logical to carry out. But above all, it should only be about something that really does need a written procedure.

Probably the single most common problem with organizational procedure manuals is that they contain far too many procedures, on far too many matters, most of which the procedure-writers should have left entirely up to the discretion of the employees and their supervisors. By choosing only the highest-priority areas of the operation for legislation, and by writing a few brief and sensible procedures to create and enforce the necessary uniformity, we can streamline the administrative system tremendously and make it highly efficient.

The same applies to performance standards, which managers rather than procedure writers should develop, and which should succinctly explain to workers whose jobs call for them what a job well done means.

By thinking clearly about these three kinds of guidance media—policies, procedures, and standards—we can diagnose the administrative system rather quickly in this regard and prescribe logical improvements in the name of simplicity and efficiency.

MAINTAINING A HEALTHY INFORMATION ENVIRONMENT

Because organizations depend more and more on information in order to function, it makes sense to take a conscious approach to managing the information environment that exists inside any enterprise. The administrative system includes as part of its operation the day-to-day flow of raw data and useful information, over and above the large amount that people pass on informally and by word of mouth. If the managers of the organization, who all play a part in its administrative processes, take an active interest in the quality of information and the efficiency with which it gets distributed to the people who need it, we can have a lively and effective administrative system.

In a highly technical organization, for example, many people need to keep abreast of developments in the industry and within their specialties. While each individual is ultimately responsible for doing this, managers and others in a position to help can gather and distribute useful information that not everyone would happen to find. In some cases a company library, well stocked with references, and well supplied with key periodicals, can serve as a valuable resource.

An organizational newsletter, or bulletin, also serves as a useful way to pass around informal but significant items of information. It also frequently conveys to the members of the organization, just by its existence, that management considers it important to promote a healthy information flow.

Standard reports, well designed, frequently reviewed in terms of their value, and properly distributed, can also play an important part in keeping various key people, especially managers, abreast of operations.

It makes sense in organizational diagnosis to examine the existing information environment, prune out the informational deadwood and useless media, and streamline and update it as necessary. This can have high payoffs in the long term, even though its effects may not always be obvious.

7

The Strategic System

A SPECIAL COMMENT ABOUT THE STRATEGIC SYSTEM

The formidable-sounding title "strategic system" applies to the steering function of the organization—its managers, the relationships among them, and the methods they use to manage. Giving a label to this aspect of the organization creates very definite implications, which you as a reader—especially if you happen to be a manager—need to be aware of.

First, it means that the systems approach to organization development holds the managers up to scientific scrutiny, just as it holds the employees, the technical processes, and the administrative processes up for scrutiny. This need not be a negative or critical scrutiny, but make no mistake—it most definitely is a deliberate form of scrutiny. This is where some managers part company with the philosophy of OD. Sometimes a manager will say, "This organization development stuff is pretty good, but sometimes it can go too far. I don't want any consultant telling me I don't know how to manage."

There is an old story that exactly exemplifies the attitude of some managers toward self-scrutiny. It concerns an elderly lady living in a small town who attended church regularly and stood firmly by her religious convictions. One Sunday morning she sat in her accustomed pew, listening to the preacher hold forth about the evil doings of some of her neighbors. When he condemned corn liquor as the devil's brew, she nodded emphatically. When he railed against gambling, she muttered an emphatic "Amen." When he got on about adultery, she clucked her tongue, shook her head, and agreed. Filled with oratory fervor that morning, he moved on to his next topic—dipping snuff. As he began to catalog the evil effects of that pastime, she sat bolt upright in her pew, set her jaw into a resolute expression of disapproval, and muttered, "Why, now he's quit preachin' and took to meddlin'!" For some managers, the line between preachin' and meddlin' comes when a consultant, internal OD specialist, or OD task force begins to take a look at their managerial styles and practices, and begins to trace out their impacts on the other three systems. Many an OD program has had its water cut off at this point, never to be restored again.

Other managers, however, have no particular qualms about examining their personal managerial styles, for they view it as a means of understanding their effectiveness better and possibly learning some new approaches or strategies. Although they certainly won't stand for being attacked or criticized without foundation, and they don't take well to consultants or other OD people who are not sensitive to their special roles as power figures and leaders, nevertheless they have enough self-confidence and ego-strength to welcome constructive scrutiny of their styles and methods.

The systems approach to OD described in this book works well with managers of the second type, those who have a fair measure of self-confidence and willingness to learn, no matter what their age or seniority. These attitudes make them and the organizations they manage "OD-ready," as previously described. The systems approach does not set very well with managers who compensate for lack of ego-strength and maturity by managing in oppressive, punitive, or otherwise toxic styles. They, and consequently their organizations, are not OD-ready.

Indeed, a skilled OD practitioner, either external or internal, will usually make a quick appraisal of the strategic system at the very outset, as part of the process of determining the general possibilities OD might present to the organization. He or she knows from experience that any OD program will only go as far and as fast as the people in charge will allow it to. If they are ready for a constructive look at the entire organization, the OD practitioner knows what kinds of approaches to propose in getting started. If not, he or she had better think the situation through carefully and decide whether to propose anything at all, and if so, what kind of a low-risk approach might gain acceptance at the outset.

As a consultant, when I am first contacted by an action person in an organization about the possibility of getting an OD process started, I first ask a series of questions about the organization and its executives. The answers to these questions tell fairly reliably the degree of OD-readiness that exists in the management group, and consequently in the organization at large. Often the person taking the initiative is the head of the training department, or "human resources development" function as many organizations now call it, or the head of the personnel department. He or she knows something about the OD process and believes that the organization could benefit from it. However, it may well be a losing situation from the start, and a few diagnostic questions will tell.

Of course, many organizations fall into the category of "almost OD-ready"; that is, some of the necessary conditions exist, but not all of them. The internal action person believes that, with a carefully chosen approach, most of the members of the management team would take well to the concept of OD, would be willing to learn about it, and would find value in it. The challenge is to package up the possibilities inherent in a very sophisticated thinking process which the managers may never have seen before, and to give them enough of a motivation to invest the time, energy, and money in trying it out.

So we can see that the strategic system of the organization—i.e., its managers—is at one and the same time an aspect of the organization that deserves legitimate study and also a key factor in determining whether any part of the organization will be studied at all. This makes it doubly important to understand the strategic system in any OD program or potential program.

COMPONENTS OF THE STRATEGIC SYSTEM

We can think of the strategic system as made up of at least the following components:

1. The top management team—the chief executive, a board of directors if one exists, and the first-level executives; those who make up the "inner circle" of the organization, including highly influential staff people or others who may not have formal managerial authority.

2. The extended management family—all other managers in the organization, seen as a connected hierarchy down through the chain of command.

3. The planning system and the plans—the scheme for determining the organization's long-range direction, laying out plans, and implementing them down through the hierarchy; this includes the plans themselves, which might consist of a master organizational plan, with short-, medium-, and long-range phases, and various departmental and unit plans which provide the "tactics" to carry out the overall strategy.

4. The written directives and other "live" media (excluding policies, procedures, and standards, which we classified under the administrative system), which managers use to give formal direction to the organization and to their individual parts of it.

5. The management information system, or "MIS," which keeps important data flowing automatically to the managers at various levels, enabling them to assess the ongoing status of the organization, anticipate problem areas, and plan ahead systematically; this may range from a crude, or nearly nonexistent system, to a very sophisticated computerized system.

THE KEY MEASURE: MANAGEMENT STRENGTH

In the simplest terms, we can consider the key measure of the strategic system to be the sum total of the skills of its managers, because all of the other elements of the strategic system depend on them. In one sense, the entire effectiveness of the organization is a measure of management strength, although we must account for a variety of practical factors beyond the control of management that affect its overall health.

Measuring management strength is not as difficult as you might surmise, even though we can't get it down to one single measure such as miles per hour or kilograms per day. We can, however, develop a reasonably objective appraisal scheme, based on known and accepted managerial competencies, and we can assess the current competency levels of the managers individually and then collectively. Probably the main reason that assessing managerial competence is not a widespread practice in business organization is that most of the assessing that goes on, of all kinds, is done by managers. Most people are understandably reluctant to set up systems that place themselves under scrutiny. Quite a few organizations have done just that, however, usually with positive results.

For example, the California Department of Motor Vehicles instituted a program in which all employees filled out rating forms, anonymously, on their supervisors. Members of a special task force assembled the results, "sanitized" them to eliminate features of the data that would uniquely identify individuals, and presented the summarized and analyzed data to the supervisors. Many of them were surprised at how highly their employees rated them; others found out useful things about their managerial styles; and a few others got stung.

It is important, in assessing managerial strength, to follow certain guidelines, to avoid creating an atmosphere of tension, defensiveness, or negative criticism. A later chapter shows how to accomplish this. When assessment of the strategic system proceeds from a constructive point of view and employs techniques that respect managers' special roles and status, it produces useful information that can help to manage more effectively.

Of course, an assessment of the strategic system involves its other components as well. We need to examine the entire planning process and the plans that it creates, as well as the means for following through on the plans. The management information system and the directive media used in guiding and controlling the organization on a day-to-day basis also deserve a careful appraisal.

All of these components taken together, and the processes and relationships that unite them, can give us a good picture of the strategic system and can help us identify ways to improve it—and thereby improve the effectiveness of the overall organization.

UNDERSTANDING "POWER PEOPLE"

Many professional people feel uncomfortable or unsure of themselves in dealing with "power people," i.e., those who exercise formal authority, usually because they have never really studied these kinds of people and learned what makes them tick. Here we will take the time to clarify several very important aspects of the psychology of these folks and to draw some useful conclusions about dealing with them.

We can make several generalizations about people who occupy positions of authority in American business organizations. First, the vast majority of "power people" are men. Men in management positions outnumber women by at least ten to one, and in chief executive jobs men outnumber women by more than a thousand to one. Power is primarily a male process.

Second, a person in authority is first of all a human being, with all the normal needs, feelings, reactions, impulses, fears, and self-doubts that anyone else has. It is easy for a subordinate person to forget this, because a managerial position usually brings with it various elements of status and various aspects of deference by other people, which make the manager seem somehow more than human. The managerial job usually feeds the incumbent's ego very well, and this enables him to act out a confident exterior, even if he doesn't really feel confident.

Third, the key to understanding how a person will adapt to having a position of authority is his self-esteem. A person with low self-esteem, which comes in a variety of forms and is often not obviously visible through his compensating social strategies, will generally feel anxious about losing power and will habitually use the power either for ego-protection or ego-building. A person with high self-esteem will generally use power more gracefully and will not let the trappings of the position seduce him into dependency on them in order to feel significant and potent.

People in power, especially at high levels, have a variety of very personal, private concerns, which subordinates seldom know about; this is why subordinates often tend to see power people as unemotional and a bit unreal. For example, a power person realizes that he can't really make a complex organization respond at the snap of his fingers, even though a typical working person believes the power person could solve certain problems just by deciding to do so. An executive often feels a sense of impotence about controlling a massive system like an organization, with so many people running this way and that, and with so much misinformation, confusion, and uncertainty. He seldom knows as much about what's going on as subordinates think, and he frequently has to deal with problems that are unclear or simply don't seem to have clean solutions. Most people at the bottom ranks of the organization make two incorrect assumptions about top managers— that they are better informed than they really are, and that they are not as intelligent as they really are. If they would reverse those two assumptions and assume that top managers are intelligent but not very well informed about organizational goings on, they could deal with them much more effectively and could sell their ideas to them more successfully.

You can size up a power person at virtually any level by knowing a few of the basic things to look for. A manager's likely effectiveness, while not guaranteed, depends heavily on at least these four factors:

1. Self-esteem, as previously explained.
2. Practical intelligence—a reasonably logical mind, a fair degree of mental flexibility and willingness to adapt to facts, and the orientation to learn.
3. A high degree of social skill—the ability to deal with subordinates, peers, and superiors positively and constructively, without abrasiveness, antagonism or undue adversarial patterns.
4. Management know-how—a grasp of at least the basic principles of management, and an orientation to look at management as a highly comprehensive role; the willingness to manage all of the organization.

While most of the foregoing remarks treat power people rather gently and considerately, let's establish one key point quite bluntly; some people do enjoy having power for its own sake. For some people, as Henry Kissinger once observed, "Power is the ultimate aphrodisiac." There are people, and quite a few of them, who gain such a delicious sense of potency from having power over others, that it becomes a virtual addiction for them. In living their roles as executives, they do not necessarily abandon all other considerations, but their power feelings are never very far from the top of their list of priorities. This dominates their behavior profoundly on a day-to-day basis. In sizing up this kind of power person, you must understand him from the point of view of this ego-feeding process; it is generally the only way to make sense of his long-term behavior.

There are many more male "power junkies" than females. Power of this type, while not completely foreign to the feminine psyche, does seem linked more or less directly to the biological experience of being male. The male phenomenon of "machismo," as the Latin cultures call it, or the highly emphasized projection of masculinity, relates closely to the kinds of dominance that are involved in the ego-serving uses of power in organizations and in governments. The "macho" behavior pattern, interestingly, is not aimed at females; it is aimed at other males. Rather than a projection of male sexuality toward females, it is really a territorial projection of physical adequacy—an attempt to overcome internal feelings of inadequacy and anxiety about being dominated or overwhelmed. Mature males, who have come to terms with their own self-esteem, have put aside these primitive anxieties and have little need to prove themselves to the outside world through primitive signalling. At the same time, they have come to terms with their sexuality and feel confident in their functioning as sexual human beings.

Am I saying that male power junkies act the way they do because they have low self-esteem, coupled with serious doubts about their potency as male creatures, and possibly substantial concern about their sexuality as well? Yes. Of course, they can't go around physically attacking other males and raping females, as the biological nature of this description would imply; in modern society they would probably get killed or put in jail as a result. So they opt for the next best thing: *abstract power—control over the resources and the punishment-reward system that other people need and depend on. They thrive on the reality of the "golden rule" of organizational life—"He who has the gold makes the rules." They get their feelings of adequacy and potency by making other people cringe. And they love it.*

As previously mentioned, this kind of a scrutiny of executives and managers is a highly personal process, and best done in the privacy of your own mind. You wouldn't want to blurt out something in a staff meeting like, "Well, Jack, the way I see it, you're a power junkie who's lacking in social skills and that makes you inept as an executive." There might be situations in which others would condone that kind of an approach, but not as a general matter. Of course, at a certain point in an OD program, you might have succeeded in creating a climate in which managers openly and honestly review their capabilities and their styles, and identify changes they might want to make. It may involve quite a challenge to get there, but a patient and positive approach usually results in the most productive process in the long run.

In summary, keep in mind, when working with executives and thinking about their roles in an OD process, that an executive is first a human being, and second a person who fills a special role. Make sure you account for this humanity first, and remember that all executives have egos. In trying to help them examine their managerial styles and needs, it makes sense to lead up to it in small, low-risk steps.

THE TOP MANAGEMENT TEAM

The top management team usually plays the most significant part in establishing the effectiveness of the strategic system in a typical organization. Here, we refer to the organization's "inner circle," which includes people who may not have formal managing authority but who nevertheless have significant influence by virtue of special roles or unusual expertise in some area. We might also include in this category executive assistants, executive secretaries, advisors, and others who make up the "executive household."

We can examine the effectiveness of the top management team just as we would any other team, looking for indications that tell us how well its members collaborate and how well they focus their energies. In this case we consider them as a functioning unit in and of itself, rather than simply individuals who are in charge of portions of the organization. They have special activities and processes that characterize them as a unit, and it is these processes we study when we look at the management team.

We can consider the effectiveness of the management team as indicated by at least the following six factors:

1. *Leadership* of the team by the chief executive; in this case he or she serves as a leader of leaders, the head of the management team as well as the head of the overall organization.

2. *Team spirit* among the members; the extent to which they get along well with one another as human beings and friends, as well as with coworkers, power people, and chiefs of the various divisions of the organization; their interpersonal commitment to working together, and to cooperating and making compromises.

3. A workable *goal-setting and planning process*, by which they convert their understanding of the outside world and of the organization into a logical form of direction for the organization.

4. Functional _cooperation_ among individuals as leaders of the various divisions of the organization; the extent to which they maintain effective inter-unit collaboration, cooperation, and compromise; and the extent to which they encourage their subordinates to do the same.

5. A _collective problem-solving and decision-making_ process, by which they can wrestle with the issues facing the organization, study the available facts, combine and evaluate various points of view, review the available options, and make determinations that they can put into action.

6. A _follow-through_ capability; the habits and methods by which they convert great thoughts into crude deeds; their ability to transfer solutions out of the conceptual realm and reduce them to management directives to the people who have to get all the work done that is necessary to make them real.

These aspects of effective mananagement teamwork apply, to some extent, at virtually all levels of the organization, down to the smallest working unit or section. Assessing team effectiveness objectively and constructively can play a key part in nearly any OD program.

THE EXTENDED
MANAGEMENT FAMILY

The strategic system extends from the chief executive all the way down to the grass-roots level of the organization, in the form of the managers who constitute the chain of command. I call this the extended management family, as distinguished from the inner circle, or top management team. Middle managers and first-line supervisors tend to feel that they belong to two groups at the same time. Not being part of the inner sanctum of leadership, they feel, at least to some extent, like working people. And not being strictly workers either, and having some formal authority, they feel like part of a special subculture, i.e., part of "management."

Along with the top management team, the extended management family plays a key role in establishing the effectiveness of the strategic system. Make an estimate of the overall effectiveness of an individual manager, say on a judgmental scale of 1 to 10, add to it the various "scores" of all the other members of the management family, divide by the number of managers, and think of the total as aggregate management strength. Management strength is an organizational resource, just as capital is a resource, just as skilled working people are a resource, and just as an effective product design is a resource.

As mentioned previously, we can't assess management strength in strictly quantitative terms, like miles per hour or volts of electricity. But we can make a reasonably objective qualitative assessment of an individual manager by assessing the extent to which he or she possesses certain concrete skills which we recognize as important in managing effectively. The discussion of the next section, coupled with a later chapter, will show how to do that. By treating aggregate management strength as a resource which we can assess, we open up the way for constructive training and development approaches which can improve it. Once we can conceive of the strategic system in fairly specific terms, we can target the extended management family for development as one of the high-payoff areas in an OD program.

UNDERSTANDING MANAGERIAL STYLES

Here we will examine a scheme for assessing, in broad terms, the general way in which a manager approaches the job of management. Having a framework like this will enable us to size up the various managerial styles in an organization, to size up the approach of any one particular manager, and more importantly to communicate with managers in a constructive way about their styles.

For this discussion, we will distinguish between managerial style and leadership style in the following way. By thinking of management as a broad, multi-role job, and leadership as one of the roles involved in it, we can clear up quite a few misunderstandings. The fact that leadership is only a part of management explains why a person can be a highly charismatic leader and an inept manager overall. It also explains why a person can be just "so-so" as a leader, i.e., basically competent but not necessarily inspiring, and still function reasonably well as a manager overall.

First, let's study the overall management style in terms of the various roles a manager must play at any level of the organization. We can think of the effective, "comprehensive" manager as filling four simultaneous and interrelated roles:

1. A *Strategist*—one who thinks through the purposes of the organization, examines the outside environment, considers the expected or possible future the organization is likely to encounter, and establishes the overall direction it must take; the strategist is the one that helps the organization adapt effectively to its changing environment.

2. A *Leader*—one who can influence people effectively, enabling them, guiding them, helping them, persuading them, and—in certain situations—directing them in the work they must do to meet the organization's goals.

3. A *Problem-Solver*—one who can think logically and flexibly, and help others to do so, in dealing with the many situations, issues, problems, dilemmas, and opportunities that present themselves every day; the manager's job is not necessarily to solve problems, but to get them solved.

4. An *Administrator*—one who creates and implements systems and repeatable processes that help people work, communicate, and collaborate efficiently; one who gives standing guidance to the work processes by means of policies, procedures, and standards as necessary.

We can think of a well-rounded manager as one who can balance all four of these roles, as illustrated in Figure 7-1. We will explore this four-dimensional managerial scheme in greater depth in a later chapter, as an assessment tool.

FIGURE 7–1   An Effective Manager Has Four Roles

Because the role of leader gets so much attention in management, and because many managers could profit by an explicit review of their leadership styles, we also need a framework for thinking about that special role. In selecting the leader role for special study, we do not imply that it is necessarily more important than the other three, just that it warrants more careful thought and study because of the complexity of its human dimensions.

We can simplify a great deal of the behavioral science theory that describes leadership, at least from the managerial point of view, in terms of four factors that continually recur. One or more of these factors seem to play a part in virtually every behavioral theory or scheme dealing with leadership style. We are going to use a distillation of many theories all put together, to reduce the matter to simple and manageable terms. The four factors that characterize a person's leadership style are the following:

1. *Shared Goals*—the extent to which the manager, as leader, gives the group members a sense of the "big picture," spells out for them the purpose and aims of the group, and allows them to share the process of setting goals and determining the course of action they will take in achieving the goals.

2. *Teamwork*—the extent to which the manager gets the group members together occasionally to help them work as a unit; helping them to identify useful ways to work together and help one another; keeping them informed of matters affecting them as a group; building team spirit and a sense of belonging on the part of the members.

3. *Autonomy*—the extent to which the manager grants freedom of action to each individual, allowing him or her to decide on the best way to accomplish the job within general guidelines; the effectiveness of the manager's delegation.

4. *Reward*—the way in which the manager rewards people for the work they do, in both tangible and intangible ways; use of positive feedback on results; use of pay and promotion; use of praise and public recognition; use of special perquisites or privileges, such as special assignments and the like.

Actually, we can think of these four factors as continuum scales, that is, a manager can use too little or too much of any of them. Too little use of shared goals, for example, would amount to purely dictatorial leadership; the manager simply tells people what to do, without soliciting their ideas or viewpoints. Conversely, the manager could overuse shared goals, by trying to run a miniature democracy; he or she could consult the employees on so many matters, large and small, that they don't feel properly led. The same idea holds true for the other three factors, as illustrated in Figure 7-2.

	TOO LITTLE	JUST RIGHT	TOO MUCH
SHARED GOALS	Manager merely dictates work to be done	Manager and workers share ideas and establish goals in cooperation	Manager relies too heavily on workers to decide what to do
TEAMWORK	Manager does not have group meetings; deals with workers individually	Manager uses group meetings to clarify goals, assign responsibilities, and solve problems	Manager wastes the time of the workers in too many meetings; puts too much emphasis on group activity
AUTONOMY	Manager overcontrols workers; gives them no chance to use their own judgment	Manager allows each worker to proceed on his or her own according to established goals	Manager gives workers too little direction; they don't know how to proceed in many situations
REWARDS	Manager seldom compliments workers or recognizes their achievements; criticizes too much	Manager recognizes effective performance and gives positive feedback; demands good performance	Manager hands out praise, pay increases, etc., without regard to performance; tries to be "nice"

FIGURE 7-2   Managerial Leadership Has Four Key Components

These schemes for evaluating managerial style and leadership style can be useful in organization development in several ways. First, they can give the person who is trying to get an OD program started a preliminary understanding of how the managers manage, and how they are likely to respond to the idea of such a program. Second, during the course of an OD program, they can serve as simple and useful ways to help the managers assess their own various styles and to understand how they affect the organization. And third, they can serve as a basis for management training programs which they might want to undertake as part of the developmental process at the appropriate stage of the OD program.

EVALUATION

Returning to the four dimensions of organizational health described in the first chapter, i.e., evaluation, adaptation, graduation, and innovation, we can see now how they fit into the strategic system. A healthy and properly functioning strategic system will include a natural means for carrying out these processes on a relatively regular and systematic basis. For an organization in which these processes do not exist or have fallen into disrepair, an OD program can play a useful part in getting them established or revived.

The evaluation process calls for two important activities. The first is a periodic review of what's going on "outdoors," i.e., the current trends and likely developments in all important aspects of the organization's operating environment. The second, based on the first, is the systematic identification of key changes the manager will have to make in the way the organization does business to enable it to adapt to the shifting environment.

We can carry out this systematic evaluation by thinking of the organization's operating environment in terms of a number of important "subenvironments" (which we will simply call environments, for semantic convenience)—i.e., smaller and more specific areas of the environment that we can study more easily than we could by attacking the whole thing at once. A typical organization, either profit-making or nonprofit, has at least the following environments outside its doors:

- Customer
- Competitor
- Economic
- Social
- Technological
- Legal
- Political
- Physical

All of these terms have fairly straightforward connotations, except perhaps the term "physical environment." This refers to the geographic, territorial, and meteorological aspects of the physical surroundings in which the organization must operate. These may be relatively unimportant for many organizations, but for a ski lodge, for example, factors such as transportation, weather, and distance from population centers may have crucial significance.

An extra category of "special environments" can account for any particular feature of the organization's outside world that managers want to give special attention. This might include a parent organization, or a government agency that plays an unusually significant part in the business, or the taxpayers in the case of a county administrative headquarters.

The evaluation process based on this environmental framework centers mostly on the technical system of the organization, although it has implications for the other systems as well. From the point of view of the technical system, the purpose of the evaluation is to spot situations, impending events, trends, and possible happenings that will either make trouble or present opportunities for the system as it presently operates.

One of the most effective ways for top managers to use this evaluation approach is to hold a planning conference periodically—at least once a year—at which someone who has conducted a thorough study of the organization's environments presents these findings. The managers then discuss the implications of the environmental analysis and develop a strategy for steering the organization in what they consider the proper direction. Out of this strategy comes operating goals for the organization, and a plan for meeting them. Thus, the environmental analysis feeds directly into the planning process. Based on this analysis, or perhaps a part of it, is the careful evaluation of all four systems of the organization, which helps determine the necessary constructive changes that management needs to make for the organization to adapt to the expected future.

ADAPTATION

There's not much to say about adaptation. It's more a matter of emphasis than technique. If the managers have developed an effective follow-through process, they can convert the desired changes into real changes. An organization adapts on a day-to-day basis, more than in one giant leap. The managers must identify the opportunities, big and small, for communicating the plan down through the chain of command, for helping the middle-level and lower managers understand and implement it, and for reinforcing the importance of the changes.

If the management team lacks an effective follow-through capability, then the first order of business is to develop one. This the team can do, for example, by setting up a system of special projects, one for each of the outcomes it wants to promote. By assigning each project to one single individual, either within the top management team or in a position to report to the team, and by imposing clear expectations and deadlines, they can get the results they want.

Sometimes a training workshop for managers, focusing on project management and follow-through, can help them develop the collective discipline to keep the organization adapting as it should.

GRADUATION

Every organization of any size needs a "graduation" process—a means by which top management can find the leaders of tomorrow. There needs to be a way to identify people who have the potential and the interest to become managers, to give them developmental opportunities, and to have a pool of capable people to choose from when vacancies in the management ranks open up. If the organization is in a rapid growth mode, the graduation process is all the more important. Even if not, the availability of capable leaders almost always affects an organization's long-term effectiveness.

When an organization lacks a graduation process, management will sooner or later probably face the dilemma of trying to find a qualified individual to fill a fairly high-ranking spot and having no obvious candidates to choose from within the organization. The chief executive may say, "We really don't have anybody qualified to do a good job in this position, so I guess we'll have to go outside." This is equivalent to saying, in my opinion, "We failed to graduate people into positions of management readiness, so we'll have to gamble on an outside person." Hiring from the outside is a controversial point in the management field. Some managers insist on their prerogative of hiring anybody they choose to fill a key spot, either from within the organization or from outside—it makes no difference. Others believe that bringing someone in from outside the organization, over the heads of those who would like to have a shot at the job, tends to damage morale and commitment. Some companies have a firm policy of giving first chance at a managerial job to people in the organization and only going outside if that avenue fails.

In the absence of a graduation process, even the means for

deciding whether one of the people in the organization can fill the job do not exist. Usually the manager who "owns" the job, i.e., the one in whose department it resides, will take a quick look at the people working in the unit that needs a new manager and, if none of them is currently the manager's fair-haired boy or fair-haired girl, will simply decide the matter on the basis of whether it appears that one of them could presently do the job. If the answer is no, then they are doomed to another period of stagnation, because once the manager locates a new person for the job, the situation returns to its previous state, with nobody getting developed for anything.

Frequently, the manager simply isn't too impressed with any of the available people, sometimes only because of overfamiliarity and "boredom" with them. The idea of engaging a search firm sounds like a scientific way to go about it, and all the expectations rig the game in favor of the incoming person.

Having a graduation process prevents these and a variety of other pitfalls. Whenever I work with an organization on a long-term basis, I usually try to sell the top managers on instituting a graduation process, based on a policy of developing people ahead of time and on requiring certain conditions for promoting someone into management. I usually recommend a written policy from management that says that nobody gets promoted into management without the following conditions being met:

1. The person wants a management job, or at least he or she thinks so, and would like to try it.

2. The candidate has had some formal training in management; this might take the form of an in-company training program, attendance at a management course at a university extension or similar institution (for which the company might pay the costs), or any equivalent means of learning what the job of a manager is all about.

3. The person has had an opportunity to demonstrate reasonable social and leadership skills, such as in coordinating a special project, leading a special team or task force, or some similar situation in which he or she dealt with other people in a leadership capacity, and they came away untraumatized.

4. The person competes for the job in a relatively formal way by having his or her qualifications reviewed by a selection committee in competition with other qualified people; the decision to appoint the person should not rest solely with the manager who owns the job—this prevents the selection of the fair-haired boy or girl in a rigged game.

A top management commitment to a graduation process amounts to saying to the employees, "You get ahead on merit around here, and there is a fair chance that, if you work hard, learn as much as you can about management, and prepare well, you can make it." This approach also helps enormously in eliminating misunderstanding and hard feelings in the area of equal employment opportunity (EEO). It enables top management to pick the person best qualified for the job. To enhance the possibilities of women and minorities, the proper avenue is not to promote unqualified people, but to systematically increase the number of qualified people in those categories.

A management position is one of the most valuable resources the organization has at its disposal. To waste it on someone who can't handle it, by promoting unqualified fair-haired people or by thrusting unprepared technical experts into management because they did their technical jobs well, is to detract from the organization's potential effectiveness and to make life less than comfortable for those who have to live and work under inept, and perhaps toxic, management. It has many costly side effects. An effective graduation process helps ensure, even though it cannot guarantee, that the aggregate management strength of the organization is adequate to meet its needs.

INNOVATION

The last key dimension to be discussed is innovation. It is the process by which people in an organization find new and better ways to achieve worthwhile results. Just about anyone can function as an innovator, in almost any situation. A person can often find a better way to do something that has been done the same way for years. But few people do. Very few people, including managers, ever function at anything like their potential as problem solvers and innovators. Why? Usually because the social and intellectual climate in the organization rewards certainty, convergent thinking, and tried, true, and trusted solutions.

The styles of the managers of an organization usually have a great deal to do with the extent to which people come up with new ideas and share them with their leaders. This is an area in which American managers have much to learn from their Japanese counterparts, who place great emphasis on employee initiative and group problem-solving in increasing productivity.

An American innovator, Charles Kettering, had strong views on the matter of encouraging new ideas. Kettering was a prolific inventor and served as head of General Motors for a time. After he retired from GM, he traveled about, lecturing to educators, urging them to teach the skills of divergent thinking, idea production, and other creative skills to students. Kettering had this to say about the climate for innovation in most organizations:

> Man is so constituted as to see what is wrong with a new thing, not what is right. To verify this, you have but to submit a new idea to a committee. They will obliterate ninety percent of rightness for the sake of ten percent of wrongness. The possibilities a new idea opens up are not visualized, because not one person in a thousand has any imagination.

The area of creative problem-solving and the whole range of practical thinking skills is recently coming into its own as a high-payoff form of training for people in organizations. By sponsoring these kinds of activities, and by encouraging and rewarding innovative actions on the part of employees, management can revitalize the innovative process in the organization, with obvious benefits.

THE THREE BOTTOM LINES

For a number of years, the term "bottom line" has been a popular and somewhat overworked metaphor in organizational life. It does, however, have its applications. Originally, the term referred to the financial results of management's efforts—specifically to the last line on the corporate profit-and-loss statement, which shows how much more money the company has taken in than it has spent. Indeed, the successful manager must be bottom-line oriented, giving a great deal of attention to the economic health of the enterprise. This applies to nonprofit organizations as well, although for different reasons.

I like to think of the executive in today's organizational world as having three bottom lines to tend to, in a sense, with each requiring an appropriate share for management attention. One of them is the traditional and well-understood economic bottom line, and the other two deal with key results which are not denominated in units of currency. The three bottom lines for today's organization are:

1. The *Economic Bottom Line*—the financial performance of the organization taken as a whole; its economic health as proven by the fact that it
   acquires capital faster than it expends it.
2. The *Human Bottom Line*—the sum total of the conditions in the
   organization as perceived by the "citizens" of that organization; the
   quality of life as they evaluate it.
3. The *Social Bottom Line*—the sum total of the organization's impacts
   on the society and community of which it is a part; the extent to which it
   behaves fairly and humanely as a good neighbor to the people of the
   country in which it operates.

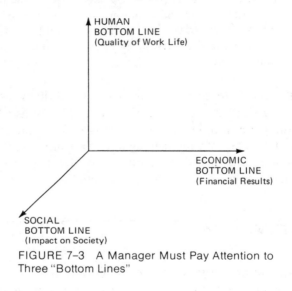

FIGURE 7–3   A Manager Must Pay Attention to
Three "Bottom Lines"

Figure 7-3 illustrates the interlocking relationship of these three
bottom lines.

To the hard-bitten, "old school" manager, there is really only
one "true" bottom line—the economic one. "Listen," he will growl,
"without a profit, nobody's got a job. All these other things are
secondary to making a profit." He is partially right and partially
wrong. He is absolutely correct in his conviction that profit—or at a
minimum, break-even performance in the short run—is the first condition for continued survival of the company. He is wrong in considering the human and social bottom lines as secondary. A disaster
along any one of these dimensions can sink a company.

It is only when the human and social bottom lines are not giving
the old-school manager trouble that he can forget about them or
consider them "secondary." In the rare circumstance when a company

is figuratively rolling in profits, the executives tend to pay less attention to the economic bottom line on a daily basis for the same reason. But when some disturbance flares up on the human bottom line, such as a unionization attempt or an employee walkout, or when a crisis occurs on the social bottom line, such as a class-action lawsuit claiming 25 million dollars in damages for discriminatory hiring practices, it gets the attention of management very quickly. Even the old-school manager has to come to terms with an upheaval of that magnitude.

The creative attitude toward management in today's environment recognizes the legitimacy of all three bottom lines and affirms the executive's responsibility to manage all of them. It is certainly not necessary to consider these three dimensions as mutually antagonistic or conflicting. They may be in conflict from time to time, but over the long pull the imaginative executive can integrate them quite successfully. This is, indeed, happening daily in many organizations throughout the world, although many more still have a long way to go.

PUTTING IT ALL TOGETHER

I hope that, by this stage in the development of our systems view of the organization, you have begun to detect the key relationships that tie these concepts together. For example, you may have thought about how the four roles of the manager—strategist, leader, problem-solver, and administrator—might relate to the four systems—technical, social, administrative, and strategic. We can also tie these aspects to the four dimensions of organizational health—evaluation, adaptation, graduation, and innovation.

We can indeed knit all of these points of view together into an integrated systems picture of the organization and the way it is managed. As should now be apparent, the manager plays a part in each of the four systems by virtue of the four roles he or she must play in managing comprehensively. The role of strategist, of course, ties into the strategic system; the role of leader ties into the social system; the role of problem-solver ties into the technical system; and the role of administrator ties into the administrative system. And the four dimensions of organizational health, while they relate to all systems to some extent, relate closely to certain ones in particular. Evaluation relates to the strategic system, adaptation relates to the administrative system, graduation relates to the social system, and innovation relates to the technical system.

Figure 7-4 unites these concepts into a convenient framework, which can serve us well as we go about the process of diagnosing an organization and identifying the kinds of improvements in its operation that offer high payoff.

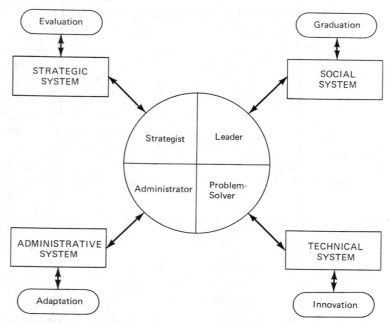

FIGURE 7–4 A Healthy Organization Has an Effective Interplay Among Systems, Processes, and Managerial Roles.

8

A Systems Approach to Organization Development

AVOIDING THE "HAMMER SYNDROME"

Now that we have a logical and comprehensive systems approach for describing an organization, we can put together a systems approach to developing it. This chapter deals with the approach, the methods, and the tools we can use in systems-oriented OD.

Having explored a very broad picture of the organization as a sociotechnical system, we can now see even more clearly why it is so important to match the "fix" to the problem and to avoid the "hammer syndrome," previously attributed to Abraham Maslow. To review that notion: Maslow remarked that "When the only tool you have is a hammer, you tend to treat everything as if it were a nail." To lend more color to the metaphor, picture a young child who has been given a plastic hammer as a toy. The child will go about the house pounding on things, including things that don't need or deserve to be pounded.

Walls, doorknobs, television buttons, the cat, kneecaps of adults—all get the same treatment. The availability of the hammer makes the child into a pounder.

By analogy, the availability of only one mode of change agentry, such as T-Group training, makes the would-be OD specialist into a pounder with that particular hammer. Just as the child eventually needs to learn about many tools, and to learn when and when not to use them, so in the practice of organization development we need to learn which tools to use and when. We need an effective means for determining what technique or tool is best suited to the situation that has presented itself. The systems approach to OD gives us not only a diversified tool kit to work with but, more importantly, also gives us a way to think through the requirements of the organization and to choose our tools intelligently.

SETTING A CLIMATE FOR CANDID PROBLEM-SOLVING

In order for the OD process to catch on with the key people of the organization and to begin to produce useful results, there first needs to be a "climate," or a condition of acceptance of the idea and positive expectations about the outcome. This climate is what we have been calling the condition of OD-readiness. It involves the managers especially and all others who will have first-hand parts to play in getting an OD process started.

The most basic aspect of the condition of OD-readiness is a climate in which key people are willing to engage in candid problem-solving. They need to be willing to level with one another, to confront important issues of all kinds that are having an influence on the organization's effectiveness, and to forthrightly consider realistic options for solving them. If this condition exists, and there are no problematical "sacred cows," then an OD process has an excellent chance of producing a highly effective form of organizational renewal. If, however, several key people don't want to play, or if they want to keep certain sacred cows immune to scrutiny, then the outcome of the process will probably be distorted to a significant degree.

This sacred cow syndrome deserves careful thought. Professor William Dyer of Brigham Young University calls it the "don't upset mother" syndrome. He uses the analogy of a family situation, involving several generations and various kinds of personalities. In this imaginary setting, there is an aging and frail mother who for years has used her weakness and fragility to tyrannize the others. The members of the family come to be very apprehensive about doing anything that might "upset mother," including confronting mother with her toxic influence and negotiating with her for her to play a more constructive role in the family. Similarly, says Dyer, a typical organization will have certain aspects of its operation that people don't like but are not ready to deal with. This could involve any of a vast number of possible situations, such as an alcoholic executive who isn't meeting his responsibilities, a dishonest relationship with a customer or supplier, a condition of malpractice in making or delivering a product, or a long-standing dangerous work situation that would be costly to fix. Whenever someone in an action position tries to sell the others on coming to terms with it, the reaction is one of evasion or passive resistance. Certain key people say, figuratively, "Now, let's be careful here. We don't want to upset mother."

In consequence, an organization can have one or more painful issues or problems at near-boiling, yet managers and other key people engage in a collusion not to deal with them. While no management group is going to be willing to turn the entire organization upside down, change its fundamental characteristics, or dismiss themselves from power, it is necessary that the members be basically willing to call a spade a spade, to deal with the big issues, and to make big changes if necessary. Sometimes it becomes necessary to upset mother in order for the organization to move ahead.

The problem of creating an atmosphere of candid problem-solving, if it does not already exist, usually falls into the lap of the person who comes up with the idea of organization development in the first place. The other key people may not share this individual's conviction that planned change is necessary, or they may feel the pain or recognize the opportunities, yet not know anything about OD or what it might offer.

Basically, there are three types of people, distinguished by their positions or roles in the organization, who can plausibly act in the capacity of a change agent, i.e., an action person who undertakes to trigger interest and commitment for an OD program. The three typical kinds of change agents are these:

1. The *Chief executive*—obviously the most influential of all possible change agents; this person can usually create a problem-solving climate in short order if he or she knows how or has the support of a capable OD practitioner.

2. A *Key manager*—usually a member of the top management team, but conceivably a respected middle manager who can get the attention of top management or a significant number of other managers and key staff people.

3. A *Staff specialist*—someone with no formal authority, but who serves in a role that could make him or her a plausible change agent in the eyes of managers and key staff people; he or she might be the director of training (or "human resources development" as it is increasingly called), the director of personnel, or a person in a special staff assignment created for the purposes of OD or for some purpose that he or she can develop into an OD responsibility.

Reviewing a key point, about which contemporary OD practitioners often disagree, we are saying here that just about any reasonably placed person with energy and ability can conceivably get an OD process started. The person does not have to be an external consultant with formal training in the behavioral sciences, as some scholars and external consultants with formal training in the behavioral sciences contend. We do have to recognize, however, that the "leverage" the change agent can bring to bear depends fairly directly on his or her proximity to the sources of power within the organization. As previously mentioned, the most influential change agent is the top manager, assuming of course that he or she knows how to facilitate change. All other change agents must either derive their influence from the support and sponsorship of the top manager or from a coalition of other managers or key staff people who recognize and value the possibilities they have to offer.

Establishing the problem-solving climate usually depends to a great extent on the first few tangible steps in a would-be OD process. It is usually at this point that the change agent succeeds in capturing the attention of key action people and inspiring them to some extent with the possibilities, or falls short of that ideal to some extent. The short fall may range from only slight to complete. It is not unheard of for a staff specialist to lose his or her job, or to risk losing it, merely by proposing an OD program. For some executives, OD is a dirty word, a substitute "gimmick" for weak management, or a threat to their sense of control. In the typical case, the staff specialist may begin to talk about and advocate an OD program, and succeed in selling a number of key people on the spirit of such an effort, if not necessarily the form of it. Getting from initial interest to full commitment usually depends on the change agent's ability to propose a concrete approach that looks appealing to the key action people. It is at this point that some staff specialists fumble the ball, often because they don't have enough expertise to put together an overall program when called upon to do so. They may believe in the approach, but not know exactly how to go about getting started. When top management asks for a program plan describing how the entire process will unfold, they may get stuck.

And occasionally, the ideal circumstance occurs. The chief executive will learn about organization development, become intrigued with its possibilities, and decide to implement a program. At this point, success depends on having someone on the staff or available as a consultant who has the expertise to get it going. But with the personal commitment, and especially the initiative, of the chief executive, the battle is ninety percent won.

A simple and low-risk way to get an OD program started, if the organization and its managers seem reasonably ready, is to hold an exploratory meeting on the subject. The top management group can get together for a few hours and discuss the possibilities of a program. It is very helpful at this point to have someone available who fully understands the OD process and who can answer questions, deal with concerns, and give some recommendations about how to proceed. For example, management might have a staff specialist or an external consultant give a lecture or briefing on the OD process and answer any questions that may arise. If, as a result of the exploratory meeting, there seems to be sufficient genuine commitment to the process, it is wise to appoint a specific person or a task force to come up with a concrete plan of action for review and approval by management in the near future. The plan should incorporate the four phases of the OD process presented in this chapter and show how to carry them out.

THE BASIC FOUR-PHASE OD PROCESS

Now we come to the particulars of the "how-to-do-it" portion of our subject, the four-step process that serves as the foundation of virtually any organized effort to bring about planned improvement. Not all OD processes will be equally extensive or elaborate, and in fact some might be quite modest or quite specifically targeted. But a logical approach would dictate some form of these four steps in virtually any case. The four steps are really nothing more than the simplest logical progression in problem-solving: figure out what the problem is, decide what you have to do to change things, put the "fix" into effect, and then compare what happens with what you wanted to happen. If the key action people in the organization agree on this overall approach, they can hardly go wrong in the long run. It will keep their energies focused on recognizable targets and will help them keep the entire process in perspective as it proceeds, even if it extends over a period of several years, as many large-scale OD processes do.

Once more, this time with feeling, here are the four phases of the systems approach to organization development:

1. The Assessment Phase—the process by which the leaders of the organization make a thorough and objective analysis of the present state of affairs in all four of the key systems and identify the disparities between what is and what ought to be.

2. The Problem-Solving Phase—the process in which they make decisions based on the findings of the assessment phase, determine what concrete improvements they want to make in the way the four key systems function, and determine what specific actions are necessary and what they will cost.

3. The Implementation Phase—getting down to work; the process of putting into play the various improvement projects, each with an action person appointed to spearhead it and with concrete expected outcomes and deadlines.

4. The Evaluation Phase—a replay of the assessment phase, but narrowed down to the specific areas of change undertaken in the implementation phase; here we compare what we accomplished with what we set out to do; if we are not entirely satisfied with the results, we replan the program and continue the implementation phase.

Figure 8-1 diagrams these phases as a flow process.

Actually, implementation and evaluation should be going on in parallel fashion for a large portion of the program. If the management team members are fully involved, they will be reviewing results right along. However, it does not help to schedule a full-scale formal review of the program at some strategically chosen date.

Some executives like to conceive of OD as a more or less cyclic process, one in which the evaluation phase becomes the basis for a new assessment and a new beginning. At this point, someone is probably saying, "This is nothing more than good management. Every year we get together at our annual management retreat, and we work out our plan for the upcoming year. We plan and manage in a cyclic

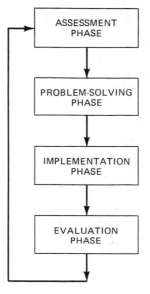

FIGURE 8-1
The Systems Approach to Organization
Development Has Four Phases

process, and we make improvements in the organization each year. So, what's the difference between OD and just good, sound management?" This is a good question, and one that deserves a thoughtful answer.

Once a process like organization development becomes a cyclic institution in the organization, we have to question whether it is still achieving its original purpose of comprehensive planned improvement. It is one thing for OD to be a continuous on-going process and quite another for it to have become a part of the annual "weather cycle" of planning. The tell-tale sign is usually the time line. If OD is an annual process, locked to the annual planning process, I question whether management hasn't made it into one more ritual. A program plan of exactly one year for an OD process is usually grounds for considerable suspicion. Phrases like "installing an OD system" are also suspect.

This is not to say that OD can't be done effectively on this basis. But experience seems to show that the ad hoc quality of OD is one of its key benefits. It provides a way to "wake up" a somnolent organization and give it an energy boost, or a kind of a renewal. OD seems to work best when executives consider it as a large-scale option—an ad hoc process and a managerial technology, rather than an annual ritual.

As the OD program develops and gains full acceptance and endorsement by top management, it may be advisable to incorporate the program as an element of the organization's long-range master plan, as one of the key result areas in a management-by-objectives

THE CATALYST FUNCTION

We all know that long-term initiatives like OD, which lack any sort of a "crisis" flavor, and which depend on a great deal of voluntary interaction among organizational departments, typically die on the vine after a few months if management doesn't create some special mechanism for keeping them alive. Despite the best of intentions, managers in an organization tend to get sucked into the daily quagmire of crisis and confusion, and quickly lose their energetic commitment to any nonemergency matters, no matter how enthusiastic they feel about them at the outset. There are very few organizations in which a process as broad, conceptual, and long-range-oriented as OD will survive or amount to anything without a special effort to make it happen.

One of the most effective ways to concentrate the attention and resources of an organization on a particular result area is to create a catalyst function—to appoint a person or a task force with the expertise, energy, resources, and authorization to see the effort through. The catalyst person or group does not substitute for managerial involvement or managerial problem-solving and decision-making. It simply keeps the program moving on a day-to-day, week-to-week, and month-to-month basis. This can mean the difference between a high-payoff OD program and one that degenerates into a third-priority "off-line" activity that managers fall out of love with and end up giving lip service to.

As a management consultant, I am emphatically committed to the use of a catalyst function for problem-solving processes like OD, in almost every case. This catalyst function can take any of the following three forms or a combination of them:

1. A staff specialist, appointed to spearhead the program, with a reasonable range of authority and resources as well as clearly defined responsibility;

2. An external consultant, engaged to develop and implement the program, usually working closely with top management;

3. An OD task force, consisting of a small group of talented,

energetic, and personally committed individuals who work as a team to develop and recommend solutions and to follow through on implementation, in a cooperative effort with the other members of the management team.

As a consultant, I am also emphatically committed to the task force approach. Whenever I am engaged by the executives of an organization in any long-term developmental program, I try to persuade them to create a special-purpose task force to work together with me in developing and implementing the solutions. This has several advantages. First, it integrates their intimate knowledge of the organization, its products or services, its history, and its culture with my expertise in implementing the OD process.

Second, it creates a natural form of advocacy among key leaders within the organization itself. The program does not "belong" to a consultant; it belongs to them, and by extension it belongs to all of management. This process of "syndicating ownership" of the issues and the solutions invariably plays an important part in rolling out the planned-change process through the organization.

And third, it makes their commitment binding because they realize that they will have to live with the solutions we create; this is not just an academic exercise or a case study—this is the real thing, and they are putting their reputations as practical problem-solvers behind the solutions we propose.

ENGAGING AN EXTERNAL CONSULTANT

How can a management consultant, writing a book about organization development, be expected to be objective about the matter of engaging consultants? He cannot. That is understood. Let's proceed from there. An external consultant can play a productive and worthwhile role under one or more of the following conditions:

1. The concept of OD is entirely new to the organization, and top management wants professional assistance.
2. There is no one person on the staff with sufficient expertise to develop and implement the entire program.
3. Top management may be relatively new or inexperienced, and not well-versed in management methods, as in the case of a small and fast-

growing company founded by technical entrepreneurs; they may feel the need for overall assistance in developing their management strength.

4. Conditions within the organization lead top management to want the benefits of an external, unbiased perspective.

5. Organizational staff resources are overcommitted, and it is unlikely that someone like the training director or other potential catalyst person could spearhead an OD program in addition to his or her other commitments.

6. The OD program will involve various managerial learning processes or workshop activities, which management considers best provided by a consultant who works in close conjunction with the other portions of the program.

Given that some circumstances favor the use of outside expertise, under what circumstances should management not engage a consultant? Here I will offer a few blunt suggestions that consultants rarely make in conversation with managers for fear of creating misunderstandings. These observations seem less blunt in print than when spoken, but they are no less important or worthy of thinking about.

First, don't engage a consultant for "cosmetic" effect, i.e., to convey the impression that management is undertaking a scientific approach and that Dr. Knowsalot's presence is proof of an enlightened effort. If the organization is not reasonably OD-ready or at least capable of becoming so, don't swindle a management consultant into thinking it is. Both you and the consultant will eventually be disappointed.

Second, don't "use" a consultant for dirty duties, such as providing reinforcements in a palace war, hatcheting executives or managers, or forcing people out of the organization by "scientifically" eliminating their jobs or departments.

Speaking to the chief executive: if you are presently in the process of getting rid of somebody whom you no longer want as part of the top management team, and the process has reached the point of no return, please get it taken care of before engaging a consultant. Start with a clean slate and an above-board agenda for what you want the consultant to do.

Third, don't confuse training consultants with OD consultants. Don't assume that team-development workshops, leadership training, stress-management training, or any other training option will be the nucleus of your OD program until you have completed a reasonable diagnosis. If a consultant offers a particular hammer, and only that hammer, wait to see whether it will be useful and will fit in at some appropriate point. You might want to engage several different training consultants if you need them, for individual assignments of a specialized nature. But don't get the prescription before the diagnosis.

A few final comments regarding consultants, in case you decide to engage one: take special care to establish the proper working relationship between the consultant and the organization's action people, especially the OD task force. Choose someone who can appreciate the realities and quirks of your organization and who has the personal skills to form a compatible psychological link with your key management people. Make up your mind clearly what role you want the consultant to play, or if that is difficult to do, get the consultant to work with you in defining it. Don't use an open-ended "retainer" contract without building in definite goals, actions, and outcomes. Approach the consultant's assignment as a project, with the expected results clearly identified at the beginning. Even the most complex or confusing OD program consists of distinct phases and basic processes needed to carry them out. Get these processes defined and down on paper. Then both the managers and the consultant can have certain legitimate expectations of one another, and they can review results against expectations from time to time.

SETTING UP AN OD TASK FORCE

An OD task force has proven to be one of the most reliable and straightforward ways to get an OD process going in an organization, and especially to keep it going. A properly selected "tiger team," properly led, and properly chartered by management, can play a crucial role in all four phases of the process by acting as the catalyst function previously described. I consider the OD task force so fundamental to the success of a program that the remainder of this book proceeds from the assumption that one will exist.

There are only a few basic considerations in forming an effective task force, but they are extremely important. First, the task force must have the recognition and acknowledgment of the management group and the various other action people in the organization. These people must believe in the mission of the task force and accord them the consideration and cooperation they will need in getting their job done.

Second, it is important to select the members of the task force carefully and with a logical rationale. The group needs, first of all, an effective leader, operating as a chairperson. This person should know how to get the group organized, get it targeted on high-payoff actions, work out a plan, and coordinate the efforts of the various members in a humane but decisive way. The other members should be highly regarded action people who have, as individuals, demonstrated that they can go after a problem energetically and effectively, and get things done. They may be managers, or they may be influential staff people. They should not be "miscellaneous" people, i.e., chosen from among the lower ranks simply because they weren't busy when the time came to appoint the task force. Equally important, the members of the task force should serve voluntarily, not under coercion. They should be ready, willing, and able to give it their attention, energy, talents, and above all the necessary time. No one should serve on an OD task force against his or her will.

The task force should include people chosen for a balanced mixture of skills and areas of expertise. At least one person, not necessarily the chairperson (but preferably), should have reasonably extensive expertise in the OD process. This could include formal training as an OD practitioner, experience in other OD programs, or at least extensive experience in the area of human resource development and intimate familiarity with the literature and concepts of the field. It may be wise to engage a highly qualified consultant for this role. It may also be wise to include someone intimately familiar with the technical system, and possibly someone to provide insights on any other areas of significant specialization or complexity. The task force should virtually always include a well-qualified professional staff person from the personnel or human-resources department. Other areas of expertise will depend on the early indications of what the OD program will likely require.

Does it go without saying that the task force should be small? It should be just large enough to include the essential talent needed for the job, and no larger. A good rule of thumb is five to seven people. When a task force has more than about seven people, it usually begins to have organizational problems of its own. If the members of the task force decide they need to augment their capabilities in various specific areas or functions, it usually works well to identify special resource people who come in on an ad hoc basis, share their knowledge or expertise, and depart.

The task force should be a well-knit group, with clearly defined membership. It must not be a "bus stop"-type of committee, i.e., a group where people come and go, where the exact membership is not clear, or where some members don't show up for action. Every member should be a full-fledged, active, contributing member, willing to take assignments and complete them by promised deadlines. Each person should think this over before getting deeply involved with the task force because it will involve significant demands on his or her time and will certainly have an impact on his or her regular job. If a member "fades out" of the action and can no longer carry out the commitment to the task force's goals, it is perfectly appropriate to ask that person to drop out formally and to surrender the space on the task force to another person who can.

The very first task of the task force is to develop itself into an effective team. The team leader should have the capability to pull the group together, develop a high level of rapport and cooperation, and get the "goals and roles" of the group clearly defined. If the OD task force cannot function effectively as a team, there is no way in heaven or on earth that they can help the rest of the organization function more effectively.

This last point deserves further emphasis. If the members of the task force fall into interpersonal wrangles, role disputes, power politics, or other kinds of "gamey" interactions with one another, then they can't very well get an effective program going, nor can they exemplify to other units in the organization a method of working effectively. It is highly ironic, if not laughable, to think of an OD task force that can't "get its own act together." The members of the OD task force, and the task force itself, should function as responsible role models for other people in the organization. It may pay off well to engage a consultant for the purpose of training and developing the OD task force to get it off on the right foot.

And finally, the people on the task force should have a plan. They must, as the old truism says, "Plan the work and work the plan." They need to develop a written plan for their own activities, in some depth, possibly with a time line extending out a year or more and with the immediate phase planned in more detail. Their own plan of activities should reflect and support the overall OD program plan, which they must develop and present for management review and approval. With an effective task-force plan, each member can plan his or her work accordingly, having a fairly good idea of the amount of time the work of the task force will require. A good plan will also enable them to work effectively and know just what their priorities are and what they need to accomplish at each meeting.

More and more organizations now have a person specially appointed as an internal OD specialist. Some organizations even have a small unit called the "OD Department." This trend probably grieves a number of "old-school" OD practitioners who feel that "true OD" requires an external change agent in the catalyst role. This trend now seems so strong, however, that it will probably become the norm before very long. To make sure our theory keeps up with practice, it makes sense to acknowledge this approach as important and relevant, and to offer ways of implementing it effectively. Here are some observations and suggestions about the role of an internal OD specialist or department.

In some cases, heads of training departments have simply gotten their departments renamed "OD Department," without changing in any way the missions they perform, or the way they relate to their organizations. This sometimes conveys the impression that there is more organization development going on than there actually is. Abraham Lincoln had a favorite story he used to tell about this "renaming" subterfuge. Lincoln would ask someone, "If you call the dog's tail a leg, then how many legs does he have?" When a person would answer "Five," Lincoln would say, "No—he has four. Calling a tail a leg doesn't make it a leg." If you're going to rename the training department and call it the OD department, then why not actually make it an OD department?

The question also arises of where to place this function—Which organizational block seems like the appropriate home base? The answer depends on the particulars of the organization. In some cases, the training department comes under the personnel organization. In this case, converting it to an OD department can be a clean fix. In some cases, the training department might be separate from personnel, especially if the work of the organization requires a great deal of skills training. Of course, in small and growing companies, the personnel function and the training function can land in all sorts of strange places, such as under the finance director or under a vague conglomeration of activities called the "administrative department." In those cases, it's anybody's guess what they will do with an OD function.

In some cases, top management creates an OD unit separate and distinct from personnel and from training. This almost invariably causes frictions and feelings of competitiveness among these units. As a general matter, people in the organization seem to want to see OD as a "personnel"-type of activity, with a great deal to do with the people and the culture of the organizations. While they will accept and support a systems-oriented approach, in the end they seem to want to place it generally in the human resources development area for want of any other logical place. After all, an OD department under the manufacturing division would look a bit peculiar, unless it served only the requirements of that division.

Another option is to make the OD-specialist position an ad hoc assignment, reporting to the chief executive, and having a certain pre-established duration, such as one year or two years. This has the advantage of giving the OD person wider latitude of operation, since he or she doesn't represent any specific organizational group. One of the problems any OD-department head must continually face is the problem of "role contamination," or having to contend with being one of the boxes on the organizational chart, while trying to perform a function that involves inducing changes in all of the boxes. If there is a feud between personnel and another division, and if the OD function comes under personnel, members of the other division will see the OD specialist as "one of them"—i.e., as coming from personnel, rather than as serving in a change-agent role.

In a number of organizations with internal OD specialists or units, the function unfortunately gets buried too deeply in the organization to have much of an effect. Perhaps one energetic person sold management on the idea of having an OD function and ended up over in the corner of the training department, which is in a corner of the personnel department, which is in the southwest corner of the building. This is what makes the life of an internal change-agent challenging, although potentially frustrating.

If we want to create an institutional form of OD, we need to think carefully about how to get the best results for our money. An internal OD specialist needs to be well selected, well trained, well chartered in his or her mission, and well located with access to management and access to the leaders of the organization the OD function is supposed to serve.

CLARIFYING THE ROLE OF TRAINING IN ORGANIZATION DEVELOPMENT

Most OD programs sooner or later involve various types of training processes as means for solving certain kinds of identified problems. It helps to clarify the role of the training department and the training process, so the task force members and the managers know what options they have and how to make the best use of them.

When a consultant or other highly qualified OD practitioner plays a key part in the program, he will usually propose a certain amount of group activity, carried out in a "shirt-sleeves" workshop-type situation. Part of the diagnosis, or assessment phase, may involve some intensive management-team meetings in which the managers analyze the external environment and analyze the organization's current functioning. With the consultant coordinating this process, it often takes on the appearance of a training seminar, or at least a workshop form of meeting. This is especially true if the consultant teaches the management team members some new concepts or techniques for long-range planning, problem-solving, or follow-through.

It is important, however, not to confuse OD with training. The fact that the managers are attending lots of workshops with a consultant does not necessarily prove they are engaged in a full-scale OD process. Training can be a part of the OD process, specifically a problem-solving option, but it is only a part.

If the organization has a training department, but not a formally identified OD function, the head of training should most certainly serve as a member of the OD task force. As a specialist in the human side of the organization, he or she can offer a great deal of help in that area. And in addition, he or she can tell whether or not a training program is a useful option for the task force to consider in dealing with a particular problem or issue.

In this way, we can accomplish something that many training directors fervently hope for—to give focus and direction to the training department's program and to put it on a results-oriented basis of accomplishment instead of mere training activity.

ASSESSING TOP MANAGEMENT "SUPPORT"

We've stressed many times the significance of top management's participation or involvement in an OD program. This can range from one hundred percent when the chief executive gets the idea, to zero when management has no idea someone is trying to get a program started, or knows about it but has no use for it at all. Actually, there could be a negative end of the scale as well, i.e., when top management is definitely antagonistic to the program and wants to squelch it. The middle of the range is probably the most common case.

When you listen to an internal OD specialist describe his or her efforts to get a program underway, you can almost "measure" the true level of top management investment in the program by listening to the choice of words used. Whether the staff specialist realizes it or not, he or she tends to state the true conditions fairly accurately. The most commonly used terms for this, and their "true" meanings, are these:

1. "Top management is *interested* in this program"—they know about it, and they haven't made any move to kill it.
2. "Top management *supports* this program"—they said we could do something along these lines, provided we didn't make trouble, and it didn't cost anything.
3. "Top management is *involved* in this program"—one or more people in the top management team have attended some of our meetings, and they seem to like what we're doing; they're giving us some advice and occasional direction.
4. "Top management is *committed* to this program"—they're paying the bill, and they expect to get their money's worth.

While these "definitions" are admittedly a bit cynical, they do point out a basic fact of life in organizations: the number one indication of significant commitment on the part of top management is money. Sooner or later, any major effort with ambitious objectives is going to cost money or staff resources, or both. Management's willingness to invest precious resources and money in an undertaking like OD, or any other broad-scale program, is a fairly reliable indication of its significance and potential value to them.

The important thing for the OD practitioner, either external or internal, is to make an honest assessment of the level of management support and to face the facts at the outset. If management commitment seems seriously lacking, the OD person needs to consider seriously whether to try to push ahead with an attempted program, or whether he or she can do something in the early stages to win a significant level of commitment. This usually involves gaining access to the thinking processes of one or more well-placed executives and showing them how an OD program can relieve some of the pains that concern them in managing the organization.

OBJECTIVES-ORIENTED OD

Just as the concept of management-by-objectives makes sense as a general practice, so an approach of organization-development-by-objectives makes sense; that is, the result of the early stages of the process should be a clear definition of "point B," or the target condition of the organization which we want to reach somehow, over some time period. The more explicitly we can spell out the improvement we want to make, the more readily we can identify the actions, projects, tasks, or management directives needed to make them. Too vague a result-condition generally results in no results or, at best, marginally-impressive results.

For example, it is usually a waste of time to set a goal under an OD program such as "To improve communications in the organization." This statement is much too vague and nebulous to use as a guide for action. We should take a beginning statement like that and break it down into a succession of more concrete, action-oriented goal statements. These might include something like, "Significantly reduce the conflict and working-level friction between the Nursing Department and the Administration Department." A deadline and a prescription for concrete results also helps a great deal.

Although we can't claim that the second example is specific enough that we can measure it in acres or miles per hour, nevertheless it is relatively definite and we will know when we get there, at least in qualitative terms. Other useful and fairly specific OD goals could include these: "Increase the time available to sales agents for actual sales calls by ten percent, by the end of the current quarter"; "Create a career-development and mobility program for women and minority employees and have it operating by June 30"; and "Reduce the organization's 'union vulnerability' rating from 8 points down to less than 5 points, within ninety days."

These are, of course, merely examples of the kinds of OD goals the people on the task force might come up with, depending on the diagnosis and on the priorities they decide to set for various areas. Because every organization has its own peculiar needs and issues, it is impossible to catalog all the kinds of changes the people of a particular organization can think up. The reasoning process behind OD goal-setting is more important than any specific goal or problem-solving project. Just as in management, where it is very important to help the employees understand the "big picture" and to work toward well-specified goals or targets, so in OD it is very important for the OD practitioner or other would-be change agent to package the idea in this way for sale. He needs to create, or help create, the "big picture" of the OD effort and to organize it in terms of definite outcomes, in the form of objectives which the various action people can understand, accept, and work toward in their various special capacities.

THE TIME LINE OF AN OD PROGRAM

Before we proceed to study each of the four stages of the systems-oriented OD process, let's put everything together into a general time line of activities to make it easier to understand at a glance. Let's assume a hypothetical organization and a hypothetical program, and see how the events would unfold along the way, following the four-phase process.

Most of what we've covered so far in this book emphasizes the comprehensive nature of the OD process and pictures it as something that we target at the entire organization, as an overall entity. However, it is perfectly possible, and frequently done, to target the OD process at one specific problem area and to use it as a problem-solving process in a more focused way. We can call this a "single-issue" form of OD. It is also sometimes called a "single-thread" OD program. For example, management might choose to try to solve the problem of extremely low morale in an organization of professional people. We could use the same four-stage process—assessment, problem solving, implementation, and evaluation—and simply focus the attention on the morale situation. We would still need to use effective fact-finding techniques in the assessment stage, an effective solution-finding and planning process in the problem-solving stage, a well-thought-out and well-managed program plan during the implementation, and a replay of the fact-finding process during the evaluation to see how well we achieved our purposes. So, let's not hesitate to use OD techniques on a single-issue basis, provided we keep the same level of discipline and scientific attack that the grand-scale process calls for.

Now, let's sketch out a fairly typical OD program, in skeletal form, for a typical organization, say a small, rapidly-growing firm in the microelectronics business. Let's assume it to have about 400 employees, a single location for its plant, and about 50 million dollars in sales. The organization has grown to the "indigestion" point in less than four years after its creation by three electronics engineers, all three of whom are now the top executives of the company. It is still a privately-held corporation. The engineers who founded the company are almost completely lacking in management experience or training, having acquired a "survival" knowledge of management as they went along. To some extent, they have become one of the organization's problems because they have not learned to shift from their early roles as inventors into the new roles they must play as executives. Because of this, the organization suffers from a lack of clearly defined structure, minimal leadership at mid-management and lower levels, an administrative system that is in a shambles, and no long-range planning process whatever. This description will give us enough substance to go on; we can make up the rest as we go along.

Without a great deal of elaboration, let's just tick off the kinds of steps that might go in an OD program for this company:

1. The chief executive, with the consensus of the management team, engages a management consultant to help the company.

2. The consultant meets with the management team, gets agreement on the general approach to the OD process, based on the systems approach we have been studying, and they draw up a letter contract which specifies what the consultant will do, what management will do, roughly how long the program will take, and how much it will cost.

3. At the consultant's request, management appoints an OD task force of six people—the head of personnel, a key engineering manager, the manager of administration, a key manufacturing manager, a key marketing person, and the executive assistant to the president. They elect the personnel director as chairman of the committee, and the consultant serves as a member with the special role of outside resource person reporting to the chief executive.

4. With the assistance of the consultant, the members of the task force undertake a team-development process to prepare themselves for their new roles; this consists of a half-day shirt-sleeves session. followed up by three meetings of about an hour each. The outcome is a well-developed set of goals, roles, and working relationships, and a general plan and time line for the conduct of the OD program, divided into the four stages of assessment, problem-solving, implementation, and evaluation.

5. The task force presents the general plan and time line for the OD program to top management; management grants approval, along with several imposed requirements and priorities, and approves a budget of

$25,000 for the program in its first phase. Future funding is dependent on management's evaluation of results.

6. The assessment phase begins with a series of task force meetings and top management meetings for the purpose of pooling observations; this goes together with a staff-study report of the organization's external environments (customer, competitor, economic, legal, social, technological, political, and physical), the findings of a climate survey questionnaire given to the employees, and interview results and findings as a result of the consultant's thorough investigation of the four key systems of the organization. The final meeting of the assessment phase has the OD task force present a written report, giving the compilation and interpretation of the fact-finding process, and putting on record the management team's agreed-upon evaluation of the baseline condition of the organization, or its "point A" starting point. Copies of this assessment report go to all members of the management team, the members of the OD force, and other key managers involved fairly directly in the program. Management also publishes the summarized results of the employee climate survey, making the findings available to all employees. It has taken about three months to reach this point.

7. The problem-solving phase begins with a three-day, concentrated management workshop-meeting in an off-site conference center, and with a shirt-sleeves setting dedicated to deciding what constructive changes to make to the company. With the consultant coordinating the workshop activity, the management team and the OD task force go through all of the findings of the assessment phase, review the analyses of the four key systems in the company, identify the changes they want to make in the company, organize them in priority order, and develop specific plans for the various change-projects that will be necessary. These plans include the following: a productivity-improvement program (technical fix); an "executive visibility" program to put the executives in closer touch with the employees (social fix); a complete redevelopment of the entire administrative structure of the company and an organizational realignment for more efficient marketing (administrative fix); and an intensive program of management development, starting with the executives (strategic fix). The problem-solving processes produce more change-projects than these, but these are enough to get the idea of the kinds of changes management and the OD people want to make. It takes about one month to complete the problem-solving phase and have the approved plan available.

8. The implementation process in our hypothetical organization spans a period of slightly more than seven months and includes all of the high-priority change projects identified during the problem-solving phase, as well as some others added later as the program proceeds. This phase sees the management development program get underway, with a series of team-development workshops and training seminars conducted by the consultant, and a series of basic-management courses conducted by the training department for new and prospective supervisors. It sees a special adjunct team created to augment the OD task force in the specific area of productivity improvement. It sees a very successful climate-building program sponsored by top management to re-establish the sense of community among the employees and to reinforce the cooperative relationship between management and the employees. It also sees an adjunct task force created to support the OD task force in the area of administrative systems and procedures. This group simplifies and reorganizes the process of record-keeping, correspondence and filing; introduces a "word-processing" system and a training program for the administrative people to learn to operate it; and lays out a plan and takes the initial steps to fully computerize the company's accounting, payroll, personnel-management, and production-control systems.

9. The evaluation phase, after a period of more than ten months, is a concentrated three-week effort in which the people on the OD task force review the status of all change projects under the OD plan against their original objectives, and report the status and accomplishments to top management. They make a formal presentation to the management staff and offer a plan for extending the OD effort further, this time in certain selected areas of high payoff. As part of the evaluation process, top management approves the extension of the OD program for a tentative period of fifteen months to account for implementation of the long-range solutions, such as the computerization of the administrative processes, development of a career-path system, creation of an employee handbook, and a productivity analysis of automatic component-insertion machines for manufacturing.

10. After the initial thrust of the first year or so, the OD task force continues to facilitate the continuation of the change projects. It makes the evaluation process nearly continual and reports status to top management on a regular basis. As the program proceeds, more and more of the solutions and discoveries, as well as the continuation of

VW —

The Personal Side of
Interpersonal Competence.

Communication the message =
1 Emotion
E Content
S Skill.

- Self Awareness
  Assertiveness / aggressiveness
P. 156 pp -178 / passiveness
Prac. Psy in Const

the implementation process, find their way into the general management planning process the management team has created. At this point, OD as an ad hoc proposition begins to blend with the ongoing management process.

9

The Assessment Phase

ASSESSING
ALL FOUR KEY SYSTEMS

Again, it is appropriate to stress the importance of a comprehensive understanding of the organization if we are to prescribe helpful improvements to it. As noted consultant and author Warren Bennis puts it, "Before you decide what you want, you must first find out what's so." Most managers are fairly well acquainted with the technical system of the organization and usually less well acquainted with the other three key systems. An effective OD program will not exempt any of the four systems from scrutiny and will not proceed under the assumption that any one of them is necessarily the most important place to start. An objective assessment will treat all four of them with the same initial interest and will account for the special approaches needed to understand each of them on an individual basis.

A comprehensive assessment of the entire organization has at least three benefits. First, it tends to eliminate "solution biases"; that is, it delays the decision about which "fix" to use until all of the relevant facts are in. This prevents having some vocal advocate of a particular solution, such as sensitivity training, productivity studies, or reorganization, from selling it prematurely before we know that this is what the organization needs.

Second, a comprehensive and thorough assessment clearly maximizes the payoff possibilities. It enables us to surface those situations or conditions in the organization that are most in need of improvement and that offer the greatest possibilities for valuable results. These results may include cost savings, increased profitability, improved morale and loyalty to the organization on the part of the workers, or increased administrative efficiency. Settling too early on a specific area for problem-solving may lead to preoccupation with the "noisier" problems, which may not necessarily be the ones offering the greatest opportunity for pain relief or the highest possible payoff.

Additionally, a comprehensive assessment helps us understand inter-system dynamics, clarifies "political" relationships in the organization, and identifies areas of interaction among the four systems that we can improve upon. This insures against a truncated definition of a problem, based on too narrow a picture of the processes involved.

And finally, a comprehensive assessment encourages the managers to think comprehensively about their organization and gives those involved with it a thorough understanding of the "big picture," which enables them to manage more comprehensively and, perhaps, more scientifically.

FACT-FINDING METHODS

A scientific approach to assessment dictates that we employ all available means for finding out what we need to know about the organization. We can go about this systematically by considering, first, the kinds of information we need, and second, the places and forms in which we might find it.

Concerning kinds of information, we can subdivide the possibilities into two categories—"hard data," or objectively verifiable measurements and variables, and "soft data," or judgments, opinions, perceptions, predictions, guesses, assumptions, and inferences. Soft data can be just as important and useful as hard data, and we can be just as scientific about using soft data as hard data, provided we have a clear idea of the uncertainties involved.

In looking for hard data, we can usually find many useful items readily available in the four key systems of the organization. For example, we can conduct a fairly thorough review of the technical system's processes and capture the more important variables that define how much of the product or service is being produced, how, and at what costs in terms of labor, materials, and resource utilization. A straightforward review of the technical processes, with effectiveness as a focus, can look beyond the obvious considerations and identify opportunities for payoff.

Similarly, a thoughtful look at the social system, the administrative system, and the strategic system can give us a useful starting point for a comprehensive assessment.

It is important, in this respect, to appreciate the value of analyzing the obvious, because we usually get to the nonobvious by that avenue. For example, just by looking at the number of employees in the organization, their age and gender statistics, their educational levels, the amount of training they have had, the various lengths of tenure with the organization, and their rates of turnover, we can answer a variety of questions about the kind of organization it has become. A very young work force, for example, is likely to have different preferences for benefit systems than an older population. There may be significant differences in certain value systems between these two groups, and these differences may play a part in the way the employees respond to management-induced change.

Similarly, looking at the hard numbers that define certain aspects of the strategic system can enable us to make some inferences about how the senior managers and middle managers approach their jobs. Knowing how well trained and how experienced the first-line supervisors are can enable us to make some useful inferences about potential effectiveness of the various work groups.

In gathering information with which to make an assessment of any of the four organizational systems, it is important to distinguish the wheat from the chaff; that is, we need not wade through mountains of data just for the sake of saying we did a thorough job. We need to look for the relevant information. We need to approach the data-gathering process with an investigative frame of mind, passing over that which offers little to enlighten us and keeping alert for that which can help us understand the essence of the organization we are studying. This makes the assessment process manageable, while it also allows us to follow a fairly scientific approach.

"Soft" data requires a somewhat different approach to the investigative process. Here we are dealing with inferences, opinions, value judgments, and perceptions. These kinds of inputs can be invaluable in forming a workable picture of the organization in all four of its systems dimensions, but we need to keep them clearly identified as soft inputs and frequently remind ourselves that we are making interpretations from them.

Probably the most familiar of the soft-data gathering techniques is the questionnaire. We can question a wide variety of people about a wide variety of topics of importance to the assessment. For example, we can question the organization's customers or clients to find out what they think of the organization and its products or services. We can question field people, such as sales representatives, to get their specialized perspectives on the operation. We can question employees to find out what they think of the organization as a place to work, their managers, and the way they are treated. The "climate survey" is probably the best-known OD technique of this type. It is simply a questionnaire which management sends to the employees, asking them to state their perceptions, judgments, and opinions about working for the organization and to evaluate key factors from their various individual points of view.

Interviewing is another useful way to gather soft data about the organization and its processes. It frequently helps to follow up a climate survey with "focus-group" interviews, which involve people with distinctive points of view. For example, it might be helpful to interview several different work groups as intact units. It might also help to interview a cross section of employees who do the same kind of work. Interviews with supervisors and managers about significant topics can also provide useful subjective information for the assessment process. Effective interviewing requires highly developed questioning skills. It is important to assign people to this process who can do it effectively. For example, the interviewer does best when he or she asks open-ended questions, listens for key themes and concerns, and continues to develop the flow of information without "shopping" for certain kinds of answers, and without steering the people being interviewed too forcefully. It is also important in interviewing to "listen" for unspoken concerns, implied opinions, and feelings that the people do not feel free to share without coaxing.

In summary, the fact-finding process in many ways forms the heart of the assessment phase, and it is critical to the development of a shared understanding of the organization. It is important in any organizational assessment to make fact finding a distinctive, relatively formal process and to give it the priority and careful attention it deserves. The people on the OD task force must do more than simply sit down and dredge up assumptions and inferences from their minds. They need to make a specific project out of data gathering. They need to rough out a statement of the kinds of things they want to find out, identify the kinds of information—both hard and soft—it will need in order to make those determinations, and figure out where and how to get the information.

A carefully planned and carefully executed fact-finding process has several advantages. First, it tends to prevent the people involved in spearheading the OD process from going off on tangents and trying to solve problems that don't exist at the expense of problems that do. Second, it helps to assure that all the people involved in the process, managers and OD people alike, are proceeding from the same data. Making the starting point explicit and getting agreements on basic facts and conjectures tends to eliminate many misunderstandings and disputes, and it tends to produce more clear-cut agreements on what needs to be done.

In working with management teams in various organizations, I've discovered an additional, subjective effect of fact finding that strikes me as very significant and very helpful. I've found that merely putting some specific information down on paper and giving it to managers to consider causes a very important thing to happen—it leads them into a more or less scientific frame of mind. Typically, the manager who makes "visceral" judgments, guesses, and unsupported inferences about various aspects of the organization becomes fascinated with facts and figures presented to him or her by a consultant or other catalyst person. Such a manager often starts asking penetrating questions that lead to further investigation. The manager may say, for example, "How come you didn't ask the employees how they felt about rotating shift work when you sent out the climate survey?" Rather than feeling defensive in the face of such a question, the OD person has cause for joy. A manager who is in a questioning frame of mind can exert a very powerful influence for constructive change.

ASSESSING THE TECHNICAL SYSTEM

In assessing the technical system of any organization, especially when using a systems point of view, it is very helpful to diagram it out. Here, we are talking about the primary productive axis of the organization, the central flow of events that constitutes its reason for being. While we recognize that all or most of the functions that make up a modern organization are necessary to its operation, in the analysis of the technical system we are trying to identify the key variables in its effectiveness. A systems diagram of the technical system can take the form of a simple flow chart, showing how materials move through the primary facility and what happens to them at each stage. For a service-oriented organization, the diagram would show the sequence of processes, events, and interactions that combine to produce whatever results the outside world is willing to pay for.

Those who do not understand the thinking process behind the systems approach, or who have little patience with analytical thinking, may tend to dismiss the diagramming process as sterile and theoretical. Yet, time and again, such a simple "straight-through" analysis can uncover critical factors in productivity and technical effectiveness that managers have not clearly seen. For example, a review of a manufacturing process for industrial valves identified several stages at which the semi-finished products sat idle. Then there was an end-of-the-month rush in the shipping department, that traditionally led to a great deal of costly overtime work, resulted from an ineffective product-flow process. Managing this process more effectively reduced overall costs and also helped to reduce errors due to the hysterical pace. This problem had existed for several years before a simple analysis of the process showed where the bottleneck was.

An assessment of a large and complex technical system needs to proceed in small, manageable steps. Here, we need to subdivide the overall process into more easily understood chunks and to focus attention on those aspects that seem to offer the highest apparent payoff. In all cases, the people who do the technical assessment should be those who have the technical expertise to understand the processes.

We can waste a great deal of time and resources by having technically naive investigators asking sophomoric questions about processes they barely understand. This is not to say that an outside perspective is not helpful—it certainly is, and it is generally warranted. It is important, however, to get the right balance of expertise and perspective, combined with a systems approach that values results rather than preconceived solutions.

Using a systems diagram also helps people to focus their thinking on causes and effects. A straight-through analysis will get them thinking about how the technical system works in its simplest form, and it will invite them to look for key factors that warrant further investigation. We can get a great deal of "mileage" out of one simple model such as this. For example, we can annotate the diagram to show various periods of time involved in the overall process, how many people are involved, the rate at which costs build up as the process moves to maturity, and the interactions between various organizational units at various stages.

Productivity improvement programs generally have the greatest probability of success with this systems-mapping process, because it quickly identifies the key variables involved in productivity and helps us to keep from getting bogged down in secondary or irrelevant concerns. Productivity, defined in some concrete and specific way, can often serve as a "focus variable" in our analysis, because it enables managers to target their efforts toward identifiable outcomes.

Once we have a clear picture of the overall technical system, or at least the most significant portion of it, we can supplement our knowledge with inquiries into selected key areas. Productivity studies, studies of key capital equipment and facilities, cost studies, and product-design reviews can all provide information that will help us pinpoint the most promising features of the technical system that will benefit from planned improvement.

The final result of the assessment of the technical system should be a written summary, usually developed by the OD task force, of the basic features of the technical system that seem to warrant detailed attention and problem-solving. This statement need not be extremely extensive or elaborate. It should, however, provide all the key people involved in the OD process with an agreed basis for deciding what constructive changes to make. The assessment does not have to identify specific changes or solutions to problems, nor should it. These will come out of the problem-solving phase, which will focus on the problems the assessment process isolates.

ASSESSING THE SOCIAL SYSTEM

In assessing the social system of the organization, we are trying to understand the people who inhabit it from the point of view of a miniature society. We want to know as much as we reasonably can about who they are, what they are like with regard to their roles as workers, what they need and want out of their participation in the organization, and what kind of a "culture" exists among them. This takes us into the exploration of matters such as authority, values, norms, and rewards. We need to understand the social "climate" that exists in this particular culture, and we need to know something about the perceptions the people have of the organization as a place to work, and their feelings about the way they are treated by those in authority.

Many of the personal facts and intimate details of a working person's life are none of management's business. Executives have no right, in my opinion, and indeed no need to pry into the private lives of the people of the organization. In assessing the culture and climate of the organization, we are dealing only with work-related perceptions, values, opinions, and feelings. These variables are indeed the legitimate concern of top management and of managers at all levels. Reasonable and humane methods for gathering this information are entirely in keeping with good management practice.

We can assess the social system of the organization by starting with the obvious hard information and progressing to the more subtle, soft kinds of information. In terms of hard data, the basic demographics of the citizenry of the organization can tell us a great deal about the people as a kind of "society" at work.

For example, a manufacturing company may have a very high proportion of women workers. This will have certain implications for interest, views and values, and personal needs and preferences for work styles. Very young working women who don't have children may not be so interested in subsidized day care for children. Older working women may have a greater preference for part-time work or for job-sharing situations than younger women who are just beginning their adult lives.

As another example, in a work force made up of very young people, retirement plans and seniority-oriented benefit systems may have very little appeal and may not serve as very strong deterrents to turnover. For these people, liberal vacation plans, opportunities for leave without pay, and rapid mobility opportunities may be much more important.

For these and many other reasons, the age and gender distributions of the work force are very important elements of information. It is not uncommon for the executives of an organization to have only a fuzzy notion of the kinds of people working there and to know relatively little about their concerns, values, and preferences. Starting with hard demographic data can give a very clear focus to the assessment process for the social system.

Many aspects of work life in American organizations are anachronistic with respect to the realities of the present-day work force. For example, life insurance, medical insurance, and retirement plans typically aim at the male head of household who works full-time and has a dependent spouse who doesn't work. Yet that had ceased to be the profile of the "typical" American worker by the early 1970's. Although this kind of worker accounts for about seventy percent of hours worked in the United States, he is far outweighed in numbers by other workers of a more diversified type. Sixty percent of the total work force are women, working either part-time or full-time. College students, semi-retired people, and career women also show up in large numbers. There are more and more dual-career couples in the United States, and they have different values about jobs and benefit systems.

Looking at demographic data can tell us other interesting things about our particular work force as well. For example, there might be a significant disparity between the percentage of women in the overall organization and the percentage of women in management jobs. There may be a significant "pile-up" of people in a certain age range, such as we see in the American population at large, and this might mean that many of them will become frustrated and disillusioned when they find they don't get ahead as rapidly as they had expected because of the heavy competition of numbers. We might find the average age of the engineering or technical work force to be quite high, which would invite investigation into the possibility that a number of them are technically obsolescent and that our product designs may become progressively less competitive.

Once we have established a reasonable profile of the social system in terms of the people who comprise it, we can move to the softer kinds of information, such as the perceptions, opinions, beliefs, judgments, and expressed desires of the people. This we determine mostly by using questionnaires and interview processes. A climate survey questionnaire, in particular, will give us some more or less standardized subjective data to think about. We can follow up on this with well-thought-out interviews to round out our perceptions of the employees' perceptions.

Some of the factors we need to explore in gathering soft data about the social system include the ways in which power and authority play a part in daily life there, the feelings people have toward the executives and other managers, their perceptions of the quality of work life in the organization, the perceptions of women and ethnic minorities about opportunities for advancement, and any opinions or strong feelings that would suggest the existence of the primary enabling conditions for unionization. We also need to find out as much as we can about organizational values, as the employees see them projected by management.

It is very important to analyze the information that describes the social system, organize it, and assemble it in written form so that top management and the other people involved in the OD process can understand it, think about it, and arrive at an interpretation of it that they can use to guide their efforts in the problem-solving phase. Typically, this is one of the useful functions the OD task force can perform, acting as spearhead and central catalyst function for the OD effort. Computer programs such as the Assessment Survey Kit (A.S.K.) enable you to process questionnaire answer data quickly and economically, if you have access to a small "desk-top" computer. (A.S.K. is published by Karl Albrecht & Associates, San Diego.)

ASSESSING THE ADMINISTRATIVE SYSTEM

Although the administrative system hardly seems glamorous, or worthy of the attention that the technical and social systems usually get, nevertheless it may hold extraordinary potential for increasing the overall effectiveness of the organization. The administrative system is the "central nervous system" of the organization. It provides the pathways over which vital information flows. No organization of even modest size can function effectively without these pathways. And when the pathways become obstructed, distorted, or interrupted, the other systems of the organization begin to suffer.

In some kinds of organizations, it may be convenient to treat certain production-related paper processes as part of the technical system and to reserve the definition of the administrative system for those processes that serve the entire organization. The distinction is not particularly important, provided we do account for all the significant aspects of the control and information flow in the organization we are studying.

One simple approach to the administrative system is to make a survey of the various paper media the people use. An early value judgment can determine whether the organization has become a "paper mill," and whether this aspect warrants first attention in problem-solving. An overabundance of forms, reports, files, and copies is often a tip-off that the people have become the slaves of their tools. In making a quick check of this point, just note the number of file cabinets and copy machines in a particular building. If people are lined up for long periods of time waiting to make photocopies, it may well be that they have adopted ways of communicating and relating to one another that value formality, protective record-keeping, and "saving string."

Policy manuals and procedure manuals should nearly always warrant a healthy suspicion. Probably a majority of organizations, industrial as well as governmental, have evolved cancerous "systems" of policies and procedures that hardly anyone uses and that very few specialists understand. Most organizations have the means for creating new directives, policy statements, and procedure guides, but very few seem to have automatic means for eliminating those that no longer serve any useful purpose. The result is that the "procedure manual" may have grown to hundreds of pages, and may include many obsolete procedures dealing with work activities that are best left to the judgment of those doing the work. Often, the only people who consider the procedures important are those who have the job of writing and publishing them. It is almost always a mistake, and frequently a costly one, to create a "procedures department." Such an administrative monster will usually proceed to do what its name implies—write and publish one document after another, purporting to legislate this or that aspect of employee work behavior. Procedures people seldom know when to stop and almost never conclude that they have completed their mission. Typically, they continue to pump out paper long after it has become obvious to nearly everyone else that they are part of the problem, not an avenue to its solution.

Actually, the administrative system has only three basic purposes, and these can serve as criteria for evaluating its effectiveness. The purposes are the following:

1. To provide a flow of routine information to top management, from which they can infer the overall health of the organization.
2. To provide a flow of information from top management to the various levels of management, and to the people at working levels, letting them know what is going on above them and what to expect from top management in the future.
3. To provide a flow of necessary work-related information between organizational units and functions.

This means that if some information activity is not serving one or more of these basic purposes, it is probably wasting energy, wasting money, and obstructing some other useful process. Examples of wasted information activities include keeping ancient information in overstuffed file cabinets "just in case," writing many self-protective memoranda designed for the "C.Y.A." function, i.e., "cover your assets," and creating new forms when several existing forms could be consolidated or eliminated.

We can often use the same systems-diagram approach in understanding the administrative system that we use with the technical system. It is not necessary to sketch out all of the information flow processes and activities in order to understand the administrative system fairly well. We need only to zero in on those that seem to represent inordinately high cost, long process times, or levels of complexity that make it difficult for the action people of the organization to use the information effectively. We can analyze these in the same sense that we analyzed technical processes and identify those factors that invite detailed treatment and improvement during the problem-solving phase.

If the organization relies heavily on computers to process information, then these activities deserve the same close scrutiny that any other high-cost processes get. Too often the data-processing people of the organization operate in their own private "temple," immune to logical scrutiny or evaluation. It is usually appropriate, during an OD assessment phase, to think carefully about the role of computers in managing and operating the organization and to make evaluations and determinations that treat the computer as an expensive element of capital and an important aspect of administrative capability.

Other aspects of the administrative system include the various routine reports and other media that transfer information, the management information system, or MIS, as data-processing people often call it, and the "company bugle," or house newsletter, if one exists.

Above all, the formal structure of the organization should be clear in terms of the lines of command, functional subdivisions, and jurisdictions among managers. Some executives overdo this process, with too-rigid structures, while others underdo it with vague and confusing organizational concepts that the people at working levels cannot understand. An organizational structure needs to be fairly flexible and open to change, and it also needs to be reassuringly definite. Top management should spell out the levels of authority that exist and should clarify the kinds of decisions and the magnitude of the resource commitments that each level can make without prior authorization from above.

One of the most useful tests of the administrative system's efficiency is its response time in conveying important information. For example, how long does it take for a directive or a communique issued by the chief executive to find its way to the lowest level of the organization? How long does it take for a significant fact to make its way from the lowest level of the organization up to the executive suite? In some cases, this time lag is nearly infinite. In others, there may be a relatively small lag and relatively less distortion in the process. Some straightforward fact finding, especially by interviews, can usually provide realistic answers to these questions rather quickly.

Just as in the case of the technical system and in the case of the social system, the OD task force should write up a summary of the findings of the assessment of the administrative system and make it available to everyone directly involved in the OD process. This gives them something specific to evaluate, and it points the way to a problem-solving process that can achieve the maximum in the way of high-payoff improvements, with only a reasonable investment in energy and resources.

ASSESSING THE STRATEGIC SYSTEM

Assessing the strategic system of the organization sometimes involves rather delicate considerations, especially when the matter of evaluating managerial strength comes up. This is the aspect of organization development that is so sensitive to top management readiness. No executive in his or her right mind appreciates being held up to critical scrutiny and certainly will not appoint a task force if that promises to be the primary outcome. This means that the approach to the appraisal of the strategic system must offer the executives some important benefits, and it must provide assurances that they will come through it unscathed and still firmly in charge.

Generally, this means that the only people authorized to evaluate the managers are the managers themselves. The OD task force must offer an overall approach to the assessment that enables the executives to think constructively about the extended management family and to make their own judgments about its overall effectiveness. Usually, this needs to be a relatively low-key process, and one in which the chief executive and the second-tier executives decide to a great extent how to go about it.

Probably the most constructive role for the OD task force in this process is one of providing information, making suggestions, and carrying out specific evaluative tasks that the top management team may assign. For example, a consultant or OD specialist may offer some useful conceptual models or criteria for assessing management strength. Also, the task force may work with the personnel people to gather some overall descriptive data about the managerial family. These facts might include the total number of managers, the relative proportion of males and females, statistics on formal management training, age and experience distributions, and tenure statistics.

Occasionally, the executives of an organization may be perfectly inclined to deal quite explicitly with the matter of management effectiveness. The chief executive may want to examine his or her own managerial style and the styles of the other members of the executive team, either with the help of an expert consultant or without it. The people on the OD task force should be prepared for this possibility and should know how to respond to the requirement. As a practical matter, however, they should also be prepared to see the process of assessing the strategic system handled behind closed doors, or barely handled at all. This is a practical fact of organizational life and should be dealt with flexibly and realistically.

It might also happen that top management wants to make a thorough assessment of managers at various subordinate levels, down to and including the first-line supervisor level. There are precedents for this seemingly preposterous undertaking and workable techniques for carrying it out. For example, the personnel department can provide an objective assessment of each manager's background, experience, training, and performance if the organization has a performance appraisal system for managers. A useful adjunct to this objective information would be to have the employees in a group evaluate their supervisor, submitting their evaluations to a third-party team who "sanitizes" the information before presenting it to the supervisor in order to eliminate any data that would uniquely identify any particular person. As a policy matter, top management may elect to have this evaluative data delivered directly to the managers concerned, with no one else having access to it. A further sanitized version of the composite findings could go to the OD task force and to top management, as useful data in deciding what management development programs may be needed.

It also makes sense for the members of the OD task force to make their own practical and realistic assessment of the chief executive's style, and the styles of the second-tier executives. This will help them maintain a clear perspective on the OD process, assess the kinds of solutions they can sell, and identify aspects of the strategic system they need to affect in order to get the OD program underway.

Once the OD task force has a reasonable understanding of the organization's managers as people, the next step is to assess the tools and processes of setting strategy, planning, and carrying out the plan. The entire strategic planning process of the organization—if it has one, and a surprising number of organizations do not—needs careful scrutiny. The plans themselves, the ways in which they are prepared, the goals and the ways in which they are set, and the extent to which the planning process allows for concentration of resources on high-payoff areas, all deserve thorough and dispassionate scrutiny.

Just as in the cases of the technical system, the social system, and the administrative system, a written summary of the strategic system can help top management and the OD task force develop a course of action for making worthwhile changes. As we've already noted, the readiness of the top management team for the kinds of thinking processes involved in organization development will determine to a great extent the proper means for expressing and interpreting the findings.

HOW TO ANALYZE MANAGERIAL STYLES

Usually, the single most important factor in the overall "personality" of an organization is the managerial style of the person who heads it. To a somewhat lesser degree, the managerial styles of the second-tier executives also combine to shape the culture and climate of the organization. A person who is interested in applying OD techniques in an organization will do well to spend some time assessing the styles of the people at the helm.

The members of an OD task force might want to make an appraisal of executive styles as part of the process of formulating a workable approach to OD in their particular organization. This could be a relatively private, low-key matter, or it might have a clear sanction from the executives. Commonly, the situation will be somewhere between these two extremes. In any case, an honest and fairly objective assessment of managerial style is essential to an understanding of the overall organization, its ways of operating, and its effectiveness.

Here we will explore several simple conceptual schemes, or models, that can help us to organize what we find out about a particular group of managers and help us to make sense out of it. In assessing managerial styles, either on the part of executives or lower-level managers, we are looking for a few key factors. These have to do with the ways in which they use their formal authority, the extent to which they have accumulated "earned authority" as individuals, the extent to which they think and manage comprehensively, and the ways in which they habitually relate to the people who report to them.

Let's consider a prototype of the most frequently found manager in a business organization, and use that portrait as a convenient basis for discussion and analysis. The most commonly found manager in American business is a male between the ages of about forty and fifty-five, with some years of experience in a technical or line function, a college degree plus a smattering of additional schooling, and about ten years or more in a management or leadership job. We will refer to such a person as "he," primarily because this is by far the most common gender to be found in management jobs at present. All of the concepts we will explore here apply just as well to executives as to managers at various other levels in the organization, and just as well to female managers and executives.

Let's begin our appraisal by trying to guess how this person handles power, authority, and interactions with people. Researcher David McClelland claims that three general needs, or appetites, serve to describe virtually all people when it comes to human interaction, whether formal authority is involved or not. The first of these is the need for *affiliation*. The second is the need for *achievement*. And the third is the need for *power*. Affiliation simply means an appetite for involvement with and connectedness to other people on an on-going basis. Achievement refers to accomplishing things that one deems worthwhile and important. Power means the desire to wield influence, in and of itself, over other people and their actions. McClelland describes these social motives as "driving forces" that tend to shape a person's behavior toward others.

By observing a manager as a person, an interactor, over a period of time, you can probably form a fairly reliable impression of his preferences for each of these three kinds of gratification. A power-oriented manager will treat other people quite differently over the long run than an achievement-oriented manager will. An affliation-oriented manager will be different from the first two types. An extreme orientation to one of these forms of gratification will usually make for a very distinctive and recognizable style on the part of a manager. He may very well appear rather lopsided in his dealings with other people, especially subordinates. No one has shown any one of these three orientations to be "better" than the others for managing effectively. This knowledge simply helps us to make sense of the consistent patterns of behavior we observe in the managers we want to study.

A second useful angle for appraising the manager is his use of formal authority over the long run. We can identify four general levels of control-orientation which a manager can choose from, consciously or unconsciously, in running an organization. These are the following:

1. *Autocratic*
2. *Parental*
3. *Participative*
4. *Collegial*

The autocratic style emphasizes virtually total control by the manager, with virtually all key decisions in his hands, and most of the communication process consisting of one-way directives rather than shared problem-solving. The parental style, referred to as "paternal" if the manager is a man and "maternal" if she is a woman, is a more benevolent form of control. The message is "I still make the rules and I do the thinking, but I'll treat you kindly." The participative style involves much more interaction between manager and subordinates, and much more delegation of authority and freedom of action. The collegial style (from the word "colleagues") implies a situation of minimal use of authority, such as might be found in small groups of highly qualified people working more or less autonomously. It seems questionable whether this could be a workable style for managing larger, traditional organizations.

These four levels help to describe the range of choices in imposing formal authority, from overcontrol to undercontrol. One can argue that each style has its place, in certain organizations, at certain times, and for certain people. Each manager tends to choose one of them over the others as a long-run orientation. This choice tends to color his interactions with subordinates to a very great extent, on a day-to-day basis as well as over the longer term.

In a sense, the employees of an organization also adopt "styles" in their reactions to being managed. Each of the four authority styles tends to invite employees to respond in certain ways, and over the long run they may come to prefer a certain way of relating to the manager as a matter of habit. For example, the autocratic style of management eventually tends to develop *obedient* employees. The parental style tends to develop *dependent* employees. The participative style tends to develop *self-directed* employees. And the collegial style tends to develop *autonomous* employees. Again, the judgment about the relative benefits of any of these modes for a given situation depends on many situational factors.

Figure 9-1 shows how styles of managing correspond to styles of being managed. The squares along the diagonal of the matrix diagram

EMPLOYEE STYLE

	Obedient	Dependent	Self-directed	Autonomous
Autocratic	X			
Parental		X		
Participative			X	
Collegial				X

EXECUTIVE STYLE

FIGURE 9-1
Executive Style and
Employees' Style
May Be Matched
or Mismatched

suggest that there will be some form of compatible "match" between manager and employees, although it says nothing about the relative effectiveness of the relationship. It is also interesting to speculate about differences between the style the manager offers and the style the employees have learned to deal with.

For example, an executive who takes over the top spot in a company, in which the people have been conditioned to respond obediently to an autocratic manager, may face a great deal of inertia and resistance in implementing a participative style of managing. The people of the organization may not be ready to take more responsibility and freedom of action overnight. These are some of the kinds of considerations that OD techniques can help to clarify and remedy.

Another simple and useful framework of appraising managerial style is based on the four general roles a manager must serve if he is to function in a comprehensive way. As previously described, these are the roles of:

1. *Strategist*
2. *Leader*
3. *Problem-Solver*
4. *Administrator*

The strategist role deals with the future, with the reasoning process that establishes the organization's purposes, and with the actions that affect its destiny. The leader role deals with influencing people at various levels in strong positive ways, and helping them to convert their aspirations to actions. The problem-solver role deals with helping people to adapt to obstacles and redirect their energies according to priorities. The administrator role deals with creating and maintaining the formal processes by which people in large numbers collaborate by exchanging information. These four roles correspond nicely to the four organizational systems in our approach to OD—the strategic, social, technical, and administrative.

You can make a useful appraisal of a manager's style simply by arranging these four roles in a forced-choice sequence from highest to lowest, according to your judgments about how extensively the manager you are studying emphasizes each role in his overall pattern of managing. A manager who strongly emphasizes one role much more than the others will have a very distinctive orientation that will usually carry over from situation to situation. For example, one who emphasizes the administrative role will show a strong preoccupation with systems, methods, processes, information flows, and media. One who emphasises the leader role will be heavily oriented toward influencing people and getting action. A manager who is lopsided, i.e., who emphasizes one role and lacks skill in the others, seldom manages as effectively in the long run as one who has learned to serve each of the four roles. Understanding the role orientation of an executive, or a manager at any level, can give you a great deal of insight into his patterns of managing and can help you understand how he needs to see the world.

One more conceptual framework along these lines, aimed at the leader role, should round out our knowledge of managerial style and equip us with enough thinking tools to make a fairly reliable appraisal of the management dynamics in an organization. We can divide the leadership process into four component processes, based on the way the manager uses his authority in the day-to-day process of giving direction to subordinates. As previously described, these four component processes are:

1. *Shared goals*
2. *Teamwork*
3. *Autonomy*
4. *Reward*

These four aspects give rise to the acronym "STAR," an intriguing term for a highly effective manager.

Shared goals refers to the process of dialoguing problems and solutions with subordinates and arriving at goals that have high"ownership" value for the people who must accomplish them. Teamwork refers to the process of building group solidarity, trust, and collaborative problem-solving capabilities, and knowing which activities warrant group action and which warrant individual action. Autonomy refers to the extent to which the manager grants freedom of action to the person responsible for getting the results. Reward refers to the sum total of the reinforcements the manager provides, either positive or negative, monetary or other, conscious or unconscious.

Each of these four aspects of managerial leadership needs to be adjusted to the needs of the individual, the situation, and the nature of the task. No one mixture of shared goals, teamwork, autonomy, and reward will suit all situations and all individuals. However, the overall pattern of a manager's actions will usually show a distinctive orientation toward each of the four components, and the combination of these trends will usually make for a distinctive leadership style.

With a few basic conceptual schemes like these, it is possible to make sense out of what managers do. By knowing the primary patterns that show up in an executive's style, we can understand many things. For example, we can understand the personal needs and values that have impelled him to certain actions in the past. We can, to some extent, predict the way he will probably manage in the future. And, when it comes to selling him on a certain course of action, such as an OD program for the entire organization, we have a better idea of the way he needs to think about it, the ways in which he might respond to it, and the benefits we must create in order to make it worthwhile within his distinctive frame of reference.

HOW TO CONDUCT A CLIMATE SURVEY

A climate survey can be a very useful process for helping management understand the people of the organization if it is well carried out, and it can be a disaster if it is poorly carried out. If we observe certain common-sense rules in assessing the social climate, there is very little risk of a negative or unpleasant outcome. Essentially, we want to gather some useful information about an important aspect of the organization, and we want to gather it in a business-like, humane, and realistic way.

It is worthwhile to review the more common mistakes managers can make in using climate surveys and to spell out some "do's" and "don't's" to guide our efforts. First, I prefer to use the term "climate survey" as opposed to the cruder term "attitude survey." The second term tends to conjure up notions in people's heads of angry, disgruntled employees, and of managers placing themselves at great psychological risk in opening the floodgates and releasing this anger. Using the term "climate" suggests a more benign state of affairs, and it implies an internal social setting that always exists.

Probably the most common blunder managers make in doing climate surveys is to ignore the effects of the process itself on the very feelings and perceptions they want to assess. The mere act of sending out a survey questionnaire to the employees starts an irreversible chain of events. For one thing, a questionnaire tends to raise expectations in the minds of the employees. "What's going to happen as a result of this survey?" they ask. Someone says, "Management is finally beginning to listen to us." Someone else thinks "Maybe they'll finally catch up with my boss, and realize the S.O.B. should be fired." As the famous Hawthorne studies of the late 1930s showed, any attempt to measure key aspects of a social system has a perturbing influence on the system itself. To some extent, the researchers at the Western Electric assembly plant were measuring the effects of their own intervention into the daily life of the workers.

Many a naive manager has traveled the same disastrous route: send out a survey questionnaire, unknowingly raise expectations, analyze the results and find them horrifying, destroy the results or quietly file them, and pretend that nothing has happened. But something has happened. Rightly or wrongly, the employees have interpreted management's action in sending out the questionnaire as a covenant—an implied promise to listen with an open mind and to do something constructive about their concerns. Usually, the first question the employees ask is "Are we going to see the results of the questionnaire?" If management then covers up the whole process and declines to publish the results, the result is usually a near-fatal loss of trust and credibility. In such a case, it would have been far better not to have done the survey at all.

A survey questionnaire I recently reviewed, used by a savings and loan institution, had a novel question at the end. It asked, "Do you think anything positive will come of this survey?" The answer given by the employees was a resounding "No." Did anything positive result? You guessed it. Six months later, after management had forgotten all about it, the employees were still saying, "I told you so."

On the subject of specific questions, here is a question that should never be asked on a climate survey: "Would you prefer to have a union in our company?" In all likelihood, the National Labor Relations Board would interpret the results of that question, if affirmative, as tantamount to a vote by the employees in favor of having a union election. A union leader, armed with that data, would probably have very little difficulty getting an election held.

Let's review the steps in carrying out a climate survey effectively:

1. First, know why you're doing the survey; decide in advance what you want to find out and how you plan to use the data.
2. Appoint someone with the necessary expertise to design the questionnaire properly; don't just put together a hodgepodge of questions and hope for the best.
3. Allow enough time and resources to develop an effective questionnaire; test the questions on a sample group of employees, and refine them if necessary; make sure the people you want to survey will really understand the questions and will know how to answer them unambiguously.

4. Get the managers at all levels involved in the process; brief them ahead of time to make sure they understand what is going to happen and make sure they can explain the process to the managers of their units; carry out the process through the chain of command—i.e., have the managers distribute the questionnaires, collect the completed answer sheets, and send them in to a central collection point.

5. Make the questionnaire anonymous; make whatever provisions are necessary to assure the employees that their answers will not identify them or make them vulnerable to recrimination; allow people to identify themselves if they choose to, but make anonymity the norm.

6. Process the results as quickly as possible, summarize them, and put them in a written form that is easy to understand.

7. Present the results to top management for an initial appraisal, and distribute copies to all managers; make no interpretations at this point.

8. Have the managers share the results with their staff members and discuss them briefly; make sure all employees know what the results of the survey are.

9. After the various key people involved have had a chance to review the results, convene a conference to discuss their interpretations and to arrive at a plan for capitalizing on the information.

10. Repeat the survey in exactly the same form in the future, say every six months or every year, to identify trends and changes that reflect the results of various OD interventions.

One of the keys to getting good questionnaire results is to state the questions skillfully. This is a combination of art and science, and it takes a little careful thought. Here are some simple suggestions for arriving at effective questions.

1. Use numerical scales whenever possible; give the person a choice between two extremes, such as 1 through 5.

2. Focus each question on only one factor; avoid "compound" questions or complex mixtures of issues and concerns.

3. Avoid leading or loaded questions; don't "shop" for certain kinds of answers.

4. Focus each question on the individual; get his or her own perspective or opinion on the matter.

5. Word each question carefully to eliminate ambiguity, obscure terms, or misleading implications.

6. Do ask for narrative responses following the numerically-oriented questions; give people a chance to express their ideas in their own ways, in addition to numerical form.

7. Keep the questionnaire fairly brief; twenty questions or so will usually give you a great deal of information to think about; don't go into elaborate details or isolated issues that are best explored by interviews or other data-gathering methods.

8. Make the physical design of the questionnaire attractive, simple, and easy to understand; consider having a detachable answer sheet that lends itself well to computer processing of the data, and permit the employees to keep the questions if they like.

9. Test the design and layout of the questionnaire to make sure a person who hasn't seen it before will really know how to fill it out and what to do with it when he or she is finished.

10. Include some simple and well-worded instructions as part of the introduction to the questionnaire; consider also explaining why management is conducting the survey and what they plan to do with the results.

Computer programs such as the Assessment Survey Kit ("A.S.K."), published by Karl Albrecht & Associates, enable you to process questionnaire data quickly, easily, and economically, if you have access to a small "desk-top" computer.

BUILDING AN EMPLOYEE-SENSING SYSTEM

It is a fairly simple matter to apply the techniques of climate assessment on a regular basis by means of an "employee-sensing system." This is simply a routine process of surveying, interviewing, and thinking, which provides management with useful information about the status of the social system. More and more companies are setting up such systems, typically after finding that their first-time experiences with climate surveys are highly positive and productive. TRW, Inc. is probably the best-known proponent of routine employee sensing. That company uses what its executives call a "one in five" method, which means that they survey all employees in a given division by questionnaire, and then they contact at least one-fifth of them for follow-up, indepth interviews.

In a TRW division, typically the division manager would request the services of an OD team to come in and conduct a survey. The team members would interview the managers and other key people, talk with some of the employees, and identify key issues to be "sensed." They would prepare a questionnaire, administer it, process the data, and present the results to management. Then they would begin holding interview meetings with groups of employees, usually representing a mixture of job specialties and areas of the organization. They would normally carry out the interviews in small groups, usually five to fifteen people, and they would spend most of their time asking open-ended questions and recording the results. In reporting the narrative results to division management, they would typically identify the various recurring themes they heard, rank them in order of frequency and intensity, and supplement them with selected verbatim comments. They would compile all of their findings into a comprehensive report to division management, which would be free to use the results as it saw fit.

This is probably as reasonable a model for a sensing system as any. It has the advantage of making the process more or less routine and eliminating any ominous overtones or implications that might accompany a first-time climate survey. Managers also benefit from this approach, because they get important information about the employees, in a psychologically safe "routine" context.

An easy way to start, after first having conducted a successful climate assessment and having mastered the practical considerations, is to have the personnel department set up a routine procedure on a scheduled basis, say every six months or every year. It helps to use the identical questionnaire each time if possible, to make it possible to compare data from one period with results from previous periods. The routine process should also include a written report to top management and the release of the results to the employees.

It is also possible to supplement the regular sensing questionnaire with various special-issue questions to find out about these topics as they arise. For example, the executives may want to know how the employees would feel about a program of flexible working hours, options for benefit plans, or the effects of previously implemented changes.

10

The Problem-Solving Phase

A "CATALOG" OF OPTIONS FOR ORGANIZATION DEVELOPMENT

Our broad systems view of the organization and its implied systems approach to OD make possible a wide range of options for improvements. The traditional, human relations school of OD has held that something is an "OD intervention" only if it attempts to change the social culture of the organization, dealing with issues of power, values, norms, and rewards. But, with the broader definition of OD as a comprehensive process of planned change in the organization's total functioning, almost anything goes. In a sense, nothing necessarily is or is not an OD fix by definition. Whatever we think is necessary and helpful for organizational improvement consequently falls under the heading of OD options.

Here is a wide-ranging list of interesting options for OD:

1. Administrative Systems Development/Redevelopment
2. Annual Management Retreat
3. Behavior Modification Programs
4. Capital Improvement Projects
5. Computerization
6. Cross-cultural Training and Awareness Programs
7. Debt Restructuring
8. EEO/Affirmative Action Program
9. Employee Action Committee
10. Employee Activity Programs
    a. Education
    b. Fitness, Smoke-stop, Health Enhancement
    c. Spouse and Family Programs
    d. Others
11. Employee Assistance and Counselling Programs
    a. Personal
    b. Career Development
    c. Life Planning
    d. Therapy and Problem Counselling
12. Employee Newsletter
13. Employee Recognition Award Program
14. Employee-sensing System
15. Employee Suggestion System
16. Executive Development
17. Executive Visibility Program
18. "Inter-Groups"
    a. Inter-departmental Committees
    b. Union-Management Committee
    c. Others
19. Job Posting/Advertising Program
20. Job Restructuring
    a. Autonomous Work Groups
    b. Flextime
    c. Job Enlargement
    d. Job Enrichment
    e. Job Rotation
    f. Job Sharing
21. Management Development
22. Mentor-Consultant Resources
23. Merit Compensation Systems
24. "Out-placement" (job-finding) for Displaced Employees

25. Planning Processes
    a. Strategic
    b. Long Range
    c. Operational
26. Productivity Improvement Programs
27. Quality Circles
28. Quality-of-Work-Life Programs
29. Reorganization
30. Special Benefit Programs
31. Special Task Forces
    a. EEO/AAP
    b. OD
    c. Technical Problem-Solving
    d. Women's Opportunity
    e. Others
32. Team Building
33. Training
    a. Job Skills Training
    b. Personal Skills Training
    c. Management Training
    d. Laboratory Training
    e. Team Training
34. Work Simplification Programs

TEAM BUILDING

The process of team building is probably the best-known feature of organization development and possibly the one that shows the most promise for increasing the effectiveness of many contemporary organizations. Effective intragroup collaboration and problem-solving is becoming increasingly important as organizations become more complex and more information-intensive, and as teamwork steadily becomes a more valuable asset.

In order to understand how team building works, it is first necessary to have a clear idea of what team effectiveness really is. We can say a group of people have worked effectively as a team, under some circumstances, if they have met two important conditions. First, they have accomplished something of value; they reached the worthwhile goal they set for themselves or had presented to them. And second, they maintained or increased their sense of cohesiveness, or group integrity and willingness to work together.

A good test of a group's cohesiveness is simply to find out whether the members would enjoy working together again on some project in the future. If they accomplished their current objective but now despise one another as a result of painful interactions and frustrations in working at cross-purposes, they haven't functioned very well as a team. Conversely, if they got along famously with one another but failed to achieve their objective—assuming it was a reasonably achievable objective—then they also have not functioned effectively. Both conditions are necessary for effective team operation.

Whether the members of a certain group of people work together routinely as part of an intact work unit, or they have just come together to work as an ad hoc problem-solving group or task force, they can learn some basic techniques for good teamwork. The process of team building usually employs an outside person in the role of a coach, working with the team members for one or more concentrated sessions to help them build both their problem-solving capability and their cohesiveness.

The key to team building is helping the people learn to monitor their own interaction processes, rather than having them preoccupy themselves solely with the "content" of those processes, i.e., with the specific subject matter or problems they are dealing with. This "content-process" distinction is rather subtle and difficult to grasp for some people at first, and this is how an external consultant can be resourceful to them. The consultant can observe and participate as they go about their task, and can help them develop process-type techniques and ground rules, such as ways to clarify objectives, agree on roles and interactions, disagree without fighting, problem-solve collectively and collaboratively, focus their energies on outcomes, and commit themselves to concrete plans.

We can specify the basic conditions for a team to function effectively, in terms of three primary factors: goals, roles, and a plan. Taken in order, they are:

1. *Goals*—The group must have a clear-cut purpose or outcome which its members have set about to achieve. If it does not have a definite and concretely stated objective, then their first objective must be to establish their group's objective.

2. *Roles*—Sooner or later, they must figure out what has to be done and divide up the work amongst themselves. They need to establish a clearly defined role, or task assignment, for each member, including the role of the team leader. The group members need a clearly identified leader who has the skills to coordinate their activities while maintaining positive interpersonal relations. They need an agreed basis for dealing with one another when they meet as a group, as well as when they work on their own.

3. *A Plan*—It is important that the team members spell out the timetable of their actions, with their various tasks clearly related to the objective they want to achieve. The plan should be more than a few spoken words. If the objective is at all ambitious, the plan should be thoughtfully prepared, briefly written, and distributed to all members of the team.

By keeping these three key points in mind, the team members can analyze their own processes and develop ways of working together that maximize their chances of achieving their objective while maintaining humane dealings with one another.

The traditional human-relations school of OD held for many years that people could not really function effectively as a team unless they delved deeply into interpersonal issues of power, influence, and emotional responses to one another. This made team building, by definition, essentially an encounter process. This is probably the one form of extremism that gave the traditional school of OD a permanent black eye and the uncharitable label of the "touchy-feely" movement. During the 1950s and 1960s, a small number of managers went through various "sensitivity groups," or "encounter groups," hoping to learn the skills of effective interaction in the group setting. This kind of intensive group-dynamic training still goes on to some extent, but it appears to be fading out for lack of impressive results.

Contemporary team building has become much more of a comfortable, nonthreatening process of teaching and coaching, and is now gaining acceptance with managers as a result. In the team-building sessions I conduct for client organizations, I present a model of team effectiveness and identify the key skills in getting there. Then we go through a process of acquiring and using those key skills, usually in the context of the task the group has set about. I also make extensive use of a stepwise problem-solving procedure, or "model," which helps the team members to explore the problem thoroughly before closing in on solutions.

It is possible, of course, for a group of people to discuss and analyze their team processes without the aid of a consultant or external facilitator and to make significant improvements in the way they operate. Historically, the use of outside consulting assistance, either on the part of a professional consultant or someone from an appropriate department in the organization, has proven to give the most effective results. And now that we have developed team-building techniques oriented to teaching and coaching, in workshop style, the process need not be psychologically threatening. It makes good sense as an investment in organizational effectiveness.

DEVELOPING THE MANAGEMENT TEAM

Because so many aspects of the organization's effectiveness depend on skillful management, it often makes sense to focus first on the top management team as a starting point for OD. An internal OD specialist may not always be able to sell this approach, but an external consultant often can, perhaps only because he or she has been engaged by top management and formally acknowledged as a catalyst-person or change agent.

We can consider top-management team development as an aspect of OD in two different ways. First, it may be appropriate to undertake a management team-building project in order to enable the team to function effectively during the problem-solving phase of the OD program. By increasing the members' collective ability for problem-solving as well as other forms of interaction, they become much more capable of developing imaginative solutions during the problem-solving phase. In the second approach, management team building may be indicated as one of the intervention strategies selected during the problem-solving phase of the OD program. This means it goes on the agenda of things to accomplish during the implementation phase, rather than becoming a part of the problem-solving phase.

Developing the overall management team—i.e., the entire extended management "family" of the organization—usually makes sense as well. Unless the organization has had an on-going management development program, it is rather unlikely that the members of the overall management group will be as highly skilled and capable as they could be. Most organizations have a rather wide variation in levels of skills among managers, from incompetent to outstanding. It is surprising how long incompetent or oppressive managers can remain in the jobs to which they were appointed before upper management discovers the mistakes and takes action to remedy them. Meanwhile, the employees of the misplaced managers often pay a high price in reduced effectiveness, low morale, and lack of collaboration.

It is possible to evolve the total management strength of an organization to an impressively high level by making sure the following three primary conditions exist:

1. The chief executive is a competent and effective manager who manages comprehensively, models effective managerial behavior for subordinate managers, and maintains high expectations for their performance.
2. The organization has an effective screening and selection program that makes sure only well-qualified and well-prepared people get promoted into managerial positions.
3. The organization has a management development program that helps to provide well-prepared candidates for managerial jobs when they open up.

The third of these conditions merits special consideration. It is possible to arrange the circumstances in an organization to maximize the number of highly capable people who get management jobs and to minimize the number of misplaced managers. We can do this by setting up a relatively formal managerial selection and placement program—the "graduation" process described previously, in which a person must pass through four "gates" to be considered eligible for promotion to a supervisory job.

Setting up a process like this requires that top management plan fairly far ahead in developing management strength. The chief executive must answer the question, "Where will we get tomorrow's leaders, and what must we do today to develop them?" Very often, promotion decisions in organizations are made in an atmosphere of default, i.e., a supervisory job opens up and there are no highly qualified candidates available, or at least visible. Because management didn't plan for the inevitable need for new managers, a middle manager will usually end up choosing some favored employee from the ranks, often with little regard for demonstrated managerial ability. Without identifying and training high-potential people well in advance of the need, it becomes a matter of "pot luck." Even worse, the managers may tend to go outside the organization to hire new managers, a practice which almost always creates resentment, frustration, and a sense of betrayal on the part of eligible people in the organization. When an executive says, "We just don't have anyone qualified for this job," he is saying, in effect, "I didn't do my job—I didn't anticipate or plan for today's management needs yesterday."

In addition to a selection system, the organization also needs a "rescue system." There must be some reasonable and humane means for identifying those managers who are not living up to the requirements of their jobs, and who should be removed or given assistance or remedial training. The longer a manager who has "bombed out" stays in the job, the more damage he causes, and the longer the delay is in getting the group back to a productive mode of operation. The manager suffers, the employees suffer, and the organization suffers. It does not necessarily have to mean a devastating loss of face for a person to be removed from a managerial job and returned to a job in which he or she can perform effectively. An effective approach to this problem is to have a formally recognized trial period, or probationary period, during which both the new manager and his or her senior manager both make an assessment of the situation. Either the executive or the newly appointed manager should be free to decide that a managerial job is not the best way to use this person's capabilities. Making the placement process and the rescue process explicit, public, and humane tends to remove the negative connotations generally applied to them and tends to encourage executives to act more quickly and decisively in problem cases.

Management strength is always a key element of the organization's total capability and total effectiveness. An effective executive will create the conditions that identify, develop, select, and promote effective managers. A job in management is one of the most valuable resources the organization has. It must not be wasted on incompetent, underdeveloped, or underprepared people. It is top management's responsibility—and opportunity—to get the most effective people into managerial jobs.

CREATING A PROCESS FOR COLLECTIVE PROBLEM-SOLVING

One of the ways in which we can get constructive change throughout an organization is to "light many fires." This means we have to mobilize and enable as many people and work units as we can to solve problems effectively and adapt to changing circumstances. The day in which the autocratic, parental, or dictatorial manager could direct an organization by sheer force of personality is gone. Most modern organizations have become so knowledge-intensive in their work processes, so diversified in their functions, and so complex in their internal workings that the executive simply has no choice but to depend on the independent actions of many people and many units in getting the organization's objectives met.

As a general and an emperor, Napoleon was struck by this consideration. He is supposed to have confided this to one of his advisors. "Do you know what amuses me most?" he reflected, "the utter impotence of pure force to organize anything."

If we really want an adaptive, problem-solving organization, then we must authorize and condone adaptive, problem-solving behavior on the part of the managers and their employees. We need to require of managers at all levels that they manage participatively to some extent, that they stimulate problem-solving processes in their units, and that they take the initiative in finding new and better ways to achieve results.

One of the ways in which we can make the top management team more effective as a problem-solving resource is by teaching the executives certain innovative skills, preferably in the context of the team-building process. In the team-building projects I have conducted, I have had very gratifying results in using a systematic problem-solving process, or "model," as a way to enable team members to collaborate much more effectively than they otherwise would. Typically, I teach the members of the team to use a simple two-step process—first, a "divergent" thinking stage of sizing up a problem, and then a "convergent" thinking stage of closing in on acceptable solutions.

Untrained groups usually lose a great deal of energy because they unconsciously mix divergent and convergent thinking processes indiscriminately. One or two people may be trying to understand the problem and its component issues, while others may have made up their minds and are advocating solutions. People frequently argue, debate, and battle back and forth, because they don't use a shared, conscious, stepwise approach to their problem-solving. By having the group members deliberately stay in a divergent mode of thinking and talking for a certain period of time, with no one killing anyone else's ideas, it is possible to get them to consider a much broader view of the problem, and to develop many more effective options for solving it. Then, when they move to the convergent phase, they can choose a course of action more confidently, and put it into effect with less dissension and wasted motion than if they had decided, as groups typically do, based on the strength of personalities.

A well-designed training seminar on problem-solving techniques, especially for managers and other staff professional people, can be an excellent investment in organizational effectiveness. When people learn collaborative problem-solving techniques and have a chance to put them to use in real-life situations, they develop a greater concern for high-quality solutions, based on thorough appraisals of the dominant issues, disciplined fact finding, and careful consideration of alternatives. Members of management teams and work groups who have been trained in methods for collaborative problem-solving virtually always report that they have improved the quality of their decision-making processes and that they achieve higher-quality solutions to the problems they choose to attack. This team problem-solving process, I have found, is a foundation for improved work-group performance, similar to the well-known "quality circle" concept in Japan.

WHAT IS OUR BUSINESS?
OD AND STRATEGIC PLANNING

A broad view of the organization development process allows for the treatment of issues that have absolutely fundamental significance for the organization and its destiny. Recognizing that every organization needs a strategic planning process, we can apply OD techniques in creating such a process if one does not presently exist, or in improving an existing process if it needs improving. In the broadest sense, we can call strategic planning one of our options for developing the organization, although the traditional human-relations school of OD would not generally condone such a broad definition.

The fundamental question we have to answer in getting a strategic planning process underway is the question posed by management consultant Peter F. Drucker, namely, "What is our business?" The answer to this question usually seems straightforward and fairly simple, but it seldom is. Most executives and action people in a typical organization will tend to answer this question in terms of what the organization currently does, i.e., its current mode of servicing its market. Unfortunately, according to Drucker, this conception of business mission frequently confuses means with ends.

The executives of a publishing firm can say, on the one hand, "Our business is publishing books." On the other hand, they can say, "Our business is providing information." Another conception is to say, "Our business is human competence," especially in the case of a publisher of materials such as those used in industrial training. There is a conceptual contrast between these two ways of stating "what our business is." The narrower statement implies a means of doing business. The broader statement implies the greater scope within which executives need to make strategy decisions.

We can distinguish these two conceptions as the "mundane" statement of the business mission and the "creative" statement. The mundane statement is almost always easy to find; the creative statement many times is not. It often requires a broad-minded assessment of what is happening in the organization's environment, and a creative judgment about the organization's "next move" in adapting to the changes in that environment.

An effective strategic planning process needs to have at least the following components:

1. Some means for making a comprehensive assessment of the organization's environment, and for identifying those likely trends, changes, or "unique events" that will shape that environment in the long run.

2. A means for making a comprehensive assessment of the organization itself, as an adaptive entity, and for pinpointing "out-of-kilter" conditions; recognizing the disparities between what is and what ought to be.

3. A process by which the executives undertake an honest, open-minded, and imaginative look at the relationship that currently exists between the organization and the environment; they assess the quality of the "environmental match"—the extent to which the enterprise is attuned to the major flow of events in the environment that will affect its health and survival.

4. A means for converting these great thoughts into crude deeds; a process of inferring, from the environmental and organizational analyses, those strategies, organizational interventions, changes, new programs, new concepts, and management actions that will keep the enterprise adapting successfully.

Out of the creative statement of "our business" arises the strategic "thrust" of the organization—the figurative "next move" that may be necessary to align it or realign it with the changing environment. This may simply be a decision to continue on as is, holding course and speed until further notice. Or, it may involve a difficult and painful redefinition of what the organization is all about. It could lead to an entirely new approach to the customer or the market in general, a new conception of the product or service, or a new way to go about delivering it.

In considering the organization's environment, the top management team must account for all major outside forces, factors, and trends that will affect it. It usually helps a great deal to subdivide the overall environment into various logical components for greater concentration and logical analysis. As previously described, we can think of a typical organization as having at least the following eight environments or subenvironments:

Customer
Competitor
Economic
Social
Technological
Political
Legal
Physical

In addition, the executives may choose to identify certain specialized environments or environmental factors that affect the organization, such as a parent company, a key shareholder or group, or an industry-specific influence they want to plan for and deal with.

In any case, the ability to set strategy is the primary test of the effectiveness of the strategic system of the organization, i.e., its managers. The part that organization development can play in this process is to help the managers assess their current strategy, help them assess their current process for setting strategy, and help them get a more effective strategic planning process underway if that is what the organization needs.

STREAMLINING THE STRUCTURE

If the organization has some structural peculiarities that need correcting, an OD program is an excellent context in which to do it. Adjustments to the structure can range from modest realignments of functions or responsibilities, all the way to wholesale redeployment of major functions and resources. In either case, we must certainly treat changes to the organization's structure with the careful deliberation they deserve. The idea of a reorganization usually creates quite a lot of concern and apprehension since it may involve gains and losses of "turf" for various individual managers, and redefinition of the ways in which various working people relate to one another.

Executives also vary significantly in their willingness to change the organizational structures over which they preside. Some executives will procrastinate indefinitely on a major change, while others seem almost to relish the idea of rearranging the enterprise. Frequently, the organizational structure reflects the personal desires, needs, and values of the chief executive, and what may look illogical from external points of view looks quite logical to him.

For the sake of this discussion, we will assume that the enterprise is somewhat malorganized, that top management recognizes that fact, and intends to restructure it in a logical way by means of a fairly rational thinking process. This may be an untenable assumption in many cases. If there is not a strong commitment to a rational structure, then the OD person must learn to get along with irrational structures. Actually, any time an executive works out a structure for the organization, it seems perfectly rational from his or her point of view as the presiding person. It may only appear irrational from other points of view which are more comprehensive and less emotionally invested.

In any case, we must remind ourselves that the structure chart, i.e., the "power diagram," is usually the personal emotional property of the chief executive, and it has a great deal to do with his or her feelings of control and efficacy. To change it involves much more than simply rearranging functions and relationships. To the executive, it means redefining the allocation of power and influence among the members of the inner circle, and it has many social ramifications. Reorganization can indeed be approached rationally within this conceptual framework. It is important, however, to maintain the broad view of the organizational diagram as a power diagram as well as an aspect of the administrative system.

Assuming we are prepared to take a fairly rational approach to defining the organizational structure according to the findings of the assessment stage, we can identify certain ground rules or guidelines to follow in revising the structure. Some of the major considerations include:

1. Structure should follow strategy; the deployment of resources should relate fairly directly to the strategic thrust, or "next move" the organization needs to make in its environment.

2. Keep it simple; if a newcomer to the organization can't understand the organization chart after a few seconds' explanation, then probably the people working there don't understand it either; seek the most "natural" arrangement of resources that circumstances allow.

3. Balance the relative amounts of circumstantial power across the various functions; don't let one major unit be the tail that wags the dog by an arrangement that gives one executive a clear-cut power advantage over the others.

4. When possible, minimize the number of levels in the organization; don't let the total number of levels, including highest and lowest, exceed five if possible; for larger enterprises, create natural administrative subdivisions, with no "tactical" unit within them having more than five levels.

5. Arrange the chief executive's span of control—i.e., the total number of people reporting to him—to maximize the organizational impact of his limited time and availability; a span of control of eight or more invites speculation about the executive's getting spread too thin, while a span of control of three or less suggests too "tall" an organizational structure with too many levels.

6. Start from scratch and define the organization the way it really should be, rather than patch up an existing hodgepodge of boxes and relationships; make a logical comparison of several plausible options for the structure, and choose one of them for clearly identified logical reasons.

7. Organize for the future, not the past; choose a structure that will equip the enterprise to adapt to foreseeable changes in its environment and in its primary ways of doing business.

8. Test the new organization on paper; subject it to a thorough "what-if" analysis to identify potential problems, areas in need of further definition, and obstacles to implementation; make sure it has the promise of working well.

9. Work out the new organization thoroughly before inflicting it on the people; clear up as many of the question areas as possible, and define as many of the functions, responsibilities, and ranges of authority as possible before making the changeover.

10. Manage and facilitate the changeover to the new organization as carefully as you would manage any other very important project; plan the changeover, let people know about it in advance, explain it to them, help them deal with their concerns about it, and be willing to spend time and money if necessary in getting the transition made as effectively and humanely as possible.

ORGANIZING AND MANAGING FOR INNOVATION

The executives of any organization need to think very carefully and imaginatively about the adaptive capability of the organization—its capacity for innovation to meet the needs of tomorrow. A portion of today's profits must be allocated to developing tomorrow's products in the face of rapidly changing markets and competition. Innovation is becoming necessary for survival, and it doesn't come for free.

Yet, many organizations have in-built blockages to innovation—illogical structures, procedural or jurisdictional tangles, missing functions, managerial obsolescence, or other factors that prevent them from allocating talent and resources to the future. It is fairly common to see a rather staid, conventionally organized company cruise along at an "adequate" level of profitability, only to find that its environment has changed so much that it no longer can cope with the competition. If the company's executives refuse to invest part of today's profit in tomorrow, they are likely to find themselves cruising right into the ground.

Further, there is a fundamental conflict between organizing for operation and organizing for innovation. When you arrange an organization for productive efficiency, i.e., making or doing something for the millionth time, you unavoidably create a setting that is antagonistic to things that are new, strange, unusual, or unproven. Organizing for operation means doing things over and over again the same way, without mistakes. Organizing for innovation means trying to do things that haven't been done before. The functions, procedures, decisions, resource allocations, and day-to-day work processes are quite different for the two kinds of different orientations. As management consultant Jay Galbraith observes, "In the operating organization, you want to eliminate failures. But in the innovating organization, you want to accelerate failure—you need to fail early and often in order to solve a new problem." By that, he means that mistakes and false starts are fundamental to the innovative process; if you're not making mistakes, you're not innovating.

The formal procedures, organizational structures, and habit patterns of the people working in the operating organization generally act to squelch unproven new approaches to the product or service they are providing. Operating people almost always get so completely caught up in the preoccupation with repetitive efficiency that they consciously or unconsciously resist ideas or people that threaten to complicate the operation or increase the ambiguity involved. This is an advantage from one point of view, and a disadvantage from another. New ideas, approaches, or possibilities that bubble up from the grassroots level of the operating organization tend to get squelched as a matter of course. There is a monolithic resistance to the new and the unproven.

On the other hand, an organization constructed mostly for innovative purposes is usually inept at routine operations. Seldom can a research and development department turn out a reasonable quantity of preproduction models without falling victim to the "just one more refinement" syndrome. Each organizational structure has its advantages and disadvantages, which are almost completely complementary to the other.

These two processes mix like oil and water, yet it is the executive's job to get them to mix somehow. In a conventional organization, this usually means having specially designated "islands" of innovative activity—one or more organizational units created solely for the purpose of developing new approaches. The company R&D department is probably the most familiar example of this. There are, however, other approaches to the structure that may promote innovation as well. For example, a new-products committee operating as an "inter-group" across the organization can have a form of flexibility that a conventional engineering or R&D department might not have. Organizations that provide services may especially need these islands of innovative activity within the formal structure. For example, a county department may become so fully fossilized and encrusted with the barnacles of habit that it resists the attempts of its service clients or other units to change its ways. By creating one or more islands of innovation within the organization, such as a special service-development function, the executives can get the organization moving into the future again.

Sometimes the chief executive or the second-tier executives may be so out of date, so rigid in their thinking, or so wedded to traditional approaches, that they become the primary block to innovation. In this case, progress will probably be very slow unless they begin to wake up to the future. Sometimes the entire technical system of the organization needs a good shaking out in order to get people to rethink their relationship to their environment and to get started again in developing new possibilities.

An organization development program sometimes offers a convenient avenue for rearranging the balance between operation and innovation in the enterprise. A new look at strategic issues and strategic planning, a review of executive management style, a thoughtful analysis of the organization's structure and its internal habit patterns, a review of its products or services against the demands of the market and the depredations of the competition, and training workshops in innovative thinking and problem-solving can all help to bring a fossilized organization to life again. Developing and maintaining an organization that can serve the needs of both operation and innovation is one of the chief executive's toughest challenges, and one that offers great payoffs in terms of future capability.

IMPROVING PRODUCTIVITY

A productivity improvement program usually makes more sense after we have taken care of some of the more influential factors, such as developing the management team and streamlining the organizational structure. Then we are in a position to approach improvements in the primary productive axis of the technical system comprehensively and systematically.

Improving productivity requires that we first settle on the measure or measures of productivity that we are going to use. Many managers and staff people in organizations tend to use the term "productivity" very broadly, implying some general value judgment about how well people are working. It is usually much more helpful to identify specific variables that measure specific aspects of the prime axis that we can control and improve upon. For example, if we simply say that the operations division of a commercial construction company "poured 175 floor slabs last quarter," we've said something about production but we haven't said anything about productivity. Productivity means the efficiency with which we attain a certain production level, in terms of the resources we had to spend to get there. It is much more informative to say the operations division "poured

175 floor slabs last quarter at a labor productivity of 1.44 tons per labor hour," or perhaps "94 square feet per labor hour." A specific measure of productivity, in terms of output achieved divided by input resources invested, gives us a much clearer focus on the effectiveness of the technical system.

It generally helps a great deal to create a special project aimed at productivity improvement, rather than simply to hope that all departments will somehow work together and spontaneously improve it. This generally doesn't happen. Probably the best approach in most cases is to establish a special productivity task force, with the assignment of proposing improvements in the technical system that hold promise of increasing productivity. Properly chosen people, led by a competent group leader, and armed with a fairly scientific approach, can often develop very effective improvements.

Typically, a productivity improvement task force should follow roughly the following steps:

1. Gather the facts first; study the processes in question, collect descriptive data on them, and interview people who understand them well—including the first-line workers.

2. Focus on one or two specific areas or aspects of the productive axis that seem to offer the highest potential for payoff.

3. Diagram the process as a time-sequential flow of materials, media, data, and events; figure out what feeds into what, what depends on what, and where the high-cost stages are; make sure you include all the important inputs to the process, and make sure you understand how the output depends on them.

4. Don't limit your thinking to purely technical or mechanical aspects of the process; stay alert for human factors, such as skill level, experience, morale, interpersonal relationships, and quality of supervision; pay attention to information as a raw material and make sure it is properly integrated into the technical processes.

5. Work with reliable measurements whenever possible, especially in the area of costs; develop a baseline cost summary of the process (say for producing one item) for later comparison to see whether your proposed solutions actually made things any better.

6. Work through the supervisors in order to gain their commitment to the improvement process; if there is a union involved, develop a cooperative approach with the union leaders before undertaking the project; don't present supervisors or union leaders with a ready-made plan for productivity improvement and expect them to support it if they haven't been involved in developing it.

7. Capitalize on the ideas and the motivation of the first-level working people; create a mechanism for them to identify problems, share their ideas, and suggest solutions, and to receive recognition and compensation in return; consider setting up a "share the gains" program in which the employees get a share of any cost savings that result from their suggestions.

8. Develop a realistic, stepwise plan for implementing the changes; be realistic in your estimates of the time and effort involved in moving to the new way of doing things.

One particular approach to improving productivity that has become relatively popular in the United States, and therefore merits special mention, is the group problem-solving technique that evolved in Japan, known as the "quality circle." A quality circle, as the Japanese practice it, is simply a group of production employees who meet as a team with their supervisor, generally once a week or so, to analyze production problems and find ways to do their jobs better. They will often have the consulting support of an industrial engineer who helps them solve the problems they identify.

As American firms have implemented the quality circle concept, it usually starts out as management's idea rather than as a grass-roots phenomenon. Typically, a company will have a quality circles coordinator on assignment, usually from the training department. This person will work with supervisors, trained quality-circle facilitators, and middle managers to set up quality circles in the organization. Many companies also have steering groups for the process, usually made up of managers, supervisors, consultants, and possibly key production employees. These programs are usually quite successful in those instances when supervisors and employees take them seriously and perceive some potential benefits to themselves from them. I believe the American version of the quality circle that eventually survives will eventually become less imitative of the Japanese approach, and more distinctly American. It will probably involve team training in innovative problem-solving techniques, as well as training for supervisors in the methods for conducting problem-solving sessions.

IMPROVING THE
QUALITY OF WORK LIFE

Quality of work life (QWL) virtually always deserves close attention by management. Although an increase in the QWL level in an organization will not in itself guarantee increased production, productivity, or profitability, a marked decrease in QWL, on the other hand, will often lead to a noticeable decline in those economic indicators. A highly dissatisfied work force is usually an unproductive work force.

Some managers who are unfamiliar with the basics of organizational behavior, and especially the key factors involved in motivation, tend to react negatively to the term "quality of work life," as if it somehow represents a soft, coddling attitude toward the workers. The purpose of paying attention to QWL in the organization is, in addition to being humane for its own sake, to create and maintain an environment around the members of the work force that enables them to work most effectively. A QWL program answers the needs of the economic bottom line as well as the human bottom line.

Any systematic program for improving the quality of work life in the organization should begin with a fairly objective definition of QWL so we will recognize it when we achieve it. For convenience, here are the ten components of QWL discussed previously:

1. A job worth doing.
2. Safe and healthy working conditions.
3. Fair compensation for one's work.
4. Job security.
5. Competent supervision.
6. Feedback on the results of one's work; recognition of one's contribution.
7. A chance to grow and develop.
8. A chance to get ahead on merit.
9. A positive social climate.
10. Justice and fair play.

Using a fairly objective set of criteria like these enables us to make a fairly objective assessment of the quality of work life in the organization and to take fairly objective measures to improve it. A careful review of available hard facts, coupled with useful "soft" data from climate surveys and employee interviews, can give us a pretty reliable picture of the current level of QWL as perceived by the employees.

Once we have a good fix on QWL, we need to select those aspects that promise the greatest payoff and therefore merit the highest priority. It is important to make an effective start and to avoid running aground because of an overly ambitious program. It is crucially important to respond to the employees' needs as they see them, not as someone in management would like them to be.

A QWL program should proceed in well-defined logical stages with realistic objectives at each stage. It may help to make some small but highly desirable changes immediately to let the employees know that management is serious about their needs and interests and to build credibility for the program. Some of the highest-impact changes may take many weeks or months to get fully underway, and there needs to be some short-term payoff that everyone can see and appreciate while waiting for the longer-term effects.

There are differing opinions among OD people concerning the appropriateness of publicizing the QWL program to the employees. In my view, the less fanfare there is, the better off the program will be. Often, the big announcement in the company "bugle" and the employee meetings to announce the new program are really only serving the psychological needs of the managers. The employees will almost always adopt a "wait and see" attitude, and the first several weeks or months will lead them to make some general conclusions. Unfortunately, programs such as these often encounter snags in getting underway, and there may not be any impressive results to show right away.

On the other hand, if management simply begins making the changes they can conveniently make immediately and gets on with the program on a low-key basis, the employees will usually begin to notice the results and will spread the word. As more and more results become visible, management begins to gain credibility with the employees. No amount of fanfare will convince the employees that top management knows and cares about their concerns, but tangible results certainly will.

For example, if our investigation shows that item number ten on the list, "justice and fair play," is deficient in the opinions of the employees, then we might elect to create a grievance procedure and a process by which an employee can request a review of a disciplinary action imposed by a supervisor. Once the new system has shown positive results, the word gets around, and the employees' perceptions and opinions of the justice and fair play component of QWL will improve.

If the employees of the organization are not represented by a labor union, then it may become a high-priority objective of management to keep it that way. A QWL program can go a long way toward eliminating the enabling conditions that might lead them to want to interpose a third party between themselves and the management of the organization. Essentially, top management prevents unionization by providing as much or more in the way of quality-of-work-life factors as the employees believe they could reasonably expect to get through union representation.

If the organization has one or more labor unions, OD techniques can sometimes help in fostering reasonably positive relationships between management and the unions. We say "reasonably positive" here, because we must be realistic about the nature of the union-management relationship. It is, above all, an adversary relationship, based on a precarious balance of power between two groups whose primary objectives are often in opposition. The two groups may learn to cooperate fairly effectively on various matters, but make no mistake: the mission of the union leader is to squeeze the best possible deal out of the organization's management on behalf of the workers.

Before we attempt major changes in the status of the union-management relationship, we must first understand clearly the nature of the relationship. There are basically four variations of the balance of power:

1. Management has a clear upper hand, and the union is fairly weak.
2. The union has a clear upper hand, and management accedes to its demands in many cases.
3. No one has a clear upper hand, and there is a hostile stand-off between the two of them.
4. No one has a clear upper hand, and the two factions relate as cooperative adversaries.

As a practical compromise among undesirable options, the fourth state of affairs, or "cooperative adversaries" relationship offers the most possibilities. It is possible, by means of a conscious effort, to shift a union-management relationship to this status from one of the other three problematic forms. It is indeed an interesting kind of relationship, characterized by a certain amount of posturing and "show business."

Experienced labor negotiators can often read the signals in the mock battle between the factions so well, that they know when to give ground and when to stand firm. When a union group and a management group have faced each other over the bargaining table many times, they may develop a grudging respect for each other and even, sometimes, a cantankerous kind of a subterranean friendship. Of course, it is necessary for "audience effect" that they berate each other in public, call names, level accusations, and make outrageous demands. Too much of a "sweetheart" relationship between these two supposedly natural enemies would probably undermine the faith of the employees in both groups. Both sides learn to read each other's signals through the shouting and posturing and to converge on a bargain they both can live with.

As part of an OD program in a unionized organization, we need to assess the nature of the union-management relationship as it exists, identify areas for potential improvement, and move steadily in those directions. Usually, management must approach this process somewhat cautiously and delicately because certain union leaders may have such an intense commitment to an antagonistic relationship that they feel they would lose influence with the workers if they were to cooperate with anything proposed by management. If this does not seem to be the case, then management can possibly move more directly in proposing new approaches.

One of the most useful specific mechanisms for improving union-management relations is the creation of an *inter-group,* usually called a union-management committee. The U.S. steel industry, in particular, has used this approach successfully, as well as the mining industry to some extent. A union-management committee is a group of selected managers and union leaders who meet periodically to discuss broad issues of concern to both the employees and management. The purposes of such a committee can include exchanging information and viewpoints in a nonadversary situation and opening up topics for discussion that normally would not appear to relate to union concerns and yet do have implications for the employees. Typically, a union-management committee deals only with "nonbargainable" issues, i.e., those that do not relate to the terms of the contract. The committee does not negotiate. Neither constituency tries to sell the other on anything. Neither side tries to pressure the other into anything. Their whole purpose is to look for ways to make the organization a better place to live and work.

Frequently, a union-management committee will succeed in moving the relationship from a problematic status to a cooperative-adversary status, and from there it can begin to open up a wide variety of topics for investigation. These may include matters of employee health and welfare, new ways of getting the work done, ways of improving productivity, and studies of the impact of developing trends in the organization's environment. It may also happen that some topic that arises during a committee discussion will develop into a matter of large-scale interest and will eventually find its way into the bargaining process.

DEVELOPING A REALISTIC OD IMPLEMENTATION PLAN

The result of an effective OD problem-solving phase is a realistic, workable, and promising plan of action for the implementation phase. Having capitalized on the information provided by the assessment phase, and having worked through the issues and made decisions about what to improve and how to improve it, we are ready to put our conclusions down on paper and commit our energies to getting results.

Ideally, the chief executive will determine what changes to make and the general approach to each of the major changes. If the executives of the organization really "own" the OD process, then they will have been at the very center of the activity during the problem-solving phase. This is not always the case, of course, and many times an OD person or OD task force will find it necessary to sell the proposed improvements to the top management team. This is not the ideal situation to have, but all is not necessarily lost. Strong leadership on the part of the task force, effective solutions, and a good sales approach can often gain a great deal of management backing and commitment.

It is important to decide consciously on the magnitude of the OD program you intend to undertake. This is a decision requiring some imagination and judgment. It is possible to come away from a problem-solving session with a plan that is simply inadequate to make the kinds of organizational improvements management wants. Being stingy on resources and expecting the OD program to succeed without having to spend any money may do more harm in the long run than not undertaking the program at all. When results fail to meet expectations, frustration usually results.

We can define the magnitude of the program as the amount of management time and attention, staff time, and monetary commitment top management is willing to invest to make it happen. I've found the following four categories, or levels of magnitude, useful in helping managers think through the resource-commitment decision. The metaphorical terms seem to capture the idea of comparative levels that can very substantially.

1. *Slingshot*—a minimal, token effort in terms of resources; we assign it to someone as an extra duty and hope something good comes out of it.
2. *Pistol*—We think it's important enough to make a special project out of it, with someone accountable for carrying out a plan.
3. *Rifle*—We make a significant commitment of resources, both in staff time and money, to follow through on a comprehensive plan.
4. *Cannon*—We make an all-out corporate commitment to the program and to the outcomes we have decided we want; we spend whatever it reasonably takes in staff time, management attention, and money to make it happen.

There need be no particular guilt associated with choosing less than the "cannon" approach. Top management does, however, need to make a clear determination of the kind of magnitude the program deserves and be clear about that decision. In some instances, a slingshot approach may work sufficiently to get the desired results. Many smaller issues fall into this category. If a slingshot will solve it, then let's use a slingshot. On the other hand, if we're talking about a substantial, organization-wide change, spanning many months or even years, and facing strong resistance, it is unreasonable to expect much in the way of progress without a major push, with top management's complete backing. During the problem-solving phase of the OD process, top management needs to think over the possibilities and the goals, and make a deliberate judgment about how ambitious and costly the undertaking will be.

Here is a description of my favorite scenario for the development of the OD implementation plan. Once the basic data-gathering and analysis work is finished, and we have the assessment results in useable form, we convene a three-day intensive management conference at a location far removed from the immediate pressures and preoccupations of the office. Attending this working session are the chief executive, the members of the top management team, and the members of the OD task force. Working as a problem-solving team, we roll up our sleeves and go to work on the issues, problems and possibilities that confront the organization.

This is a very intensive session, with an ambitious pre-established agenda of work to be done and a commitment to finishing it no matter how long the days get. The session is a combination of discussion, analysis and interpretation of findings, problem-solving and decision-making, and planning. It may also involve a certain amount of developmental experience, such as additional team-development work, mini-lectures on various management topics and techniques, and skill-building activities. We march through the agenda in a very determined fashion, using our best problem-solving skills and techniques to reach solutions and specify actions in each of the problem areas we are dealing with.

By the end of the session, which may be interwoven with a certain amount of "change-of-pace" activity for meals and recreation, and possibly social activities with spouses, we have produced the basic elements of the OD implementation plan. My favorite way of facilitating this kind of problem-solving session is to use plenty of wall space, chalkboards, easel pads, and newsprint paper in order to get the major facts, factors, and ideas up on the wall in visual form, where everyone can see them and study them. Toward the close of the session, we put up a long sheet of paper on one entire wall of the conference room. This may be a sheet more than a meter wide and four to five meters long, taped to the wall. Starting on the left end of the paper, we begin to catalog the issues we have studied and the determinations we have made about them during the entire three days. As we progress to the right, we develop an increasingly specific and concrete definition of what we will do to put these chosen solutions into effect.

On the right side of the paper will eventually appear the basic elements of the implementation plan. These include a list of major projects, programs, actions, or organizational changes we intend to make. Beside each item is the name of the member of the executive staff who will spearhead that objective, and a deadline for his or her first major milestone, as well as subsidiary deadlines if there are some. When the team members see the fruits of their labors expressed visually, all in one place, and in a highly organized fashion, they feel a solid sense of accomplishment and a commitment to going forward with it.

The next step is usually for someone to transcribe the plan from the wall to a more conventional form. A selected member of the executive staff, or possibly someone from the OD task force, can have the assignment of writing up the plan in, say, ten typewritten pages or so, staffing it with the executive committee for concurrence, and then distributing it to all the key action people.

Here are some suggestions for making sure the plan is feasible and workable:

1. Express each of the action items in terms of a specific outcome, i.e, an objective that will serve as an aiming point.

2. Make the objectives realistic; remember that there is a mountain of day-to-day work waiting for you back at the office and that these objectives must take their places along with the others in your workload.

3. Make a conscious and honest decision about the level of resource commitment you are going to make to the program; don't lay out an ambitious development program if you know you are not willing to spend any money and if you know you will only give your attention to the program "when I have time"; bite off only what you can really chew.

4. Lay out the plan so that it fits right into the overall master plan for the organization; make OD a part of the management process and treat it like any other important medium-range program requiring management commitment and action.

11

The Implementation Phase

THE "EXECUTIVE QUARTERBACK" CONCEPT

Lack of follow-through is probably the most common problem in business organizations, and it is the most common mode by which OD programs fizzle out. Somehow, the great dreams and visions, the proposed new programs, and the intended actions that seemed so crystal clear on Sunday afternoon at the wrap-up of an intensive management meeting have a way of fading into obscurity on Monday morning back at the office, when the daily minutiae launch their attack on the executives' time. The vast majority of managers get so swept up in day-to-day operational matters that they simply have no time left for tasks that have longer-term payoffs. In most organizations, the immediate problem is the one that dominates, whether it is urgent, important, or mundane. In order to make an OD implementation plan

206

work, we need something more than luck. We need a modus operandi for the program—a way of making it work.

One of the most effective ways of making an OD program really work is the "executive quarterback" concept. This simply means that each of the members of the top management staff selects a certain manageable number of change issues or problem areas for special, personal attention. Each of them becomes a high-powered entrepreneur for that particular objective. This gives it the top-level visibility that it deserves, communicates to people in the organization that the issue in question is indeed important, and mobilizes resources for getting it resolved much more effectively than if the problem lay in the hands of a middle manager or someone at a lower level.

Clearly, any one executive can only handle a small number of high-priority, nonroutine programs. He or she must meet many demands in getting the day-to-day job done and still have some time available for working on tomorrow. I favor establishing the implementation goals and choosing quarterbacks by means of an intensive shirt-sleeves meeting of the management staff as described in the preceding chapter.

By about the middle of the last day of a three-day working session, we would typically have made a number of key decisions concerning the issues with which we had been dealing, selected certain promising OD options to put into effect, and set some specific goals for the implementation of these options. The only question that would remain is "Who will do these things?" It is crucially important not to let the problem-solving meeting come to an end until we have allocated the various key objectives to people who are ready, willing, and able to carry them out. When it comes to making major changes in the organization, and especially when the goals do not have any particular sense of screaming urgency about them, we must put them into the custody of high-powered people if we expect them to get done.

I coined the term "executive quarterback" as a metaphor for the role of a high-ranking change agent who is committed to a specific OD objective. This admittedly male-oriented figure of speech describes fairly clearly, in my opinion, a very powerful role function which can play an important part in the success of an OD effort. The executive quarterback for some change project—such as implementing a meaningful employee suggestion program—makes a commitment to his or her executive colleagues to spearhead this particular activity and to use all reasonable means necessary to reach the goal by an agreed-upon deadline.

Just as a quarterback does not necessarily carry the ball or try to do all the work, so the executive quarterback does not necessarily do the work—he or she simply agrees to see to it that it gets done. The quarterback can do some of the things involved, delegate some to staff members, have certain things done by consultants, or get fellow executives to agree to contribute specific pieces of the solution. But it is crucial to the definition of the executive quarterback's role that this person, and no other, is responsible to the other members of the executive team for producing the desired results.

This mode of operating has two chief advantages. For one, it puts enough "horsepower" behind a desired change to make it happen. People in the organization who see an executive committed to a certain goal tend to bend their efforts in that direction almost automatically. Second, it creates a distinct focus for implementing the desired improvement. Each executive can assume, unless specifically asked for help by the quarterback for some goal, that he doesn't have to worry about that particular goal. There is peace of mind in knowing that each of the action items is in the custody of one responsible person and that one needn't be concerned about those outside his own "portfolio."

Usually, it is a good idea to divide the various major implementation tasks among the members of the top staff, including the chief executive, so that each of them has one or more significant items to take care of. Top management can also assign various smaller-scale OD projects to the members of the OD task force for completion. The idea is not to load the executives down with extra work, but simply to put their energies squarely behind a small number of key result areas in the OD implementation phase. Probably the most significant advantage of the executive-quarterback approach is that it builds a sense of personal commitment on the part of the executives in favor of planned change and energetic follow-through. In addition, it may be a very satisfying experience for an executive, who is usually far removed from things going on in the organization at lower levels, to lend some personal leadership to get something done that needs doing. It keeps him involved in the organization's processes and enables him to feel more a part of what's going on.

Usually, the last part of the management meeting that launches the implementation phase is a process of making commitments. I like to use a very large sheet of paper on the wall of the conference room, as previously described, to build a comprehensive visual representation of the implementation process. On the left side of the paper, and, progressing toward the right, we have a listing of the problem areas, the decisions we reached about them, the actions we will take, and the goals we have set as targets for aiming our efforts. On the right side of the paper, we end up with the names of the executives who will spearhead the activities aimed at the goals, and the deadlines to which they have committed themselves. This becomes a comprehensive overview of the implementation phase, as well as an abbreviated plan for carrying it out.

IDENTIFYING AND RESOLVING BARRIERS TO CHANGE

Organization development is all about change. The very idea of "development" means replacing the past with the future, presumably with some benefit in mind. Unfortunately, not everyone sees or understands the benefits of the changes or "improvements" the executives want to make. Every organization has a certain amount of inertia—a built-in set of resisting forces, so to speak, that act in opposition to any significant disturbance to the status quo. Some changes meet with ready acceptance, but many meet with a kind of passive resistance on the part of the people when they don't align with their comfortable habit patterns.

A necessary part of the approach to implementing the selected OD options effectively is identifying the barriers which the organization, as a sociotechnical system, will predictably present to the executives' attempts at planned change. By taking special measures to resolve, eliminate, or weaken these barriers, we can make things happen more rapidly, more smoothly, and less traumatically for everyone.

One of the aspects of organizational change that we must learn to live with is the "nose-dive" syndrome, which occurs fairly predictably in medium and large organizations when top management tries to implement far-reaching changes. What happens in many cases is that management takes the first steps in implementing a major change, with the naive expectation that things will roll along smoothly and that the employees will immediately begin working enthusiastically in the new way. "Things should get better" is the expectation. Unfortunately, things get worse. People seem to be resisting the new way, holding on to the old way, griping and complaining, fighting with one another, and seemingly waiting for the whole thing to blow over. Productivity and morale, instead of going up, start to decline.

Instead of moving from the first plateau directly to the second, higher plateau, the "quality" of the situation takes a nose dive. In the short run, it looks like the new approach is not working at all. In retrospect, this is understandable because the people of the organization are responding to an outside force, which they see as having been inflicted on them by management. Before we can get to the second plateau, we have to endure a passage through the "valley of despair," as illustrated in Figure 11–1. I am grateful to management consultant Harold Hooke for this graphic representation.

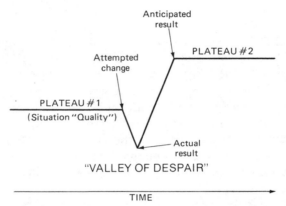

FIGURE 11–1   The Nose-Dive Syndrome Is Typical of Many Organizational Changes

This nose-dive phenomenon does not always occur, of course, but it is remarkably common in fair-sized organizations undergoing management-induced change. A very typical example is the case of a company that makes a variety of products, and whose top management wants to change the structure from a functional orientation, with separate divisions for sales, engineering, manufacturing, etc., to a product-line orientation, with autonomous divisions having full capability for all functions. Often, the management finds it infeasible to split up the manufacturing facility in this way, so they settle for a "hybrid" structure which is hard for the employees to understand. The first six months to a year after the change can be a very exasperating time for everyone. The managers reach the second plateau only after they have groped around long enough to work out new roles and relationships, and only after there has been sufficient time for a new informal organization to take shape.

It is easy for a manager to underestimate the impact that a major change can have on the daily work lives and activities of the people in the organization. What seems so simple when talked about in the executive offices gets much more complicated by the time it reaches the first-line workers in concrete form. A new organizational structure, a new set of interdepartmental relationships, a new policy, a different way of handling information, a new major item added to the workload, a new way of dealing with clients or customers—these and other changes that management may want to make all pose adjustment problems for the people who have to carry them out on a daily basis. Small wonder that employees react selfishly and from their own personal perspectives. The nose dive is really a natural and understandable phenomenon.

The term "valley of despair" in Figure 11–1 is a very apt metaphor for the situation as its worst. It is at this point in the trajectory of a major change that many managers lose confidence in their solutions. Most of the signals are suggesting that it isn't working. The original opponents of the approach are saying, smugly, "See? I told you it wouldn't work." The employees are saying, "It's so much harder this way. I think the way we used to do it was better." The performance of the technical system hasn't yet shown any significant improvement. The manager starts to re-think the situation. "Could I be wrong in this whole thing? Maybe I've gone overboard with this. It looked good at first, but now I'm not so sure."

The big problem with the valley of despair is that you don't know where it is on the time line until you've passed through it. At any one point in the process, you don't know whether things will continue to get worse, or whether the situation will finally break and start to turn upward. Living through this process takes a certain amount of patience, intellectual courage, persistence, and even a bit of stubbornness on the part of the manager. It is doubly important to think things through at the outset and to clarify the outcome you want to achieve. Then, when things begin to get discouraging, you can stick to your guns.

Obviously, one must not persist forever in a course of action that just isn't getting the desired results. It also takes intellectual courage to surrender an unworkable approach after it has had a fair try. The key point here is that it is difficult to tell what constitutes a fair try. When it comes to major organizational change, it makes sense to expect obstacles, to anticipate a nose dive in the quality of the situation, and to have to wait it out through a period in which the effectiveness of the approach is in doubt. If you understand that this will happen in most cases, then it becomes much easier to persist long enough to reach the second plateau.

In addition to expecting obstacles in implementing a significant change, we can also take the initiative in facilitating the change process. We don't have to just stand by, wringing our hands in exasperation while things grind along at an agonizing pace. We can plan out the change process we want to make happen and identify specific things we can do to help people adapt to it more rapidly. We can communicate the nature of the change much more effectively to the people. We can enlist the support of managers at all levels in facilitating it. We can arrange circumstances so that the employees discover certain rewards associated with the new way of working. The following sections explore this concept of facilitated change more thoroughly.

ANALYZING THE "FORCE FIELD"

A convenient method for anticipating the kinds of resistance our proposed change will encounter is to itemize the main organizational "forces" that will probably affect the situation. By a force, we mean any person, process, policy, procedure, tradition, value system, belief system, vested interest, or state of affairs that will play a significant part in the success of the new endeavor. Psychologist Kurt Lewin coined the term "force-field analysis" to describe the process of systematically cataloging these factors in terms of "helping forces" and "resisting forces," and diagramming them on a chart such as in Figure 11–2.

This is a much more systematic approach than most managers typically use in implementing major change. The most common approach seems to be to simply announce the change, instruct subordinates to go ahead with it, and to assume that this is all that is necessary or possible. With the force-field analysis approach, we systematically anticipate and deal with major blocks to the change. We try to eliminate some of them ahead of time if possible. In many cases, a very extensive and energetic approach to facilitating the change is advisable. This might involve orientation meetings, use of published infor-

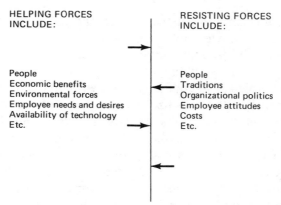

HELPING FORCES
INCLUDE:

RESISTING FORCES
INCLUDE:

People
Economic benefits
Environmental forces
Employee needs and desires
Availability of technology
Etc.

People
Traditions
Organizational politics
Employee attitudes
Costs
Etc.

FIGURE 11-2 Any Change Process Involves a
"Force-Field" of Helping Forces and Resisting Forces

mation, creation of task forces or implementation groups, engaging external consultants, or appointing a key staff person to work with the individuals who are most affected.

Inherent in the concept of force-field analysis is the idea that we can facilitate change in either of two ways. We can weaken or neutralize a resisting force, or we can strengthen a helping force. An example of the first kind of facilitation would be winning over key executives to the approach by working with them to develop a form of implementation that meets the needs of their organizations. Then they become owners and advocates of the new approach. An example of the second approach, strengthening a helping force, would be identifying key executives or managers who already favor the new approach, and giving them special roles in the implementation process. From the special vantage point of an implementer, such a person will have a strong sense of ownership of the new approach and will become a much stronger helping force.

UNDERSTANDING EMPLOYEE RESPONSES TO MANAGEMENT-INDUCED CHANGE

One of the most common "pat" statements managers and other would-be change agents frequently make is "People don't like change." This statement is sometimes true and sometimes not true. Actually, it is incomplete. It should say "People don't like change when they don't think the change will be good for them." Herein lies the all-important key to facilitating change among people working in an organization. If we are going to get them to accept and support a new way of doing something, we must somehow influence their perceptions of the change. There must be something in it for them.

Countless managers, OD people, and others acting in change-agent roles have confused and frustrated themselves by trying to make changes in the organizational setting without reckoning with the perceptions and reactions of the people who would be affected by the new approaches they advocate. We could find dozens of examples of this in a typical large organization just in the course of interviews and discussions with the people working there. This myopic approach to trying to change other people is limited in its effectiveness at best, and potentially self-defeating or even disastrous at worst.

For example, the manager of a systems and procedures department in a large high-technology company saw it as his mission to create and publish written procedural guides for the conduct of various aspects of engineering work. He appointed five full-time procedure writers to identify areas apparently in need of standardization. They began to find aspects of the work about which people disagreed and to write up their own recommended approaches to them. They would get the division head to sign off on these publications, and then they would send them to all department heads and first-line supervisors in the division. Of course, hardly anyone other than the people in the procedures department ever paid any attention to them. The managers and supervisors simply tucked them into their overstuffed loose-leaf binders along with all the previous publications. When it became apparent that the engineers were "violating" the procedures, the head of the group began to berate his peer managers for not enforcing them.

When they found that none of the engineers seemed to understand the procedures and couldn't seem to use them to find answers to procedural questions, they decided to round them all up and train them in using the procedures. Apparently, it never occurred to them that, if the engineers couldn't understand or use the procedures, there was probably something wrong with the procedures, not with the engineers. After conducting training sessions for about 400 engineering and technical people, at enormous expense, the company finally abandoned the entire collection of procedures and started from scratch. We created a simplified engineer's manual, which prescribed only the rudiments of the administrative process and relied on the various experienced administrative people in the organization to keep the engineers straight. This had been a typical case of "solution myopia," in which a would-be change agent got his means confused with his ends and refused to accept the reality of the other people's responses to his program. It is amazing at times how someone can persist in a course of action that is causing problems rather than solving them. Some people just keep making the same mistake harder. As Thomas Huxley observed, "There's no right way to do the wrong thing."

So, the key to getting people to go along with a change is to make sure it really is an improvement, as they see it.

This may mean modifying the approach to make it more beneficial to them, or compromising in the implementation in such a way that they begin to experience immediate benefits. It also means having realistic expectations about their individual, selfish responses to what is happening around them.

We can conceive of employee responses to a management-induced change as shifting through several stages, as they get more and more accustomed to the new situation. Assuming that, after the new way of operating has settled into place, the employees actually do find it more effective than the previous way, or that it has higher level organizational benefits they can appreciate, we generally see their perceptions of the new way as progressing roughly as follows:

1. Threat—The impending change threatens to disturb the status quo, and to upset familiar habits of working and relating; they don't know what to expect, but the possibilities they imagine aren't particularly inviting.

2. Problem—When the change actually arrives, it presents difficulties the employees must solve in order to get their jobs done; they must deal with an ambiguous situation, in which procedures are no longer clear.

3. Solution—Once they have learned how to make the new scheme work, they develop a degree of familiarity and comfort with it, and they can see how it benefits the organization and possibly them directly.

4. Habit—After they have been working with the new scheme for a long time, such as six months or more, it becomes so familiar that they don't recall vividly how they did things before; at this point, "the new way" becomes "the way."

The second of these four hypothetical stages, the "problem" stage, really involves only one basic kind of problem in most cases—ambiguity. Very few people can tolerate much in the way of uncertainty or ambiguity in their work environments, at least not for very long. Most people have a fairly strong need for structure and order in what they do, and they become somewhat uncomfortable or anxious when that order is disrupted or threatened. In some cases, a management change actually makes someone's job more difficult or unpleasant in some direct way, but more commonly it simply requires them to figure out a new way of working and relating. This may be mildly traumatic for them. They may have to start interacting with new people or new functional units in the organization. They may have to deal with new and unfamiliar information. They may have to produce new or different kinds of outputs. They may have to make on-the-spot determinations they never had to make before. They may encounter situations in which they have to confer with others in order to figure out how to handle some matter. Some people enjoy a certain amount of ambiguity in their work situations, but most tend to resist it.

In making any kind of significant organizational change, we need to pay close attention to the "changees," i.e., the people whose daily activities will be affected. By keeping in mind some of the simple facts we know about people and change, and focusing on the people themselves and their needs, we can develop ways to facilitate the shift to the new way of doing things. By minimizing the "lag time" of the organization in shifting to the new state of affairs, we usually minimize cost, minimize disruptions to any of the processes on the prime axis of the technical system, preserve morale and positive working relationships, and reap the expected benefits of the new approach much sooner than if we simply waited for things to work out.

DEVELOPING "OWNERSHIP" OF THE INTENDED CHANGES

Clearly, a high-priority strategy in just about any OD program is to "syndicate ownership" of the objectives and consequently of the changes that will be necessary to achieve them. Generally speaking, the more people who believe in a new way of doing something, who see its merits, and who have a personal stake of some sort in bringing it about, the faster it will happen. A great deal of change agentry amounts to identifying and appealing to the various "stakeholders" in the organization—people or factions who have something to gain or lose as a result of intended changes. This implies that the change agent's mission is largely that of turning as many people as possible into positive stakeholders or beneficiaries of the new state of affairs.

Over the long run, it seems that the most effective strategy for getting support for a new approach is not simply to try to sell it to the key stakeholders, but to have them help you develop it in response to a legitimate need which they themselves recognize. Most of us tend to support a course of action we have had a hand in developing much more energetically than one in which we played no part. We may as well proceed with the same assumptions about other people.

This implies more than giving someone a token share of the action, just to "get them involved." It means collaborating with them, working together, cooperating and compromising, and developing a workable solution that both you and they can endorse. It is tempting for managers, and even more tempting for OD people, to try to figure out what is good for the people in the organization in isolation, and then try to figure out how to sell it to them. This works to some extent, but for large-scale changes, it makes more sense to begin working with them at the "option" stage rather than at the "action" stage.

For example, the people on the OD task force may feel that the organization needs a completely new approach to employee performance appraisal. They can design and propose one to management, which the supervisors and employees could very well ignore or passively resist. On the other hand, they can go to management and say, "We think the organization needs a new performance appraisal process, and we recommend you establish a specialized task force to develop it."

The people on the performance-appraisal task force, in approaching their assignment, might interview various supervisors and employees to get their perceptions and opinions of the present situation, and identify the key factors they must account for in creating a new approach. They might design a hypothetical new process, draft new worksheets or forms if those are needed, and discuss their preliminary results with selected supervisors again. Once they have an approach they think will probably work well, they could circulate the new version to all managers, asking for comments or suggestions. After incorporating the best of these suggestions into the design, they will probably have an approach that managers are likely to buy.

The task force should probably include one or more managers, and one or more employees, as well as members of the OD group. This begins to establish a commitment on the part of a key stakeholder group, i.e., managers, and it also provides an accurate perspective on how managers are likely to view the new system. The same holds true for the employee point of view and commitment. Further, it would probably help in the implementation of the new appraisal process to hold orientation meetings for managers, to "ceremonialize" the change to some extent, and to make sure they understand it. They are much more likely to accept and implement the new system under these circumstances than if they had simply received the new forms in the company mail from the personnel department.

Another key aspect of the organization's response to change is management's credibility with the people. When the people have little faith in the executives' ability to manage, when they see their leaders as inept, unpredictable, disorganized, inconsistent, or illogical in their approaches, they are apt to view any new program or process with a certain amount of cynicism. Many managers seem to forget, or perhaps don't realize at all, that employees talk among themselves routinely, and one of the topics of conversation is the boss. Most of them have their bosses pegged pretty well in terms of managerial style and competence, and they have a pretty definite view about the competence of top management. The viewpoint often seems to be, "Whenever those guys bring in something new, things just get worse." First, it's management-by-objectives. Then it's zero defects. Then it's behavior modification. Then it's zero-based budgeting. Then it's quality circles. When it's all over, they feel, nothing has improved, and things may have gone downhill. There is an old expression that circulates among workers in many companies, couched as an abbreviation: BOHICA, which means "Bend Over, Here It Comes Again."

On the other hand, if top management enjoys a relatively high level of credibility with the employees and with subordinate managers, then those people tend to meet management-induced changes with much more of an accepting attitude. If the executives have shown in the past that they can develop logical, workable solutions, implement them competently and humanely, and account for the impacts that they will have at the working levels, then the employees will likely assume that whatever comes next will make sense, at least eventually. This predisposition on the part of employees and managers at various levels can play a crucial part in the success of management's efforts to bring about large-scale change in the organization.

BUILDING A POSITIVE FEEDBACK SYSTEM

One of the most powerful ways in which management can reinforce positive actions on the part of the employees in an organization is simply to tell them what they are doing right. Positive feedback, defined here as information coming to an employee telling him how well he is doing his job, can have a profound effect on motivation and commitment.

Most, if not all, of the cultures of the western world are oriented toward negative feedback in evaluative situations. In school, we find out how many questions on the exam we got wrong. The teacher "corrects" our papers. Many people teach their children simply by scolding them or telling them what they did wrong and how to do it right. A typical Little-League baseball practice session has an overweight, middle-aged male shouting criticisms and instructions to a group of intimidated boys who are trying to learn the skills of the game. We learn very early that it is "bad" to fail, so most of us spend our lives trying to figure out how not to fail—not figuring out how to win.

Most work situations seem to be just about the same. Those in authority occasionally tell those at the bottom when they have done something wrong. Many people at work, including many managers, see their bosses as essentially bringers of bad news. A call to go to the boss's office is, for many people, a fault-finding session. Many managers make an unnecessarily and unconsciously toxic impression on their employees because it doesn't occur to them to catch them doing something right as well as doing something wrong.

Check this out in your personal experience. If you are a manager, or a parent, or otherwise involved in an authority situation, to what extent do you give people positive feedback? To what extent do you comment favorably on something a person has done well, without a "but" coming afterward? Can you give good news without giving bad news every time? In raising your children, can you give praise, compliments, and affirmative feedback without polluting it with "constructive criticism"?

This simple technique—making a habit of positive feedback—probably goes further in building rapport, loyalty, and commitment on the part of employees than any other aspect of a manager's communication capability. It is remarkable that it is not more widely recognized and used.

In the overall organization, we can institutionalize positive feedback in many ways. We can make it a habit and a matter of daily practice. For example, in a production operation such as a factory, the managers can post production figures and related quality variables where all the employees can see them. People, including managers, like to know how they are doing. Virtually every kind of work activity can be thought of in terms of valuable outcomes which people would like to know about.

Many times, the difference between "half-empty" and "half-full" has an enormous impact on employee morale and motivation. For example, in a service organization with a very large clerical function, management installed a measurement system to evaluate the performance of the clerical staff doing the work. Each week, a clerical worker would get a computer print showing his or her "error rate." Management didn't realize it, but the employees saw the report as just one more kind of "gotcha" from their bosses. Managers, on the other hand, thought the people should be "responsible" and should want to know about their faults so they could strive to be better workers. After some debate, I succeeded in persuading the managers to change the computer program to print an "accuracy report" instead of an "error" report. Somehow, when a clerical worker read a figure like "94% correct entries," it seemed to mean something more positive than a figure like "6% errors." Concepts like these are sometimes so simple that they escape the complex minds of sophisticated people.

Building a comprehensive positive feedback system in the organization is a worthwhile and challenging project for an OD task force. It involves looking at various jobs and finding ways to inform the people doing them about the consequences of what they do. It may also involve changing the behavior of many traditionally-minded managers and teaching them to deal with their staff members affirmatively. A half-day training session for all managers on giving positive feedback is almost always a worthwhile investment. It is also easy and worthwhile to build such an element into any introductory management training program.

The strategy of "measurement and feedback" is a straightforward, simple process by which managers can reinforce positive actions by employees. The first step is simply to start observing specific variables or outcomes that have value. The second step is to present this information to the person or people doing the work. Often, that is all it takes. Once people become aware of specific measures of their accomplishment, most of them will move, consciously or unconsciously, in the direction of increased accomplishment. All management has to do is keep the information flowing and occasionally recognize a job well done. This does more to develop managerial credibility and employee loyalty than any other technique I know, and usually for little or no cost.

12

The Evaluation Phase

CLOSING THE CYCLE

Including a relatively formal evaluation phase in the OD program serves several purposes. First, it provides a sense of continuation and follow-through that probably would not be there if the program was simply an open-ended, "one-shot" attempt at making some changes. When the key people all know that six months from now, or a year from now, we will be meeting again to consider the progress we have made in our efforts to transform the organization, they are much more likely to keep after their individual objectives and not let them slide into obscurity. A long-term schedule for the activity keeps the executives and other key people involved and interested.

Second, a reasonably scientific attitude toward organizational change dictates that we compare our results with our intentions somewhere downstream and find out how well we did. This point merits some very serious thought. It helps to think of a problem-solving process as a cycle that closes on itself, with the assessment phase of one cycle proceeding out of the evaluation phase of the foregoing cycle. In the terminology of systems analysis, we call this a "closed-loop" problem-solving process.

Closed-loop problem-solving is not a very common practice in business organizations, unfortunately. It is easy to find instances in which managers agree on a certain course of action, give the instructions for carrying it out, and never check thereafter to see what happens. Many a present-day problem was originally conceived of as a solution to some previous problem. And many a present-day solution will go wrong in the future and cause problems of its own. Truly, a problem is not solved until the undesirable condition has changed, or until the desirable condition prevails. A decision by a manager is only a step in the problem-solving process, not the end of it. Without good follow-through, we not only miss out on the chance to adapt our solutions as the future unfolds, but we can't even tell how well we're doing as problem-solvers.

In almost any management situation, not only in OD, it helps to employ this futuristic, follow-through process. It is one of the most effective habit patterns a manager can form. Take a look at your own habits, for example. When you make a decision, or undertake some major commitment of time and resources, do you set up a "flag" somewhere in the future at an appropriate point, at which you will evaluate the entire undertaking and decide whether to go forward with it, and if so, how? You can use your daily calendar for this purpose. For example, if you have just implemented a new administrative system for billing customers, you can page forward about three months and make a note on your calendar to review the effectiveness of the system. You can make a similar note at the six-months' point as well. With respect to your present situation, how many key decisions, resource commitments, new initiatives, or agreements that you made in past months should you be reviewing right now? How many of your commitments should be up for a dispassionate evaluation against the original objectives that led you to undertake them?

Similarly, in an organization development program, it is important to undertake a thorough, premeditated, realistic evaluation of your progress at some formally designated point. This keeps the entire program on an honest, relatively scientific basis, and it enables you to make significant course corrections if appropriate.

FORMAL PROGRAM REVIEWS

If the OD effort has the status in the organization of a major undertaking and management has defined it and pursued it as a relatively formal program, then formal program reviews should be a part of the time-line. At the completion of the problem-solving phase, when we have solved problems, made decisions, set goals and deadlines, and assigned advocacy of results to the various key executives, we should have produced a timetable to be used for the entire process. This timetable should show all of the major tasks or subprojects under the OD program in time relationship to one another, and it should also identify major milestones along the way at which top management needs to hold formal reviews of the entire program.

Because major OD programs will usually span many months, and possibly several years in their entirety, regularly scheduled program reviews may be helpful. Every three months is often a convenient interval, giving a balance between continuing attention by management and sufficient time for things to advance noticeably. Other review points can coincide with major happenings in the implementation process, or with decision points at which management must make large commitments of resources.

Here are some guidelines for conducting program reviews:

1. Set aside enough time to do a good job; don't wedge it in between other commitments that may run overtime and push the review off the docket.
2. Devote an entire meeting to the review; don't mix it with other items on the same agenda.
3. Choose a time when all of the key executives and members of the OD task force can attend; make it a high priority for everyone.
4. Review the entire big picture; have someone give a well-organized review of the entire program and a general run-down of the major result areas.
5. Focus on facts; make sure the OD team prepares thoroughly for the meeting by gathering the facts needed by the executives in making an intelligent review; separate facts from inferences, assumptions, and opinions.
6. Question the entire undertaking from time to time; don't assume that the program necessarily still makes sense, and don't hesitate to reorient it if the situation has changed or if certain parts of it are not working out properly.
7. Wind up the review with a reaffirmation of the goals of the program and

an assurance from management of a strong commitment to the desired outcomes.

FACT FINDING REVISITED

Just as the assessment phase begins with a thorough and strategic fact-finding process, so the evaluation phase, as a miniature "replay" of the assessment phase, begins with fact finding. We need to do much more in evaluating a program—any program—than just "sniff the air" and make visceral judgments about what's going on. If we really want to know what we're getting for our time and money, and whether it makes sense to continue on the same course, we need some specific measures of success. We need to have some benchmark, or baseline condition, to compare against, and we need to have some fairly concrete outcomes to look for.

If the problem-solving phase gave us the proper focus on the issues and needs of the organizations, then the evaluation phase should be a fairly simple and straightforward process. We don't have to go as far and wide in assessing the current state of affairs because we will have a better idea of what to look for. We can target our fact-finding process against the issues, problems, and objectives we chose to work on during the problem-solving phase.

For each of the four organizational systems, the technical, the social, the administrative, and the strategic, we can go back to the key factors we examined at the outset. The assessment phase should have given us a clearly stated baseline configuration of the organization to use as a standard for evaluating future situations. For example, a productivity study would probably have identified several key factors that needed attention, such as machine utilization, labor scheduling and allocation, or employee technical skills. We can re-examine these variables to find out how much of an improvement we have achieved over the baseline state of affairs at the beginning.

As another example, if we decided to computerize the handling of information in a certain operation or department, we would have set some measurable goals or established some concrete outcomes we intended to achieve. In the evaluation phase, we need to know how things stand in those areas. Similarly, if we conducted a climate survey among the employees of the organization, we can repeat the same survey, using exactly the same questions, and compare the current results with the results we got the first time. These comparative studies may not tell the whole tale, and there may be additional fact finding necessary to understand the current situation fully, but they will go a long way in giving us a reliable profile of the organization as it is now, and it will enable us to draw some fairly confident conclusions about the payoffs we are getting from the various OD options we chose to implement.

ACCENTUATING THE POSITIVE

One of the ways in which we can get the change process to pick up speed, and minimize the time spent in the "valley of despair," is to keep people's attention on the positive aspects of the program. Without getting into a manipulative mode, or "billboarding" the program superficially, we can identify worthwhile improvements and highlight them. Using positive feedback methods, we can let the people know about their progress. If interdepartmental cooperation has improved, for example, management can take notice of the fact and comment on it in staff meetings or even in the company newsletter.

This has several advantages. First, it focuses the attention on what is working, not on what isn't working. This tends to have a positive influence on overall morale and sense of optimism. Second, it tends to create a sense of expectation and confidence that things are going to get better. This almost invariably contributes in subtle ways to the commitment people feel toward the organization, and things do tend to get better as a result. And third, the fact that management is giving positive feedback to the people in the organization tends to enhance the sense of "connectedness" people feel toward the executives.

I often recommend in such a situation that the executives select some program, project, or improvement for immediate implementation that will be a "bell-ringer"; that is, it will bring fairly immediate, visible, and positive results that people can appreciate on a personal level. By "ringing the bell," I mean accomplishing something worthwhile in the eyes of the people whose support we need. For example, discharging or reassigning one or more oppressive, toxic supervisors can give an enormous boost to the employees' faith in top management's perceptiveness and responsiveness to human concerns. Similarly, improving the quality of food in the company cafeteria may not seem like the highest-priority issue to top management, but it is a highly visible outcome and one that can ring the bell with the employees. We need not take this approach to extremes at the expense of high-priority improvements that are not so visible, but it certainly does help to "rig" the game in favor of success early on.

Management needs to accentuate the positive and talk success, but not, of course, in inane, superficial terms that tend to undermine credibility. There is a big difference between accentuating the positive and putting on a "hype." The difference is in sticking to facts. Whenever top management feeds back some positive fact or perception to the employees, they get a message they can believe in. When it's just glittering prose, they sense they are getting a "snow job." My preference is not to "billboard" the OD program, but to get it underway in a low-key, matter-of-fact style, and let the results speak for themselves. We just want to help the results do the talking.

SETTING A NEW DIRECTION

Adaptation is an important aspect of effective management. Just as strategic planning provides a steering function for the organization, so the evaluation process provides a steering function for the OD process. Indeed, the primary purpose of the evaluation phase is to discover what course corrections we need to make. It is unreasonable to assume that we can lay out a program of planned change that may span, say, two or three years altogether and expect things to unfold exactly as we predict all along the way.

Many things can change and consequently present us with a need to rethink the process and set a new direction. In some fortunate cases, a problem may be solved much sooner than we expected, and we may be able to move on from there. Some solutions, on the other hand, just may not work the way we had hoped they would. Much of the organization development process is a learning process, and learning what won't work is often just as important as learning what will.

In addition, the situational or environmental factors that lead us to adopt certain approaches may change during the course of our implementation of those approaches. Events could overtake our solution and make it inappropriate. Management's philosophy or viewpoint on OD might change. There may be a change in the makeup of the executive staff, or the chief executive might leave and be replaced by a person with different views. The nature of the market may change, or the organization's customers may start doing business in new ways. For any of these reasons, it may be worthwhile to rethink the overall OD approach and set a new direction.

As you have probably deduced by this point, the need to set a new direction brings us right to the beginning of the OD cycle again. The evaluation phase becomes, to a great extent, the assessment phase for the next adaptive lurch into the future. If things have changed so much over a year or two that the evaluation process is now dealing with factors that were not included in—or even relevant to—the original assessment process, then it is probably worthwhile to begin a new cycle of planned change and adaptation.

If the managers and people of the organization have had the benefit of the experiences of one "pass" through the OD process and have seen the fruits of their efforts, then they can undertake a new adaptation in a more highly organized way than they otherwise could. They will generally use more sophisticated methods, think more comprehensively, develop more imaginative solutions, and take a more seasoned approach as a result of their learning process. For an organization in which the executives and managers understand and have applied these concepts and methods, organization development becomes less of a special, ad hoc process and more an adjunct to a sophisticated management methodology.

13

The Future of
Organization Development

WHERE IS OD GOING?

Things are happening so fast in the organizational world these days that it's a risky proposition at best to try to forecast the situation five to ten years ahead. The best we can do is to sketch out some of the major trends we can see today, extrapolate them into the near future, and identify possible events or developments that could play an important part in reshaping those trends. When it comes to sketching the future of OD, we can see some fairly definite trends and happenings.

I think we can make the following assumptions about the organizational and business environment in which we will find ourselves in the 1980s:

1. We will see a shift toward younger top and middle managers, due largely to population imbalances across the age range that is typical of managers; there will be an increase in the number of managers aged forty to fifty finding their way into top spots.

2. Many of these managers will be more educated than their forebears, more acquainted with new technologies, and perhaps psychologically younger in terms of attitudes and values.

3. Many of tomorrow's managers will bring with them a more diversified value system than that of their predecessors; still largely materialistic, but increasingly interpersonal, individualistic, and less committed to concepts like "loyalty to your company," "coming up through the ranks," and "paying your dues."

4. The work force is becoming steadily better educated, with steadily increasing expectations about income and job possibilities; many of these people will be disappointed because the industrial base is not creating jobs that require college-level education as fast as the colleges are turning out degreed people.

5. These people will become increasingly more restive and dissatisfied with conventionally designed jobs, and less willing to obey orders without question. Young workers will probably apply social pressure for more participative management and will migrate toward organizations that have people-oriented work settings.

6. Again because of population dynamics, there will be a shortage of entry-level workers; now that almost all of the members of the post-war "baby boom" cohort have entered the work world, we will see for the first time in many years a shrinking work force. Older workers will be leaving the work force more rapidly than young people are coming in. This will make it a "seller's market" in terms of labor, and organizations will have to compete with one another even for unskilled and semi-skilled workers.

7. The maturing of the baby-boom workers will cause an unprecedented piling-up of people in their early middle years competing for a small number of higher positions. As organizations grow more slowly, many of these people will find themselves disappointed at not getting ahead as rapidly as older workers did; they will be looking for ways to develop themselves and to compete effectively for the higher jobs.

8. The American social environment, as well as that of many Western countries, will see a very powerful issue developing: corporate social responsibility. There will probably be a strong hue and cry for making corporations and other large organizations accountable to the society, not only for the effects they have on the natural and social environments but also for the quality of work life they provide within their boundaries.

9. Issues like quality of work life, productivity, and corporate social responsibility will become increasingly real for managers and will affect what they think, do, and decide on a daily basis.

10. Traditionally trained managers will have to acquire new knowledge and an understanding of the applied behavioral sciences, in addition to their conventional knowledge of plans, budgets, balance sheets, and income statements; new managers will find it necessary and useful to learn about these things. We will pretty well complete the process of integrating practical psychology and sociology into management practice, and the day-to-day actions of managers will more and more reflect this increasing respect for the social processes in their organizations.

For the above reasons, organization development as a methodology will probably find much more acceptance among managers than ever in the past, and there will probably be an increasing demand for people who have the conceptual, analytical, social, and practical skills to implement these techniques in the organizational setting. Of the three divergent "schools" of OD—the human-relations school, the behavior modification school, and the systems school—I believe the systems school will increasingly become the mainstream of OD practice. If this is true, we will probably see a developing body of literature on systems-oriented OD, with a very comprehensive philosophy.

Traditionally, OD has been the domain of the consultant, and especially the consultant who was trained in psychology or a related behavioral specialty. Many "old school" OD practitioners don't like it, but the fact is that OD is now becoming the property of people working in organizations. As of about 1980, there were more people working in organizations who called themselves OD practitioners than there were working as outside consultants. OD is rapidly becoming secularized, largely due to the huge demand among personnel and training people for new ways to make their functions effective. They are wresting OD from the hands of the "high priests," i.e., the consulting psychologists, and transmuting it into a methodology which they and their managers can apply in their own settings. I think (and hope) that the OD consultant will continue to have a valuable role to play in bringing an external perspective to the organization, in supplying needed expertise, and increasingly in training and coaching internal OD people in applying the methods on their own.

The whole area known as human resources development, or "HRD," is rapidly growing and intensifying in its activity. It is fast becoming a career field for specialists working in organizations, and it will eventually envelop all of what was previously known as the training and development function. The 1980s and beyond will probably see an ever-increasing investment of hard corporate dollars in human development and in humanistically oriented areas such as quality of work life, employee health, and personal development.

We must be careful, however, not to throw out the baby with the bath water. A corporation is still an economic creature, and it must have a favorable profit picture to survive; this is not likely to change in the foreseeable future. Rather than simply lavish money on various social benefits, executives must learn how to get a worthwhile return on these dollars. Tomorrow's chief executive must figure out how to invest money, resources, and energy in such a way as to maintain an economically viable enterprise while enhancing the quality of work life and contributing a positive impact on the environment in which the company operates. This is possible, and it will take a very imaginative approach to management.

The principles, concepts, and methods we have been studying here, under the umbrella of organization development, can indeed play an important part in bringing about this renaissance in management. As time goes on, and more and more managers apply OD techniques in their organizations, we will probably find that OD loses its exotic image and its air of specialization, and becomes simply—and appropriately—a part of modern management practice.

SKILLS OD PEOPLE WILL NEED

Organization development will probably emerge as a specialty function within organizations, much as the personnel function has emerged and developed. The role of internal OD person will probably profit from some much-needed clarity. People serving that role will increasingly be trained for it and developed as staff specialists. Looking toward that possible state of affairs, we can enumerate some of the skills that OD people will need to have.

We can divide the OD skills needed for the future into four categories:

1. *Skills of influence*—the ability to gain access to the center of power in the organization, and to induce the managers to undertake a wholesale re-evaluation of the organization and their ways of running it. This includes face-to-face communication skills, skills needed in making stand-up presentations, and the ability to sell ideas and persuade people. It also includes the ability to create and maintain positive "political" relationships with peers, key executives and managers, and others who have a part to play in the success of an OD program.

2. *Analytical skills*—the ability to make sense out of a complex and confusing sociotechnical situation, to carry out a fact-finding mission competently, and to analyze the results and figure out what they mean. This includes the skills of systems thinking, investigation, abstract conceptualization, measurement, surveying, needs assessment, statistical analysis, and organizing and interpreting information.

3. *Synthesizing skills*—the ability to develop workable solutions that comply with the reality of the findings and meet the needs of the organization. This includes bringing together disparate subproblems into an integrated picture of the need, accounting for a diversity of points of view and specialized interests, drawing on a wide variety of OD options, fitting available options to the requirements of the situation, and creating implementation programs that the influential people in the organization will buy.

4. *Implementation skills*—the ability to reduce the grand design to practice. This includes the practical skills of program planning, scheduling, acquiring funding support, budgeting, organizing task forces and sometimes leading them, carrying out various assigned tasks as a member of an OD task force, reporting results, and keeping the members of the OD task force and key managers motivated toward their goals during the "nose-dive" period.

It also helps for an OD person to have a good practical understanding of management, as well as a firm grasp on its basic principles and concepts. It is very important for OD people to know how managers think and how the world looks to them through their specialized window. Sooner or later, the ultimate change agent is a manager somewhere, with the authority and inclination to redirect resources. In order to influence that person for positive ends, it is important to understand how he or she thinks, reacts, decides, feels, and wants. Because OD people seldom have any formal organizational power, they must learn to empower themselves by working with and through those who do have it. This requires a special blend of competencies, perhaps a special kind of personal temperament, and certainly a great deal of patience and flexibility.

TEN COMMANDMENTS FOR AN OD PERSON

If you plan to act as a practitioner of this new management methodology called organization development and to operate as a change agent with and within organizations, here are some key points to keep in mind:

1. Do thy client no harm.
2. Start where the system is, and work from there.
3. Understand the organization as well as you possibly can.
4. Diagnose carefully before you prescribe.
5. Get the power people committed to the process.
6. Relieve pain when possible.
7. If something ain't busted, don't try to fix it.
8. Have a big bag of tricks; tailor the solution to the problem.
9. Don't work uphill; share ownership of the solutions with the people who must make them work.
10. Stay alive; don't get killed fighting for causes.

14

Case Studies in Organization Development

POLAROID CORPORATION

At Polaroid's film-manufacturing plant near Boston, the employees had become progressively more frustrated and angry about the treatment they felt they were getting from their management. They considered the plant manager an abrasive, oppressive, inconsiderate tyrant with little concern for their needs and interests. The situation precipitated in the form of a mass employee complaint delivered to the division vice president, asking that the plant manager be replaced or reoriented.

Polaroid's top management took the matter quite seriously and launched an investigation into the nature and history of the disturbance. They created an OD consulting team, chartered to assess the situation very thoroughly and recommend an approach. The OD team undertook a very comprehensive fact-finding process which included questionnaires, person-to-person interviews, and a review of the plant's history and work performance. Curiously, the plant had a performance record that placed it among the most productive of all Polaroid facilities. The dissatisfaction seemed to revolve around the issue of "trust," which both the executives and the employees had some difficulty defining, but which both groups felt was lacking.

The comprehensive assessment involved some interesting processes, such as hiring a consulting sociologist to write a comprehensive history of the plant, conferences between the OD team and the executives, and between the OD team and employee representatives, and sensing meetings held by the plant manager with groups of twenty employees at a time. The fixes recommended by the OD task force, and implemented by Polaroid management, included sending the plant manager to a leadership training program, conducting communication workshops for various managers, conducting problem-solving workshops for many of the managers and key employees, and continuing the employee sensing process on the part of the plant manager in order to solve the concerns about plant management being too "distant" from the workers.

As a result of the OD process, the social climate in the organization improved markedly, and the program continued further into other areas identified as promising during the diagnosis. These included improvement of the working relationship between managers and hourly workers, setting up quality-of-work-life focus groups, joint productivity-improvement projects, Polaroid's version of "quality circles," and implementation of nontraditional work structuring in the start-up of the manufacturing line for a new product.

The crisis-oriented OD intervention at Polaroid had the longer-term benefit of convincing top management of the value of OD as a general adjunct to the management process and led to a continuing commitment to regular assessments, including employee sensing, and collaborative problem-solving between managers and workers.

THE GENERAL MOTORS QUALITY-OF-WORK-LIFE PROGRAM

Since about 1976, General Motors has had an extensive corporate-wide program aimed at measuring and improving the overall quality of work life (QWL) as experienced by GM employees. It began with a systematic attempt to assess QWL by means of a survey questionnaire based on sixteen identified factors. These factors (similar to the ten aspects of QWL identified in Chapter 5) emerged from an extensive exploration of the corporate climate. What started as a voluntary surveying process on the part of a number of division executives has expanded to a near-universal policy. World-wide, over 200 GM units now use the questionnaire, and the results over the years have developed into a very useful data base which management can use in assessing current circumstances and historical progress.

Another significant aspect of the GM approach to QWL was a clearly defined relationship with the primary union that represents the workers, the United Auto Workers. Executives and union leaders worked out a letter of agreement between the company and the union, on the subject of QWL, which spelled out roles, goals, and relationships. The letter recognized the objective of enhancing QWL as beneficial to the company in terms of reduced absenteeism and turnover, and beneficial to customers in terms of product quality. GM management specifically avoided, however, using a QWL program as an instrument for productivity improvement. To implement this agreement, the company and the union established a joint committee on QWL, composed of GM managers and UAW leaders. As a result of the committee's actions, or with its encouragement, hundreds of QWL enhancement projects are underway in various areas of the organization. The committee meets periodically to review results and plan additional projects.

Although GM executives do not refer to their QWL efforts as a "program," they do have a clear-cut approach and a clearly defined means of implementation. The GM approach involves three major avenues: continuing measurement and assessment with the QWL survey questionnaire, an annual meeting of top executives to review the status of QWL efforts, and a broad-scale educational process for managers. This educational process consists primarily of familiarization sessions for plant managers and middle managers on QWL concepts and development techniques. GM also has a staff of internal consultants at corporate headquarters in Detroit, who assist unit executives in implementing their programs. The implementation of all QWL projects in GM is essentially voluntary with local executives. Top management has, however, been moving steadily in the direction of higher and higher expectations.

In addition, GM has adopted a firm policy with regard to setting up new facilities, under which behavioral scientists and OD consultants play a key part in the planning and implementation. This has led to certain highly visible changes, such as eliminating time clocks and uniformed guards. However, QWL specialists consider these improvements as far less significant than the less-visible aspects such as work-restructuring, plant layout, and inter-unit collaboration.

It certainly could not be said that all of General Motors is solidly embarked on a program of QWL enhancement. There are still recalcitrant managers in the organization who prefer to ignore the social aspects of their responsibility. And many QWL projects fail to live up to the expectations of their creators. It is, however, very significant that the Chairman of the Board and the senior executives of a 700,000-person corporation have set out quality of work life as a major corporate goal and have implemented a process to improve it at significant expense to the corporation. This represents a significant management commitment to adapt to the changing times.

SAAB-SCANIA CORPORATION

The Saab Car Division of Saab-Scania Corporation, in Trollhattan, Sweden, has had a systems-oriented OD process underway for several years. One of the company's units, a prototype-construction shop within the engineering department, had been experiencing internal problems with its structure. The shop had 200 people, mostly skilled automotive technicians and craftsmen, with a small white-collar support staff. The organization was completely unionized, including the fifteen supervisors—a fairly common situation in Sweden. When a new shop manager came in, he consulted with the company's internal OD specialists and asked for support in evolving the organization into a new structure.

At the time of the change, Sweden's government had recently passed sweeping legislation that required extensive interaction and negotiation between managers and union representatives in all cases involving significant changes to the work situation. The reorganization which the shop manager had in mind fell squarely into this category, and it was not at all clear how managers and union leaders were to interact in bringing about the change. It remained management's prerogative to decide what to do and how to implement the decision; the new law did require, however, that employee representatives be consulted and that they have access to sufficient information to be just as well informed about company operations as their bosses were.

The primary problem in the situation seemed to be a high degree of ambiguity about various aspects of the organization. A key engineer was scheduled to depart, and this opened up certain questions about allocation of responsibilities. The shop manager felt that there were too many levels of management in the organization, that unit missions were not clearly enough defined, that the roles of union leaders were indefinite, and that supervisors were uncertain about their authority and responsibilities.

Given the impact of the new labor law, and the relative ambiguity of the union-management relationship, the OD effort focused on the change process itself. The general nature and scope of the required changes were fairly clear. It became important to lay out an approach to bringing about the changes that both managers and union representatives could live with. In general, the union-management relationship was not problematical, and certainly not as volatile as would be typical of countries such as England or America. Nevertheless, it was still the classical adversarial relationship.

The general approach to the OD effort was to create a three-way relationship, involving the plant manager and his key leaders, the union leaders, and the OD consultant. The consultant adopted a strategy from early in the program, of having each of the three participating "stakeholders" clarify and state their perceptions of the situation at various points as it developed. For example, the plant manager initially felt that the process would be unnecessarily cumbersome because of the many people involved. He was accustomed to solving problems by simply issuing orders. The union people tended to see the consultant as an agent of the shop manager and expected him to help the boss force through his preconceived solutions. The consultant expressed personal concern and uncertainty about how the relationships would develop and about how the process would unfold. By making their individual perceptions and concerns known to one another, the members of the task force were able to operate from a broader perspective. Altogether, there were about thirty people involved in the process in various ways—a number which is probably unnecessarily large, even in such an unusual climate of labor-management relationships.

Some of the specific actions included a careful inventory of strong and weak aspects of the organization, a climate survey conducted among the members of the organization, and a careful definition of the new organizational structure. The task force members also created a smaller problem-solving group, which the consultant worked with in team-building activities. This group then "exploded" the problem out into its many parts and began developing solutions in each of the key areas. There were many meetings over the two-year period of the complete project, involving the problem-solving group as well as the members of the larger group.

As the new organizational structure and processes settled into place, the consultant frequently invited the key people to clarify, write down, and exchange perceptions of what was happening, and what obstacles they perceived. As they proceeded, they began to share perceptions more openly. Many of them found their initial apprehensions disconfirmed, and they began to appreciate the roles and concerns of others more thoroughly.

By the end of the period, they had succeeded in reducing the organization from four hierarchical levels to three, clarifying and strengthening the roles of the supervisors, clarifying the roles and activities of the union representatives, making the workers of the organization much better informed about its purposes and processes, and shifting the overall management orientation from an authoritarian style to a much more participative style. Side effects of the program included a one-third reduction in the rate of absenteeism and an improved reputation with the other departments for service and responsiveness.

THE U.S. DEPARTMENT OF ENERGY

Organizational history, however, is not all "happy endings." The establishment of the U.S. Department of Energy, for example, has to be one of the greatest organizational debacles in recent history. A virtual Frankenstein's monster created in 1977 by President Jimmy Carter, it exploded from virtually nothing to an agency of over 19,000 employees in less than three years.

In their haste to get going and start spending their budgeted money, the first officials of the agency hired people as fast as possible, threw together makeshift administrative processes, and started handing out contracts to eager development companies and consulting firms. The agency expanded much too fast to have any semblance of order or control, to say nothing of efficiency. Officials transferred on-going functions in from other departments, created new ones, and staffed up with people even before they knew what jobs they wanted them to do.

By 1980, the agency was spending $14 billion a year, ninety

percent of it in the form of external contracts, and much of it utterly wasted. The executives of the department at that time could not even come up with a reliable list of active contracts and contractors. Reports of gross misallocation of funds, wasted funds, and utter ignorance of what was going on abounded. The technical system consisted largely of a contracting pipeline for channeling funds as rapidly as possible to the companies. The social system was an unintegrated hodgepodge of strangers caught up in the confusion of finding their desks and finding out who their supervisors were. The administrative system was a shambles, consisting of only the most minimal procedures and controls, and a nightmarishly complex organizational structure. The secretary of the department has a span of control of seventeen major functions reporting to him, in addition to a melange of administrative assistants and special staff people. The organization was subdivided along rather awkward lines, and there was considerable misunderstanding about responsibilities and areas of operation of the various units. The strategic system was a rough assemblage of career civil servants, augmented by people hired in tremendous haste from the private sector.

The results of the too-rapid growth eventually became obvious and became an embarrassment to the Carter administration. People began to talk seriously of simply abolishing the agency and writing it off as a bad dream. When Ronald Reagan became President, he took the same attitude. The newly appointed Energy Secretary, James Edwards, took over with the mission of reducing the enormous waste, and preparing for the possibility of abolishing the organization. In his first few months on the job, Edwards eliminated over 2600 unnecessary jobs and cut the budget by $3 billion.

This was a classic case of organizational indigestion caused by too rapid a rate of expansion. A far better approach would have been for the President to appoint a nucleus organization, arranged in such a way as to provide for its own expansion over a more realistic period of time. A small, well-chosen group of executives, supported by consulting expertise in the area of organization design, could probably have worked out a realistic trajectory for the growth of the agency and could have started achieving high-priority payoffs in certain areas immediately. Apparently, those involved in starting up the organization grossly underestimated the problems and confusions associated with creating such an enterprise in such a short period of time. Any industrial corporation that went from a handful of people to over 19,000 employees in three years could be expected to have severe organizational problems in absorbing the new business and consolidating its growth. There is no reason to believe a government agency would have an easier time of it. Organization development techniques probably would have helped to lessen the Department of Energy's indigestion, but the real solution would have been to take a smaller bite.

A PRACTICE CASE STUDY

Now it's your turn. Here is a practice case study I've developed for use in teaching the OD methods in this book to managers. Try your hand at analyzing a hypothetical organization from the point of view of the four key systems and thinking about the four-stage OD process. As you read the brief description of the company, sketch the organization chart as well as you can from the information given, describe the primary productive axis, and describe the various components of the technical system, the social system, the administrative system, and the strategic system. Following the description you will find several questions to challenge your thinking about OD for this particular organization.

Description

Educational Concepts, Inc. is a publishing firm, operating in the area of books and materials. The company has about 320 people and $30 million in annual sales. The company has two locations. A headquarters building houses top management, the editorial offices, and the sales manager. The other location, two blocks away, houses the administrative functions, research and marketing, and the production department which actually produces the books and materials the company sells. Some of the printing and duplication of materials is done by subcontract, with the production division assembling and shipping the completed products.

The company is family-owned, but the newly hired president is not a family member. He was hired three months ago to fill a vacancy created when the previous president, the youngest son of the owner, left to take charge of another family business. His background is in journalism and editorial work. The company has been in a stagnant period of sales and earnings for four years and hasn't yet shown signs of improvement.

Reporting to the president are seven editors (Technical Books,

Children's Books, Elementary Materials, High School Materials, Junior College Materials, English-Language Materials, and Special Products—a new area), the head of production, the head of finance/accounting, the head of administrative services, the head of research and marketing, and the head of field sales. The personnel officer reports to the head of administrative services. The field sales force consists of sixty sales people who cover the continental U.S., and two sales representatives in Canada. The six regional sales managers currently report to the president, because the position of sales manager is vacant. Most of the sales people are relatively new and comparatively inexperienced.

The owners of the company want to see a significant increase in sales in the next 12–18 months, and the introduction of some new products that will begin to bring in revenue within 18–24 months. You have been asked by the president of the company to consult with the organization for the purpose of improving its overall operation in order to meet the stated marketing goals. The president knows little about organization development but is apparently open to new approaches.

Questions

Here are some questions to think about:

1. What are some of the key features of this particular organization that will probably need attention in an OD program?
2. What are some of the things you need to find out during the assessment phase?
3. What factors do you need to consider in getting an OD program started?

Appendix

BIBLIOGRAPHY FOR OD

The following books represent a sampling of the mainstream of contemporary OD thinking. The authors are all comparatively well known in the OD field and are considered "experts" in the matter of planned organizational change. While the newly-developing systems approach is not strongly represented in available OD literature, you may still find it profitable to explore the ideas of these thinkers.

Argyris, Chris. *Management and Organizational Development: The Path from Xa to Yb.* New York: McGraw-Hill, 1971.

Beck, A.C., and Hillmar, E. *A Practical Approach to Organization Development through MBO*—Selected Readings. Reading, MA: Addison-Wesley, 1972.

Beckhard, Richard. *Organization Development: Strategies and Models.* Reading, MA: Addison-Wesley, 1969.

Bennis, Warren. *Organization Development: Its Nature, Origins, and Prospects.* Reading, MA: Addison-Wesley, 1969.

Blake, Robert, and Mouton, Jane. *Corporate Excellence Through Grid Organization Development: A Systems Approach.* Houston: Gulf, 1968.

Dyer, William. *Team Building: Issues and Alternatives.* Reading, MA: Addison-Wesley, 1977.

French, Wendell, and Bell, Cecil. *Organization Development: Behavioral Science Interventions for Organization Improvement.* Englewood Cliffs, NJ: Prentice-Hall, 1978.

Kuriloff, Arthur. *Organization Development for Survival.* New York: American Management Association, 1972.

Lawrence, P.R., and Lorsch, J.W. *Developing Organizations: Diagnosis and Action.* Reading, MA: Addison-Wesley, 1969.

Lippitt, Gordon. *Organizational Renewal.* New York: Appleton-Century-Crofts, 1969.

Margulies, Newton. *Organizational Development: Values, Process, and Technology.* New York: McGraw-Hill, 1972.

Varney, Glenn. *Organization Development for Managers.* Reading, MA: Addison-Wesley, 1977.

ORGANIZATIONS INVOLVED IN PROMOTING OD

There are many associations, professional societies, and informal groups devoted to developing, practicing, and promoting OD. The following list gives a representative sampling of them. The list is by no means comprehensive, and it may not even be representative. I include it here as an additional item of information you may find useful in your exploration of the field.

Academy of Management—OD Division

American Association of Personnel Managers

American Productivity Center

American Society for Training & Development—OD Division

International Association for Applied Behavioral Sciences

International Registry for OD Consultants

National Training Laboratories (NTL)
OD Canada
OD Network
Société International pour le Dévelopment des Organisations (SIDO)
Tavistock Institute (Great Britain)
US Army OD Network
Work in America Institute

Index

A

Action research technique, 35
  fact finding, 35
  implementation, 35
  "sniffing the wind," 35
Adaptation, 2, 123–24, 227–28
  study of, 2
Administration, system of, assessment, 163–
    66
  computers, 165
  formal structure, 166
  paper media used in, 164
  procedure departments, 164
  procedure and policy manuals, 164
  purposes of system, 165
  response time, 166
  system diagram approach, 165
  waste effort, 165
Administration, system of, components of,
    94–97
  ad hoc growth, 94–95
  classification problems, 96–97
  data processing facilities, 96
  flow paths, 96
  media, 96
  and people in, 95
  structure, 95
Amoeba syndrome, 18–19
Anarchy syndrome, 19
Asians, 92
Assessment, comprehensive, benefits of, 155
Assessment Survey Kit, 163, 177
Attention span, problem of:
  faddism, problem of, 17
  and follow through, problem of, 17
  nature, 17

B

Barriers to change, in firms, dealing with,
    209–12
  example, 210–11
  fair try concept, 211–12

Barriers to change (*continued*)
  impact of change on work, 211
  initiatives, 212
  and nose dive syndrome, 209–10
  valley of despair syndrome, 210, 211
Behavior modification school of OD, 41–42
  changing of consequences, 42
  observing, 41–42
  reinforcers, 42
  Skinnerian theory, 41
  specifying, 41
Benne, Kenneth, 30
Bennis, Warren, 154
Blacks, 92
Blake, Robert, 31
Bottom lines, 127–29
  economic, 128
  human, 128
  and old-school managers, 128–29
  social, 128
Bradford, Leland, 30

C

Capital and productivity, 70
  and machinery, 70
Carter, Jimmy, 240
Catalyst function, in OD:
  appointments for, 138
  forms of, 138
  loss of enthusiasm, 138
  task force approach, benefits, 139
Catalyst person, OD scheme of:
  entry, 36–37
  implementation, 37
  lock-on, 37
  sensing, 37
  separation, 37
Civil rights, 92
Climate survey, in OD, 174–77
  blunders to avoid, 174
  cover-ups of bad results, 175
  observer effects, 174–75
  questions, phrasing of, 176–77
  steps, 175–76
  and unions, 175
Component of organization, excessive preoc-
    cupation with, case, 3–4
Comprehensivist style of management, 5
Conductor, analog of with manager, 4
Consultant and catalyst, OD stages:
  entry, 36–37
  implementation, 37
  lock-on, 37
  sensing, 37
  separation, 37
Consultant, external, engaging of, 139–41
  and chief executive, 140

conditions, 139–40
  points to remember, 141
  things to avoid, 140
Continuity, desire for, 7–8
  and adaptive shifts, 8
  lurches, 8
  and managers, 7
Cultural issues, 92, 93

D

Deadlock syndrome, 19–20
Department of Treasury, U.S. Government,
    240–42
  better model for, 241
  chaos in, 240–41
Diffusion, OD strategy, 36
Drucker, Peter F., 58, 98, 188
Dyer, Prof. William, 132

E

Educational Concepts, Inc., practice OD case,
    242–43
Edwards, James, 241
Employee-sensing system, building of and
    OD, 177–78
  special issue questions, 178
  starting, 178
  TRW, experience of, 177, 178
Employees, responses of to management-
    induced change, 213–16
  ambiguity, reactions to, 216
  improvement in work, communicating of,
    214, 215
  lag shift, 216
  phases of reactions to, 215
  solution myopia, nature, 214, 215
Engineer, analog of manager with, 4
Environment, changes in, organizational
    leaders' responses to, 14–16
  acceptance, 15, 16
  accommodation, 15, 16
  denial, 15
Evaluation:
  closed-loop problem-solving, 222–23
  continuity, 222
  as cycle closer, 222–23
  environments, 122
  examples, 225, 226
  and fact-finding, 225–26
  key changes, 122, 123
  planning conferences, 123
  questions to ask, 223
  return to outset, 225
Executive quarterback concept, for OD im-
    plementation, 206–9
  benefits, 208

division of tasks, 208
and loss of commitment, 206–7
nature, 207
presentation of, 208–9
Extended management, 117–18
middle groups, 117

F

Fact-finding methods, 155–58
analysis of obvious, 156
effects of, 158–59
hard, 155, 156
interviewing, 157
questionnaire, 157
soft, 155, 157
summary, 158
systems, analysis of, 156
Fads, warning about, 58 (*see also* Attention span)
Feedback systems, building of, 219–21
example, 220
half-empty/half-full contrast, 220
negative, in Western world, 219
negative, in work, 219
steps, 220–21
Force field, analysis of, 212–13
diagram, 213
implications, 213
nature, 212, 213

G

Galbraith, Jay, 193
General Motors, Quality-of-Work-Life program, OD study, 236–38
and UAW, 237
Graduation, for management, 124–26
conditions for, 125
and filling spots from outside, 124
merit, 126
problems without, 125
use, 124
Grapevines, 88–91
benefits, 89–90
layoffs, cushioning shock of, 90
nature, 89
Group dynamics school of OD:
nature, 40
NTL Institute for Applied Behavior Science, 40
University Associates, 40
Growth, rapid, problems with:
in city stage, 13
and development of founder, 14
and engineering of products, 13
in family stage, 13
"indigestion," 14

lack of structure, 13
in survivor-group stage, 12
in village stage, 13
Growth, stages of:
city, 11
family, 10
metropolis, 11
nonprofit organizations, 12
self-running property of corporation, 11, 12
survivor group, 10
village, 10

H

Hammer syndrome, avoidance of, 131–32
Hispanics, 92
Huxley, Thomas, 215

I

Inertia, 1–2, 7
fundamental, 1–2
Information environment, maintenance of, 106–7
company library, 107
newsletter, 107
reports, 107
Innovation, 126–27, 193–95
Kettering, Charles, quoted on, 127
blocks to, 193
"islands" for, 194
operation vs. innovation, conflict between, 193–94
resistance, reasons for, 194
Interplay in organization, diagram, 130
Intersystem conflicts:
high turnover, effects, 56
low wages, effects, 56
paper process, troubles with, 56–57
people vs. profits problem, 56
priority conflict, military HQ, case, 57
"I've made it" syndrome, 5

K

Kennedy, John F., 60
Kissinger, Henry, 114

L

Learning lag, 6
Lewin, Kurt, 30, 212
Likert, Rensis, 33
Linkages, OD strategy, 36
Lippitt, Ronald, 30
Lurch, management by, 2

M

Mainlining, 4–5
    effects, 5
Maladjustment, organizational, 18–22
Malorganization, symptoms of, 100–103
    absent function of personnel, 102
    example, 102–3
    power imbalances, 102
    span of control:
        narrow, 101
        problems, 101
        wide, 101
Management strength, 111–12
    example, 112
    points to remember, 112
    problems with measuring, 112
Management team, development, 184–86
    approaches, 184
    conditions for, 185
    new personnel, planning for, 185–86
    overall, 184–85
    probationary period, 186
    removal of incompetents, 186
Managerial styles, 118–21
    administrator, 119
    autonomy, 120
    factors:
        correct amount, 121
        deficiency, 121
        excess, 121
    leader, 119
    problem-solver, 119
    reward, 120
    shared goals, 120
    strategist, 119
    teamwork, 120
Managerial styles, analysis of, 168–74
    basic needs, human, 169–70
    discussion, 168–69
    employees, reactions of to management,
        171
    leadership process, 173
    managerial roles, 172
    personality types, 170
    roles, ranking of, 172–73
    style conflict, 172
    style diagram, 171
    typical American manager, 169
    use of power, 170
Maslow, Abraham, 20, 52, 131
MBA degrees, effects of, 6
McClelland, David, 169
McGregor, Douglas, 31
Media, in technical systems, 65
Minorities, 92, 93
Misplaced fix syndrome, 51–53
    country agency, case, 51–52
    hammer syndrome, 52, 53

    lack of vision, effects, 51, 52
    MBO, poor use of, 52
    T-groups, 52, 53
Mom-and-Pop syndrome, 80
    Silicon Valley syndrome, 20
Momentum, desirability of, 7–8
Motivation, and productivity, 71
Myopia syndrome, 20–21
    Social Security, 21
    and U.S. since World War II, 20

N

Nonlinear systems, 20
Nonprofit organizations, problems of:
    caretaker executive, 62
    clearcutness of mission, 59
    competition, presence of, 59
    customer role, split in, 61
    government workers, image of, 59
    managers in, typical, 61
    measures of performance, presence of, 60
    NASA, 59
    public schools, case, 59–60
    TVA, 59
    welfare agencies, cases, 60

O

"Out-of-tune" condition, 1, 2
Organization chart, rigidity of, 22
Organization, culture of:
    norms, 79
    power, 78–79
    rewards, 81
    values, 79
Organization, four key systems of:
    administration, 50
    caution, 49
    diagram of interlock, 51
    social, 50
    strategic, 50
    and subsystems, 49
    technical, 50
Organization, health, dimensions of:
    adaptation, 23
    evaluation, 23
    graduation, 23
    innovation, 23
Organization, making logical structure of:
    conditioned by strategy, 99
    implications of, 100
    naturalness of, 100
    and productive axis, 99
    reorganization, problems with, 98
    span of control, 99–100
Organizational development (OD), nature of,
    2–3

Organizational development, future of, 229–32
  human resources development, 232
  trends, 229, 230, 231
Organizational development, history of:
  encounter groups, 31
  growth groups, 32, 33
  laboratory approach, 30–31
  marathon sessions, 32
  National Training Academy, 31
  organizational culture, 34
  recent developments, 34
  re-entry shock, 33
  seminar feedback, 30
  sensitivity training, 32–33
  T-groups, 31–32
  teams of management, training of, 33
Organizational development, implementation
    of plan for, 202–5
  amounts of commitment, 203
  and executives, 202
  scenario for, 203–4
  session, planning, 204
  suggestions, 205
Organizational development, major trends in
    practice of:
  absence of framework, 38
  behavior modification school, 39
  group-dynamics school, 39
  Messiah complex, 38–39
  priest-centered vs. secular forms, 39
  shaman syndrome, 38
  systems school, 39
Organizational Development, objectives-
    oriented, 148–49
  specification of goals, 148
Organizational development, options list for,
    179–81
Organizational development process, basic:
  assessment, 136
  as cycle, 136–37
  diagram, 137
  evaluation, 136
  implementation, 136
  problem-solving phase, 136
  as ritual, 137
Organizational development, ten command-
    ments for, 234
Organizational development, use of:
  assessment, 27–28
  discussion, 24–25
  and human element, attention to, 26
  evaluation, 28
  implementation, 28
  key points, 27
  members of organization as practitioners,
    25
  network of, 25
  outside practitioners, 25

  personnel, 26
  problem-solving, 28
"Ownership" of changes, spreading of in OD,
    216–18
  credibility of management, 218
  example, 217
  and managers, 217–18
  nature, 217
  reasons for, 216, 217
  and task force, 217

P

Pain, primary:
  anticipatory management, 9
  and need for change, 8
  reactive management, 9
Paradoxical reward syndrome, 53–55
  complaints of managers, 55
  nature, 55
  punishment system, 53, 54
  reward system, 55
  unit pricing, case, 54
Parkinson, C. Northcote, 59
"Parkinson's Law," 59
Passages, in organizational life:
  compared to human growth, 9
  growth crisis, concept, 9
Pavlov, Ivan, 41
Performance appraisals, 73–74
  forms, 73
Polaroid, OD case, 235–36
Policies, clarification of, 104–6
  constancy of, 105–6
  defined, 105
  equal employment, example, 105
  problems with, 106
  purpose, 105
  work habits, 105
Politics in organization, understanding of, 86–
    88
  axis of influence, 88
  clout, 88
  coalitions, 88
  conflicts, 88
  defined, 86
  inner circle, relations in, 87–88
  necessity of, 87
  for OD, 87
  positive, 87
Positive, accentuation of, 226–27
  bell-ringing, 226
  facts, adherence to, 227
  feedback, 226
Power, psychology of, 84–86
  and egos, 85
  and human nature, 84
  and managers, 85
  new supervisors, 85

Power, psychology of (*continued*)
  OD-readiness, 86
  reluctance to discuss, 84, 85
Power people, understanding of, 113–16
  enjoyment of power, 114
  humanity of, 113
  important factors, 114
  machismo, 115
  and men, 113
  power junkies, 115
  self-esteem, 113
  wrong assumptions about by lower ranks,
    113–14
Prime axis, concept, 4–5
Problem-solving, collective, 186–88
  complexity of organizations, 168–87
  models for, 187
  need for training, 187
  seminars, 188
Problem-solving, creating climate for:
  candidness, 132, 133
  chief executive, 133
  "don't-upset-Mother" syndrome, 133
  key manager, 134
  leverage by change agents, 134
  and OD, starting of, 134–35
  staff specialist, 134
Procedure, defined, 105
Productivity, 65–67
  fluctuating, 67
  and GNP measure, 66
  measure choices, 67
  misconceptions about, 65–66
  problems of measurement, 66
  questions about, 66
Productivity, improvement of, 195–97
  measures, choice of, 195–96
  quality circles, 197
  steps, 196–97
  task force for, 196
Productivity, individual and collective:
  content-prices distinction, 69
  first line supervision, 69
  as planning variables, 68
  things to avoid, 67–68
  writing, example, 69
Program reviews, formal, 224
  guidelines, 224

Q

Quality of work life, 76–78
  aspects, 77
  and employees' perceptions, 78
  and modern U.S., 76–77
  nature, 76–77
Quality of work life, improvement of, 198–99
  components, 198
  and employees, 199

nature, 198
steps, 199

R

Rat race syndrome, 21
  in auto industry, 21
  Lordstown strike, 21
Reagan, Ronald, 241
Remote control syndrome, 21
  CETA program, 21
Response time, 97–98
  in Federal government, 97
  percolation of information, 97–98
  test, 97
Reward system:
  components, 81
  and managers, 81
  monkeys, parable, 80
  punishment, 81
Rigor mortis syndrome, 22
Rogers, Carl, 31

S

Saab-Scandia, OD case, 238–40
  and labor laws, 239, 240
  revision of structure, 239–40
  stakeholder concept, 239
Shepard, Hebert, 31
Sink-or-swim management style, 3
Skills necessary for OD:
  analysis, 233
  implementation, 233
  influence, 233
  synthesizing, 233
Skinner, B.F., 41
Slots, 22
Social systems, assessment of, 161–63
  and culture in work place, 161
  and demographic data, 162
  soft data, 163
  women, 161
  young people, 161
Social systems, components of, 75–76
Sociotechnical systems, concepts of:
  box charts, 47
  hotel, case, 48
  human systems, 48
  and primary axis, 48
  recent trends, 48–49
Solution biases, 155
Span of control, 99–100, 101
Specialists, internal OD, 144–45
  as ad hoc function, 145
  Lincoln, Abraham, story by, 144
  old-school, 144
  placement of function, 144
  as separate function, 144–45

Specialization, effects of, 7
Standard, defined, 105
Status quo, tendency toward, 2
Strategic planning and OD, 188–90
   business mission, statements of, 189
   components, 189–90
   environments, types, 190
   fundamental question, 188–89
Strategic system, assessment of, 166–68
   and executives, 167
   and managers, 167–68
   OD, best role for, 167
   points to remember, 168
   problems with, 166–67
Strategic system, and OD, 108–11
   components of, 111
   nature, 108–9
   near-readiness, 110
   and OD readiness, 109–10
   parable about self-scrutiny, 109
   and training department, 110
Structure, communicating of, 103–4
   creative confusion, 103–4
   lack, 103
Structure of organization, streamlining of,
   190–93
   executives, 191
   major considerations, 191–92, 193
   power diagram, 191
   and rationality, 191
Support, of top management, 146–47
   semantics of, 147
Systems school of OD, 42–43
   advantages, 42, 43
Systems thinking, introduction to:
   body, example, 45
   concepts about, 45
   defined, 45–46
   functions in, 46
   and managers, 47
   method, example, 45
   people as components, 46
   perspectives, 44–45
   registration in college, 46
   use, 46

T

Task force, establishing, 141–43
   conflicts in, 143
   personnel of, 142, 143
   plan, adherence to, 143
   recognition of, 141
   selection of, 141–42
   size, 142
   skills in, 142
   team, organization of, 143
Team building, for OD, 181–84
   assistance for, 183–84

development of, 183
   goals of, 182
   monitoring of, 182
   plan of, 183
   roles in, 182–83
   test of, 182
Technical system:
   assessment of, 159–60
   cautions, 159, 160
   components of, 64–65
   diagramming, 159
   example, 159
   productivity, 160
   summary in, 160
   system-mapping, 160
Time line, of OD program, 149–53
   assessment phase, 151
   case, 149–50
   and chief executives, 150
   continual evaluation, 152–53
   evaluation phase, 152
   implementation phase, 152
   and management team, 150
   problem-solving phase, 151
   single issue, 149
   and task force, 150
   team development process, 150
Top management team, 116–17
   cooperation, 117
   decision making, 117
   follow through, 117
   goal process, 116
   leadership, 116
   team spirit, 116
Training, clarification role of, 145–46
   assessment phase, 146
   caution, 146
Training, competence-based, and development:
   benefits, 72
   competence models, 73
   concreteness of skills, 72
   orientation of new employee, 71–72
   usual method, 72
Trapped administrator syndrome, 22

U

Unionization, 90–92
   conditions favoring, 91–92
   as failure of management, 90
   and OD, 92
   prevention, cases, 91
   workers' attitudes, 90–91
Unions, relations of with management, improving of, 200–202
   balance of power, types, 200
   committee bridging gap between, 201–2
   mock battles between, 201
   and OD, 200

Universities, rigidity in, 22

V

Values:
    organizational, 82–84
    reinforcement, 83, 84

W

WASPs, 92